ISMAEL 1/99

Jenna
Marie M.
Nuevo
10/31 2025 8:08pm

@ Java
Fremont

# SEEKING SPIRIT VISION

*Essays on Developing Imagination*

by

## DENNIS KLOCEK

RUDOLF STEINER COLLEGE PRESS

Rudolf Steiner College Press
9200 Fair Oaks Boulevard
Fair Oaks, CA 95628


ISBN 0-945803-33-8

*I dedicate this book to my wife Barbara,
who is the light of my life.*

# ACKNOWLEDGEMENTS

I would like to thank most especially Jennifer Blatchford who took a folder of handwritten sheets and through patience and focus turned them into a book. I am grateful to Robert Sardello for his most generous introduction and support of my work and to Mark Eisen for his clarity. Thanks to Patricia Dickson whose constant work on my behalf allows me to pursue my dreams. I would like to acknowledge my friend Claude Julien for his work in establishing Rudolf Steiner College Press, and to thank Judy Blatchford and Gayle Davis of Rudolf Steiner College for their encouragement in this project. I gratefully acknowledge Hallie Bonde for her expert tech support and attentions in the production of this book.

# CONTENTS

Foreword by Robert Sardello          i

1. Imagination: Creativity or Innovation?          1

Hypotheses in science and their sources. The difference
between creative thinking and fantasy. Onlooker consciousness. Willed thinking and the creation of a new future. The
cosmic function of the intellect in modern scientific methods.
The error of the intellect. Goethe's distinction between intellect and reason. Exact images in connection to phenomena of
the soul life. The open hypothesis.

2. Hypothesis, Apocalypse, Apotheosis          11

The polar forces of sympathy and antipathy and the sentient
soul. Mental images, anxiety, and confusion. The capacity for
recognition of the truth in the realm of concepts. Intellect and
Intuition. Modern technical science and its cornerstone.
Metaphysics and the materialistic bias of the sixteenth century. Thoughtless thinking at the wall of light. Meditative
efforts in spiritual research. The basic symptom of the onset
of apocalypse. Moral Imagination. The spiritual beings who
wish to help human beings.

3. The Abstract Predicament          21

Abstraction and the prejudice against beauty. Abstractionists
and expressionists. The shift in values between the
Renaissance and the modern period. The symptom of the
mind soul in esoteric development. Véron's categories of art
criticism. The search into primitive cultures for a counter balance to personal vision. The artist's descent into the persona
is that faced by the shaman. Ancient shamanism and the
power of image. The predicament of abstraction. Resolving
the predicament. The movement toward the New Jerusalem
and contact with the I-being. Innovation and mass produc-

tion values. Manas culture and the experience of the I Am. Stages in the development of an artist: realist, shaman, alchemist. The release of the senses to the bondage of matter.

4. The Transformation of Sympathy                               35
   Young children's mystical oneness as sympathy. The basis for the ability to think in images. Transcendence. Fanaticism. Fundamentalism. Medieval mysticism. Grasping and releasing concepts through willed activity. Goethe's distinction between reason and intellect. The archetypal Idea. The witness in the realm of angelic hosts. The experience of the I. The unfolding of consciousness in the entire human race.

5. The Black Madonna and the Mysteries of Dionysos    45
   Madonna and Child through the ages. The dark knowing of ancient cultures. The total dark idea of Goethe and Schiller. Dionysos Zagreus (the Elder). Dionysos the Younger. Dionysos as corn hero. The transformation of ancient seership into scientific intellect. Reunion with the Goddess. The task of the emerging I-being. The transformation of the ancient clairvoyance into science and the arts. The transformed Dionysos in Christian Art. Dionysos Jaccus. The Jaccus Madonna and the Black Madonna. Patron of women giving birth. Midwife between the higher self and the soul. Transcending the rigidity of the ancient binding ritual.

6. From Image to Vision                                          63
   The seer as someone able to transform images. The periodic table of Mendeleev as harmonic ordering. Shamanism and animal totems. Sophia Achamoth and the belt of lies. Mistrust in the realm of the senses. Lifting the natural world order into a moral world order.

7. The Place of the North                                        73
   The *simulacrum* and the *archeus*. Achterberg's qualities of shamanistic symbols. Imaginative power in western esotericism. Imagination and imagination. The Native American Sun Dance Wheel. Cooking and eating the shadow. The double. The intelligence of the heart. The Place of the North, give-away. The task of the new mystery teachings.

8.  The World of Imagination                                     85
    The hidden observer. The purpose of esoteric training. The
    path to the underworld in shamanism. Hypnotic states and
    shamanistic consciousness. The limits of the active alert hyp-
    notic state. Alchemists and imaginal attention. Conditions
    for a new culture to arise out of esotericism.

9.  From Dowsing to Divining                                    101
    Brain anatomy as a picture of the dowsing process. The two
    pillars in alchemy. The transformation of the salt and sulfur
    in the soul into the mercury of love and freedom. The pineal
    gland and its anatomical environment as an alchemical myth-
    ic Imagination. Jacob Boehme's inverted flaming heart. The
    heart as a sense organ. The mystery of Imagination. The vor-
    texial field of consciousness and the development of the high-
    er heart.

10. The Development of the Heart Soul:  A Modern Path     123
    The anatomy of the human being seen through the mytholo-
    gy of the Golden Legend.  The alchemy of distillation.
    Working with the two boundaries of knowledge. The path
    through the pituitary unites art and science with a religious
    veneration for all of creation. The path of the pineal opens the
    heart of the soul to rhythmic movement into and out of the
    spiritual world. Conscious surrender to the guardian angel
    and higher Imagination.

11. Imagination:  The Sacred Door                               143
    What is a mental image? Dynamic forgetting and Buddhist
    mindfulness. Alchemical transformation of the imaginal into
    Imagination. Jacob's Ladder. The alchemical *substantia* and
    the key to Imagination. Working with dreams. Unconscious
    addiction to unlawful images and violence in society.

12. The Great Tree                                              167
    Alchemical work and the transformation of the soul.  The
    three levels of polarity. The Great Tree and alchemical medi-
    ation. The first phase of alchemical meditation:  concentra-
    tion. Saturn, its image and symbol. The Moon. Exercise:
    moving an image. Mars. Exercise:  exact sense perception.

The Sun. Exercise: sacred sleep. Venus. Exercise: breathing images. Jupiter. Mercury. The method of analogy. Meditation and homeopathy.

13. Preparation for Meditation                                   233
Alchemical separation and marriage. The analog of the atmosphere. Putting fire below earth. Alchemy and the inner training of Rudolf Steiner. Exact sense perception of the plant. The purification of images. Loosening the salt body.

14. Contemplation                                                245
Living outside the body. Rudolf Steiner's protection exercises. Being awake where we normally sleep. The analog of the capacitor. The two spinal cords. The transformation of materialistic thinking into imaginative cognition.

15. The New Yoga                                                 255
Schooling ourselves to be awake where we are normally asleep. Rudolf Steiner's six basic exercises and their protections. The concentration exercise. The will exercise. Using exact sense perception to nourish the chakras.

16. The Alchemy of Goethe's Fairy Tale                           265
The transformation of metals and of the soul. Mercury. The four kings. The Rosicrucian image of the snake and the skull. The Logos. Cosmic nutrition. The mission of the Archangel Michael.

17. Seeing the Double                                            277
Possible dangers of the path. The challenge of the adept. Forming the stone. Multiplication and projection. Demeter and Persephone and two phases of the life force. The battery as an image of Bios. Technology and sub-nature. Organ clairvoyance. The double. Warmth as the vehicle of the True Self in contrast to the space around the organs. Thinking backwards and inner silence.

Bibliography                                                    307

# FOREWORD

A good book is very much like a person. You have to establish a relationship with it, be open to what it reveals of itself, be willing to enter into its complexity, honor its inner life, have a sense of its inexhaustibility, and gradually develop an intimate friendship that lasts for years. An introduction to a book, I believe, ought to be much like introducing a person, making a space, an opening, a clearing that makes the meeting between reader and book a joyful experience. A very large clearing is needed for this book you hold in your hands, for this little volume, if you are willing to take it up and work with it, will change your life, as much perhaps as the most significant person you have ever met did. While most books these days qualify only as commodities, this one, if you wish, can become a lifetime friend—a very wise friend.

If a book is at all like a person, then you ought to be prepared in this text to encounter a very complex individual, but one that hides nothing from you, one that shows you from page one what you are in for, and one that demands the engagement of your deepest and highest capacities. *Seeking Spirit Vision* begins by telling us that it is a work concerned with our soul life and how to develop the capacities of soul in a balanced way, in conjunction with the particular phenomena of the sensory world of nature. As this development takes place, the soul becomes more and more able to reach toward a knowing participation with the spiritual worlds.

While the background and approach of this text are those of Anthroposophy, Dennis Klocek gives an entirely new and fresh approach to this endeavor. He thinks anthroposophically, rather than following what has already developed in Anthroposophy and simply adding an insight here and there. Further, current writers in Anthroposophy do not, I have to say, typically work out of the realm of the soul toward spirit with any kind of careful attention to the qualities of soul. This author does; he moves from soul toward spirit rather than jumping from soul into spirit. This care makes his anthroposophical work unique, work that answers the very real need in our time to hold together the depths of the soul with the heights of the spirit. Because such care is taken to give soul its proper attention, you will find that working through the intricacies of this book, taking it slowly, which is to say soulfully, results in a healing as well as a strengthening of your soul forces.

## ANTHROPOSOPHY AS JAZZ

The meditative nature of this book can be characterized as one in which ideas are fully united with the actuality of phenomena in the world. Klocek is a most astute Goethean phenomenologist. In this tradition of scientific observation, one does not make hypotheses and then devise experiments to support these conjectures. Through a discipline of inner training of the soul, the researcher becomes capable of observing and describing the archetypal ideas forming the natural phenomena under observation. Indeed, this book can be read as a kind of instruction manual on how to become this kind of participating observer of the natural world, and, more deeply, of the intimacy of the natural world with the creative forces of the spiritual world, and of the intimacy of both with the human soul.

The kind of observational thinking involved here is what Klocek rightly calls improvisation. In this creative mode of observation and thinking, one has to learn how to step across the boundary of ordinary thought and perception which rests secure in moving toward the future based only and completely on what is already known, and thus cannot discover anything truly new. Our ordinary thought and perception, and even the enhancement of them by the methods of natural science, can give us only innovative variations of what is already known. Improvising means willing thinking into being, creating thinking rather than just using thoughts. If you really take up and work with this book, you will go a long way toward being able to engage in this mode of active thinking, which is absolutely necessary to be present to the ongoing creative forces of the natural world.

A word needs to be said about the structure of this volume because it seems to me that its structure reflects the act of cognitive improvisation. The book takes the form of a series of essays. Sometimes you will find things said in an early essay elaborated upon in a later one. But, as in musical improvisation, when you come across such an elaboration, it is more in the nature of a creative variation than a repetition. After a number of these variations you not only know more clearly what is being developed, but you also find that this knowing has a deep feeling component. For example, anthroposophists often speak of the sentient soul, the intellectual soul, and the consciousness soul. Klocek not only introduces these terms but carefully uncovers the relationships among these modes of soul life. He provides examples of how one's development can be sidetracked with each mode, shows how movement from one mode to another takes place, and presents numerous pictures of how these modes actually function in many different realms, from everyday meetings with people to quantum physics.

A great deal can be learned from this book, then, not only from what is said, but from how it is said. Much more goes on in this series of essays than one might expect from a compilation of thoughts which have been brought together in a single volume. A major aspect of the delight and wonder of reading this book derives from finding what was said earlier approached in a new way later, which amplifies, changes, deepens, and clarifies earlier resonance. Perhaps only a jazz musician could match the improvisational ability shown in this writing. To improvise in this fashion, one must know a great deal, and then give up what is known and step out into the unknown, discovering what is there rather than imposing knowledge based upon previous information.

Improvisation must be clearly distinguished from innovation. The former requires objective perception while the latter rests content taking imagination in tow and using it to create a simulated world, a double of the fullness of creation. As a way of demonstrating the difference between these two widely divergent ways of taking up imagination, Klocek takes us on a wonderful excursion into the realms of the relationships among art, shamanism, technology, and consumerism. There is no doubt that innovation now rules in the world, that consumerism has won out, and that the moments of possibility for developing toward a spirit culture, characterized by what might be called objective improvisation, requires deliberate and focused meditative practices. The remarkable contribution Klocek makes, taking us toward the realization of a true alternative to ultimately destructive innovation, centers on techniques of image-based meditation practices. What makes these techniques of extreme value is that they seek to unite inner image with outer world, a meditational way that must be accompanied with proper development of cognition.

The balance between image and cognition also forms part of the improvisational structure of this volume. Essays concerned with showing how soul life develops are interspersed with essays focused on matters such as art, myth, alchemy, brain physiology, and even Goethe's *Fairy Tale of the Green Snake and the Beautiful Lily.* The interweaving of such diverse topics is masterfully executed so that the essays are all of one piece, as if to form a unity of science, art, and religion. For example, the essay on the Black Madonna and Dionysos develops an elaborate but meaningful analogy between this mythic theme and artistic and scientific creation. Thus, through entering into the mythic imagination, what in some essays is developed in a manner that satisfies the intellect, in others is found stated in language that the soul understands—image, story, tale.

## WORLD IMAGINATION AND
## ALCHEMICAL TRANSFORMATION

While this writing is rich in imagery, images here never stand alone, but are always woven together with concepts. Soul images, by themselves, can no longer be valid guides, either to the life of the soul or to the qualities of the world. Klocek astutely develops an exploration of the spiritual being of the Sophia, or the Soul of the World, showing that through the evolution of intellect, her presence in the objective realm of Imagination became obscured and distorted. Thus, today imagination is thought of as being an inner activity of the individual soul and virtually no one considers that imagination could be present in the phenomena of nature. Further, once this obscuring of the full nature of imagination occurred, what we speak of now as imagination as an inner activity, while it may be filled with fascinating material, is considered a hindrance to coming to valid knowledge.

The kind of soul development Klocek guides us toward concerns finding a new way to bridge inner and outer imagination or, said in another way, it concerns how the individual soul can again approach Sophia, the Imagination who creates the inner form of all things. This soul development requires going through the discipline of cognitive meditative practices. Such practices, some of which are gone into in great detail in the book, gradually reduce the illusion that knowing is centered in the capacities of intellectual abstraction; instead, they consciously bring cognition into the act of perception, uniting the inner and outer worlds. These practices actively involve the soul in the act of sensing the world and make a connection with World Imagination possible.

Another significant theme intimately related to coming to World Imagination concerns alchemy and the alchemical imagination. I dare say, Dennis Klocek may be one of a very few living human beings who understand the mysteries that lie behind the strange and peculiar emblems, formulas, and writings of the alchemical tradition. I do not intend to embarrass our author by such an exclamation, so let me qualify it a bit. Certainly, there are many scholars who understand something about what alchemy was. There are also many individuals who have become interested in alchemy as a result of the work of C.G. Jung, who, while he resurrected interest in this tradition, did so in a rather one-sided manner. Jung incorrectly felt that alchemy had nothing to do with the outer world and presented the view that the imagery of alchemy came wholly from the inner soul life of the alchemists, who projected their own soul images back into the world. Then, a third group currently tries to penetrate the mysteries of alchemy by attempting to engage in its practices as they were done in earlier times. The approach to alchemy taken in this writing does not correspond to that of any of these groups.

In contrast to these approaches, Klocek's ground in Anthroposophy on the one hand, and in Goethean science on the other, makes it possible for him not just to know about alchemy, nor to try to repeat the past, nor to psychologize it, but rather to see, not *what* the alchemists saw, but *as* the alchemists saw. In other words, alchemy must be updated, seen through the eyes of the consciousness soul. Then, much of what alchemy was getting at can be retrieved, but in forms suitable for present circumstances. Klocek carries out this project in a truly astounding manner. He does so not just as someone curious about this tradition, but as someone who finds it to be central to the project of developing meditative, cognitive, perceptual soul consciousness of the natural world.

In one of the essays toward the end of the book, some specific connections are made between alchemy and the thinking of Rudolf Steiner. Also, in the essay on *The Fairy Tale of the Green Snake and the Beautiful Lily*, the fact that Goethe had a very deep understanding of alchemy and that this tale can be read alchemically is firmly established. However, in the past, alchemy worked with substances from the physical world and put these substances through operations. These operations brought about transformations of the substances, and also, due to the perceptual abilities needed to correctly execute these operations, transformations of the soul life of the alchemist. The substance to be worked on now is our own body, soul, and spirit. Goethe understood this needed shift of focus, and so does the author of this present volume. And while it may seem that Jung made a similar shift, he did not go far enough, for he saw alchemical imagery as involving only the soul/spirit and not the body.

The series of essays presenting meditation practices based on the emblem of the "Great Tree" in the alchemical tradition may well be the heart of this book. Here the actual practice of developing the kind of soul-spirit consciousness able to know and perceive the natural world as an ongoing act of creative Imagination is developed. The processes of developing capacities for creating and stabilizing inner images, coming to experience image activity rather than a pictorial content, and of making the soul receptive to creative currents of the spiritual worlds are all carefully described.

At the point at which receptivity to spiritual currents opens up, a most important meditative work is required—giving back whatever was received from the spiritual worlds. The strong temptation at this point of soul and spirit development is to take what is received and use it either for one's own purposes or to develop something of scientific or technical use. If this opening is utilized in this manner, ultimately destructive results follow. Giving back what is received prepares the possibility of developing intuition, a participation with creative spirit beings.

While you may recognize this meditative orientation as belonging to the anthroposophical path of spiritual development, it might be better described as a creative variation which provides several benefits. We gain a certain appreciation of what the alchemists were doing. Nonetheless, as you will see, it is not going back to what they were doing, as they were doing it. Because alchemy was concerned with the Soul of the World, this approach to meditative practice also keeps this intent close to the heart. Further, rather than simply going from one stage of soul and spirit development to the next, the precise relationship between one stage and the next becomes clarified, a continuity of states established. Klocek additionally elaborates a number of exceedingly useful analogies that help meditative practitioners not only to understand but also to have clear images of what they are doing. The alchemical conditions of salt, sulfur, and mercury are described as particular states of soul and spirit, of cognition, willing, and feeling. The earlier stages of meditative practice are pictured using chemical analogies, the mid-stages using the analogy of a capacitor, and the later stages are compared to the preparation of homeopathic remedies. The details of the alchemical emblem of the "Great Tree" itself serve as a pictorial geography of the worlds of meditation. All these analogies help to assure that the life of the soul is not abandoned as one develops toward the spiritual worlds.

The traditions Klocek draws upon and derives helpful analogies from are streams not addressed by most anthroposophists except in rather disparaging ways. At the same time, these traditions are of great interest to people seeking spiritual experiences these days. Does not Anthroposophy need to do more than to warn of the dangers of atavism involved in the practice of these traditions? Not only alchemy, but also shamanism, Native American spiritual practices, and dowsing, are given serious consideration in this book. Exactly what these traditions are about, seen from the point of view of someone who has evidently meditated long and deeply on them, brings us entirely new insights compared to those currently provided by the popular literature on this topics.

The service to seekers of spirit vision in the modern world provided by the honorable way these traditions are worked with in this writing is immeasurable. These spiritual traditions honor the Earth as well as the Cosmos, and what they potentially have to offer, what they can bring to Anthroposophy, is really enormous. At the same time, as Klocek so clearly understands, these traditions cannot be taken up now as they were once practiced. He clearly points out exactly why these traditions can cause difficulties if practiced exactly as they were in the past. He is not, however, satisfied with labeling them "atavistic" and therefore dangerous. Rather, he shows that these practices contain deep wisdom concerning the instinctive body, but now this wisdom must take into account the element of cognition.

## IMAGINATION'S PHYSIOLOGY
A number of the essays take us into another rather unusual domain for a work concerned with soul and spiritual development—the anatomy and physiology of the brain and nervous system. Klocek presents many details concerning brain function during meditative states, as well as descriptions of how certain functions change as a result of meditative practices. These essays need to be approached with a high degree of acumen.

The introduction of these apparently physical concerns does not in any way indicate that soul and spiritual processes are being reduced to brain states.  Nor do I think that the implication can be drawn that spiritual currents cause certain changes in brain states, or vice versa, at least not if causality is here understood in the usual way that scientists understand it.  Science restricts the notion of causality almost exclusively to that of  efficient causality, one material force affecting another material force, with both forces existing on the same plane.  If the essays on physiology and neural anatomy are read from this perspective, that of material science, they would result in serious misunderstanding.

When a Goethean phenomenologist observes the physical world of nature, we would certainly never understand these observations, which engage in soul/spiritual perception, as reducing the spiritual world to physical processes.  In fact, what happens in such observations is just the reverse; the spiritual activity forming, not causing, physical appearances is elaborated.  The careful and detailed matters concerning brain structure and functioning presented in this work have to be seen from this point of view.  I believe this point is absolutely crucial and when one is reading this material it must be kept clearly in mind.  The intricacies of brain anatomy and function can make us feel a little bit as though we are reading portions of *Gray's Anatomy.*  It is thus easy to fall back into a materialistic attitude, and that must be resisted, for the writing does not take that stance.

If the observations concerning the brain are followed through very closely, not only do we become filled with wonder concerning the wisdom of the body, we also learn a great deal about why remaining with the instinctual body in various methods of esoteric practice can be harmful.  We also learn that we could not reach for the higher realms if our body did not incorporate such a possibility in its structure and function.  For example, the essay on dowsing and divining goes into a detailed description of the  functioning of the pituitary gland in relation to these kinds of practices.  Our author gives a remarkable picture: "The pituitary gland and its surrounding tissues provide a picture of the wall between the upper world of the stars, the source of spiritual existence, and the lower world of the body, its metabolism, growth, and reproduction (p. 106)."  This gland has an upper, neurological function and a lower, metabolic function, with a thin layer of cells coated with melanin dividing the two portions of this gland. In a later essay, this image takes on even more significance as the story of Cain and Abel is imagined in relation to this gland. If we take this picture of the pituitary gland into meditation, we become acutely aware that the dividing line between spiritual work oriented toward the spiritual beings of the cosmos and the instinctual body, where we can become caught by various elemental earth beings, is gossamer.

The discussion concerning dowsing is important because it is connected not only with a whole field of alternative medical treatment, radionics, but also because the bodily processes involved in dowsing are also integral to other forms of spiritual healing, and even implicated in the process of meditation. The importance of being able to distinguish subtle instinctual experiences from higher forms of spiritual experiences is crucial. We may be aware of the importance of these differences, but the knowledge comes home in quite a different way when understood from the point of view of the organ functions involved.

The other gland specifically related to visionary states is the pineal gland. Klocek explores this gland through a series of images, so that anatomy here becomes imagination, the imagination of the heart center of the brain. Thus, terminology utilized, for example, by anthroposophists, such as heart-thinking, may be a analogy that has substance. In this book it is an imagination that prompts a consideration of the relationship between the pineal gland and the heart.

Earlier on, I remarked that following through these observations concerning anatomy and visionary states might seem as though we had entered into a medical textbook. A way in which you can know if you are reading this book as intended is by paying very close, ongoing attention to the activity of thinking that runs through this text. We do not have here a presentation of facts, flat and dead, but rather one thought-form flowing organically into another. The images employed in relation to bodily organs and functions are thus more than suggestive; they are more like inner pictures of the outer form of particular organs. Further, while at one moment we may be in the brain, the next in the heart, and the next in the midst of an image taken from Jacob Boehme, these movements are quite organic; they also can help us toward the development of a flexibility of soul that ranges between the physical and the spiritual, refusing all hard-lined divisions that bespeak one kind of dualism or another. Perhaps the height of this flexibility is demonstrated in the essay concerned with a reading of the story of Cain and Abel in connection with the pituitary gland, where we can see that an anatomical analogy of this story continues to live on within the body.

If the kind of thinking demonstrated here seems unusual, it is for the modern world, where knowledge has been cut up and divided, the pieces parceled out to various specialists. If we happened to be interested in spiritual matters, then we have certainly come across the bit of knowledge that indicates the esoteric doctrine of correspondences. We have also perhaps been intrigued with the exotic character of the saying: "As above, so below." Here, in this writing, we see actual demonstrations of these laws in operation, something that has seldom come to the light of day since the time of Paracelsus.

A reader who is a student of Anthroposophy and someone who engages in the kinds of meditation practices suggested by Steiner may well be somewhat disoriented by the emphasis placed on the body in this work. One of the essays specifically addresses this question, for Rudolf Steiner spoke both of exercises to learn to live consciously outside the body and exercises concentrating on currents within the body. This essay is nothing short of a masterpiece of investigative work into the writing of Steiner and some of his students which aids us in seeing that methods leading to out-of-body cognition and methods leading into body currents have to be held in a paradoxical tension. More importantly, until you come to this essay, the material on physiology may leave you somewhat puzzled. Are we being presented with speculation, or with the results of a great deal of inner meditative work? This question you will find answered. Incidentally, the quotation from Rudolf Steiner on pages 274–5 should be read and studied very thoroughly. You will, I think, find it quite astounding, and I suspect it also reveals something of the meditative technique of our author.

At the very end of the essay concerning in-body and out-of-body meditation practices, a comment is made that warrants a good deal of pondering: "It is hoped that these contributions are seen as a modest beginning for the destiny of Anthroposophy in America, which has as its task the transformation of materialistic thinking into imaginative cognition." All during my reading and studying of this book, the impression kept coming that indeed what we have here is a particularly American approach to Anthroposophy. Here in America, where people are so concerned with the body, with science, with electronic technology, with consummerism, and with practicality and efficiency, spiritual work must take these things into account and not simply try to turn away from them.  Klocek approaches these concerns, by first taking quite seriously what they have to offer, seeing the imagination that forms them, and then lifting those imaginations to the spiritual realm.

The great and marvelous complexity of this book can perhaps result in the reader's losing sight, from time to time, that this work, through and through, is a text of practices.  The specific essays concerned with technique are at the center of the book.  Work with these mediations can, I am convinced, lead to capacities of sustained concentration on and receptivity to the spiritual worlds.  The essays surrounding those concerned with meditation *per se* are themselves meditations, which if worked with will strengthen the practices themselves.  Very little speculation exists in this work.  The reader, however, is not invited to take up these practices unquestioningly.  To do so would be opposed to the whole tenor of what has here been so carefully developed.  Rather, we are shown new ways of doing spiritual scientific research, grounded in Anthroposophy, capable of restoring both our imagination and World Imagination.

Robert Sardello, Ph.D.
The School of Spiritual Psychology

# 1

# IMAGINATION:
# CREATIVITY OR INNOVATION?

I f we were to approach a professional scientist and challenge the experimental method, calling it a flawed premise for good science, we would certainly meet a vigorous and well-founded protest. In the realm of pragmatic physical science, the experimental method—that is, the strategy of finding a hypothesis and then setting about proving or disproving it on the basis of experiment—is effective for guiding research, and scientists are quick to defend it. However, if we challenge this well-established cornerstone of scientific work on the basis of its creative potential, it soon becomes obvious that even the creative researcher has no real insight into the *pre*-hypothesis mindset and that most scientific research focuses on *post*-hypothesis methodologies. In other words, how a researcher forms the initial hypothesis is of less interest than the subsequent experimental strategy which the hypothesis sets in motion. The sources of scientific hypotheses have ranged from happy accidents to eccentric methods such as hot baths, high-speed driving, and kite flying, to arcane inspirers such as ouija boards and UFO's. Faced with such diverse sources of inspiration, it may be advantageous to start by characterizing the differences between creative thinking and personal fantasy.

Creative thinking eludes the grasp of an intellectually fixed, abstract mindset, yet it is a definite type of thinking or cognitive state. One fundamental difference between creative thinking and fantasy is that while creative thinking is capable of improvisation, fantasy is a form of cognitive stagnation, for there is an obsessive element in personal fantasy which does not leave us free to pursue concepts in a fluid, creative manner. Goethe called attention to the difference between the fixed nature of personal fantasy and the fluid quality of creative thinking by making a distinction between *concept* and *Idea*.

The formation of concepts is primarily the function of the intellect. But in the activity of forming a concept, the intellect is called upon to touch a higher cognitive state in which the archetypal laws or Ideas at work behind each phenomenon are engaged by the thinking consciousness. Here reside the laws of nature, the energy patterns that guide and form the physical manifestations of the observable world. A scientist working to understand the behavior of matter in various conditions must be able to touch these archetypal realms of living Ideas with willed thought.

In modern science, a hypothesis must undergo a stern testing by the intellect which has learned not to unite the phenomenon and the concept subjectively. The degree of detachment present in the intellect is considered a fair measure of the objectivity of the researcher. Complete objectivity is assumed to be attained when sympathy or subjective identification with the phenomenon is held in complete abeyance. This state is known as *onlooker consciousness*. Science regards subjectivity and sympathy as suspect, as leading to a kind of tinkering and an adjustment of the experimental data in order to fit the pre-formed conclusions of the researcher. Therefore, experiments are to be conducted using the onlooker consciousness, for the analytical force of antipathy is considered the only viable tool in the pursuit of objectivity.

In the human soul, however, there are two polar states which must be in harmony to attain a true, balanced objectivity. One pole, according to Rudolf Steiner, is the will, and the other is thinking. For a person in whom the soul forces of sympathy and antipathy complement each other, research can become truly objective, and this occurs only when the sympathy in the will unites with the antipathy in the thinking to produce thinking in concepts. If this inner balance has been successful, then the scientific work rises to a higher stage wherein the soul, through the power of transcendence which links antipathy with sympathy, begins to induce universal concepts (Goethe's archetypal Ideas). These newly induced concepts can then be tested by other researchers who duplicate the experiment. Such testing puts the results back into the intellectual realm, thereby requiring the essences and primal laws that govern earthly phenomena to be revealed. This revelation is the true goal of scientific work. Having risen above simple likes (sympathies) and dislikes (antipathies), the thinking begins to see the world as it is, unencumbered by personal fantasies and prejudice.

There is an inherent danger, however, in the pursuit of higher states of thinking. This danger centers around the relationship between human will and Divine Will. In prehistoric times the human capacity for thought was embedded in the universal currents of will. Human will and Divine Will flowed in the same stream of consciousness, in a state which can be called intuitive thinking. Human consciousness was at one with divine consciousness. After the temptation in Paradise and the subsequent fall into matter and individuality, however, human consciousness felt the separation of its forces from the forces of the Godhead. In order for individual selfhood to arise, it became necessary for human currents of will to flow counter to the original will currents of the Creator and to focus upon the self. Thus, during Vedic, Persian, and Egyptian times, there was a gradual transformation in the human soul from a God-centered consciousness to an Earth-centered consciousness.

The present human consciousness is now like a swirling vortex of selfhood in a great stream. The vortex sustains itself through resistance to the prevailing motion of the whole, and the flow of Divine Will is reversed within it. In a vortex two currents meet again, having arisen by being separated by an obstruction or a resistance. In the vortex of selfhood the resistance to the flow of will from the future separates out the field of activity of the separate intellect with its resistant forces of antipathy.

The resistant antipathetic thinking forces bring a perception of the past history of the self-aware organism into direct conflict with the unfolding forces of the future. Through antipathy we can remember the history of our being. Through memory we posit the Ego or True Self. Such personal memories as we find in thinking resist the cosmic memory found in the Divine Will flowing to us from the future. The vortex of selfhood arises through antipathy, which is the foundation of thinking in the intellect. Thinking in the intellect is the force in the soul which leads to human freedom, and the human being develops intellect by personally willing the thinking. Through willed thinking, the human being can create a new future out of past failures. The tension between the forward- and backward-moving currents of Divine Will and willed thinking gives rise to the vortex of the self, an image of human consciousness, which maintains its integrity against the general flow of the great stream of Divine Will.

The consciousness which results from the dynamic balancing of will currents is capable of uniting past and future, above and below, in a rhythmical, breathing interplay. Even though it is divorced from Divine Will, the center of the vortex of self-consciousness is oriented toward the motion of the larger current, even out into its periphery. The human consciousness through states of intuition can unite itself to those peripherally located powers and reflect the broadest, most cosmic aspects of reality.

Surrounding a vortex in nature are currents which continually pulse up and down around its vertical axis. These pulsing currents are analogs for the integrating forces of inspiration which periodically connect the higher self with the lower self. The great seer Jacob Boehme pictured these selves imaginatively as two eyes, one higher and one lower. Each sees into its own world, and the task of the seer is to unite the two in a single vision. Just as in nature a vortex in a stream reunites two currents which had originally been together, part of a larger flow, so the human soul arises from a primal flow of will. In the soul, past and future streams are mingled. In Boehme's image one eye looks down to the earth and the other looks up to the cosmos. On earth the soul has a past, in the cosmos it has a future. The seer must unite past and future into a true perception of the now.

Through the vortex of selfhood the soul draws the mysteries of the cosmos and the data bits of the created world to itself. The experimental method employed by modern scientific research is designed to arrange seemingly random bits of world flotsam into manageable units. The intellect, by virtue of its power of willed thought, partakes of the future-oriented, cosmic will current in the soul, pulling into focus concepts which flow toward it from the future into the field of consciousness. When the intellect serves its primary cosmic function, it does just this and nothing more. It intuits cosmic concepts, arranges them, and then passes them back into the future where they go out of the field of human consciousness and into the hands of the Godhead. A problem develops, however, when a human consciousness infused with the temptation of its own self-will draws personally conceived conclusions out of the arranged concepts held in its vortex. The value that the I then places on the concepts in its field of consciousness rises out of the sympathy of the will force in the self-willed thinking. Concepts formed by this consciousness are then transformed from living, future-oriented units of meaning into dead, past-oriented objects of cognition. Cognizing slips from the future into the past, and the interest of the consciousness becomes fixed on its dimly reflected memories. The vortex of consciousness may pull so many concepts into its field and may hold them so tightly that its movement is impeded. It changes from a dynamic, vertically breathing vortex into a sluggish, debris-ridden eddy, a stagnating backwater isolated from the main evolutionary flow of divine consciousness. In scientific terms, the hypothesis has already been filled by the intellect with conceptual detritus.

The modern intellect, using the experimental method and enamored of its own conclusive power, reaches into its storehouse of facts and constructs a new arrangement pregnant with experimental possibilities. This process itself has elements of states of Inspiration, but most often the intellect has simply arranged pre-cognized concepts innovatively into a new order. The error of the intellect lies in the formation of conclusions which are only provable to empirical experiment. For in the formation of an experiment based on its own conclusion, the intellect has overstepped its primal function. It is in this context that Goethe made his distinction between *intellect* and *reason*.

The intellect can only order and analyze the data. It cannot really draw conclusions, and only through reason can the mind approach Ideas. These sublime Ideas of the Godhead may be pictured as concepts of concepts, or constellations of cognitive feelings. The intellect simply cognizes the concepts in its field while reason cognizes the whole field and its field of relationships. The original hypothesis that constellates within the mind of a thinker is actually the inspired door to an entire nexus of concepts that constitute the Idea. To immediately employ the intellect to form a train of experiments closes the door on the forward-moving orientation of the thought life and banishes it into the backward-moving currents of the individual's resisting self-will.

Any scientific thinker who vigorously observes his or her own cognitive states can see that the mystery and magic of the "aha!" moment of the formation or birth of the hypothesis immediately dims into a kind of post-partum blues. Where is the delicious joy of discovery, the sense of working in harmony with the Godhead? And what of the disappointment when the experimental data further tarnish the initial shining insight? Do we resort to curve-ironing and other devious intellectual ploys in order to keep the mind engaged, or is there another strategy that can be employed in pursuing Ideas?

Creative inspirational thinking springs out of the practice of the essence of mathematics. The inner experience of the orderly mathematical unfolding of a phenomenon helps to ground the consciousness and enlarges the capacity to receive creative Inspirations. Through this grounding, the mind is able to lift its focus of activity into the realm where the consciousness of the Godhead creates the laws of the world. However, after an intense effort of concentration aimed at ordering the phenomena, the mind must then relax. Relaxation allows the mind to rise into the realm of Inspiration where it can listen to the super-conscious melodies that lie behind the world's manifestations. At this point the intellect gives way to reason. The intellect can actually only work in the ordering of the concepts. It dwindles before the perceptions of the living Ideas that are the source of concepts, for the light from the source is much brighter than the small lantern of the intellect. The cognitive mode must shift from intellectual forming or speaking into reasoned listening.

The mind trained by logical mathematical principles must now recognize not the computative aspects of mathematics, but the spiritual, creative aspects emerging out of mathematical ordering. Instead of speaking about all that it has gathered, the mind must be silent and listen to the real message which is hidden, occulted in the concepts coming toward it from higher realms. Modern science here makes an error from the viewpoint of spiritual science. The new hypothesis given to a thinker is but the tip of an iceberg of constellated living Ideas. Immediately attaching the insight gained by the hypothesis to an experimental procedure forces the mind to enter into a speaking mode. The experience of the numinous character of mathematics becomes muddied in the computational speaking mode of the experiment. The results of such experiments are simply dim reflections of the sublime mysteries of higher cognitive realms. The mind, like a vortex, becomes clogged with the factual flotsam produced by the experiment and is thereafter encumbered in its ability to rise into Inspiration. It becomes enmeshed in the facts swirling around the phenomenon, while the phenomenon itself and its creative genesis become obscured by the hypothetical construct formed as a model for the experiment. The essential sacredness of number is abstracted into fixed mathematical laws that appeal to the intellect but leave the cognizing heart in hunger. The hypothesis then becomes a prison and actually works to isolate the mind from its source of Inspiration. To be more exact, it is the formation of the abstract hypothetical model that acts in this obscuring way; the initial experience of the hypothesis still remains numinous.

The implementation of an experimental procedure establishes an artificial system of logical relationships (e.g., atoms and molecules) that reflect higher laws. The intellect grasps these metaphysical constructs and can easily juggle abstract signs into new hypothetical configurations. These abstractions may be capable of predicting the behavior of chemical compounds, the velocity of moving objects, and other physical phenomena, but they impoverish the soul by denying it any relationship to the outer world other than through dimly reflected abstract signs. This alienation feeds the self-directed impulses of the lower soul and sows seeds for a technical arrogance within the thought life. Most of modern science stands at the verge of this chilling wasteland. By contrast, the soul-warming inspirative force of the initial hypothesis can be experienced as a living proof that God exists and is communicative. When this intimate, warm connection to the creative Godhead is traded for a mechanical, abstract chain of technical events, the vortex of selfhood separates further from the creative streaming currents that are the source of its continued existence.

This is not meant to imply that all hypothetical construction and experimentation can or should be done away with. On the contrary, experimentation can be a supremely enriching and empowering activity. The danger lies not in the experiments, but in the drawing of intellectual, logical conclusions from them. A more wholesome technique would be to regard the first hypothetical insight as simply one aspect of the solution. When experiments then arise as possibilities, the creative researcher can perform them in order to direct the mind toward the realm of Inspiration. This can be accomplished by converting quantities into qualities, or by focusing on secondary qualities such as color, taste, and warmth, which lead the imagination toward images or pictures of the unfolding phenomenon. Through exact images, the phenomenon can be explored as something directly connected to the soul life. Converting data into images through developing the exact imaginative forces of the mind moves the thought life from the coldness of abstract analysis into the warmth of the creative Idea. Intellect is then transformed into reason, concepts are brought into contact with their source of life and change, and the hypothesis regains its aura of numinous mystery. By transforming hard data into exact images, a mind which can connect the upper, transcendent eye with the lower, physical eye becomes able to breathe.

The questions remain of how to establish such a breathing and what the practical results would be. To a seer, the realm of

Imagination is limitless and chaotic. While the apparently random side of imaginative experience can often be observed in the dream state, there is, however, an inner consistency, even in chaotic dreams, that rests in the soul's ability to collate images and invest them with meaning. The natural world is filled with such meaningful images that can serve to regulate and inspire the consciousness. The power invested by nature in the creation of living forms can be put into service in the training of cognitive perception, the root of exact imagination. In cognitive perception we train ourselves to see exactly. This transforms into the capacity to know what we, as seers, can experience in the chaos of the imaginative world. Through this we transform imaginative experience into Imagination. This technique is accomplished by carefully observing a phenomenon and then exactly representing it as a moving image before the inner eye. Through the patterns of formative force that regulate the phenomenon the creative movements which lie behind the genesis of the phenomenon are impressed upon the consciousness of the practitioner at a level above the intellect. Through a technique of repeated exact observation, the essence of the phenomenon gradually coalesces into an Imagination that can be grasped by the self as a living creative picture. This living picture is filled with higher insight about the phenomenon because it is actually formed in the human consciousness *by* the phenomenon. It is thus not an imaginative metaphysical construct but a living Idea or Imagination which can continue growing and constellating in the higher consciousness. By contrast, the abstract concept, no matter how innovative, is held fixed by the intellect. Innovation is the clever permutation of facts which are already known. Creativity is a new synthesis which results in original or unknown ideas.

A scientific hypothesis born from the discipline of a researcher who inwardly visualizes the variables surrounding a phenomenon is often such a creative living Idea. It becomes spiritually obscured only when it is imprisoned within a quantitative or simply innovative technical procedure. What if the researcher were to design experiments and tools which strived to keep the hypothesis open? This may be difficult in the physical sciences of chemistry and physics, or in engineering, but it is quite possible in the life sciences and the social sciences. The open hypothesis is now in fact an accepted method in ecological studies, peer counseling, management training, new age medicines, and many other fields of research. Perhaps the time has come when Goethean techniques of phenomenological observation can be brought closer to the mainstream of science.

With these techniques it is possible for the intellectually closed vortex of the human consciousness to sense how its center is connected to the grand spiral motions of the cosmos and how its small confluence is an exact image of the grand workings of the universal mind. For each small vortex and eddy in a stream sings the song of the whole stream; each is growing and contracting, pulsating to the rhythms of the whole nexus of currents in each brook, creek, stream, river, and sea on the face of the planet. And the waters are sensing the swinging motions of the moon and sun and planets, which in turn are images of the great swirling dance of the universe. All of this knowledge and more is accessible to a mind whose vortex of self can remain open and responsive to the creative images continually brought into being by the dance of the Father.

# 2

# HYPOTHESIS, APOCALYPSE, APOTHEOSIS

If a person were to observe his or her inner life for a single day, the polar forces of sympathy and antipathy would be seen to stand behind the vast flow of feeling and thought within the soul. In order to illustrate the effect of these polarities, consider a situation in which a well-dressed, attractive person suddenly approaches you in the street and offers you fifty dollars. Most people would immediately assume an inner questioning attitude in an attempt to create some psychological distance between themselves and the stranger. They would begin to analyze and question the motives of the other. This scrutiny would most often be accompanied by vaguely sensed but definite feelings of mistrust or antipathy toward the other. In the antipathy there would be no hate, just a healthy scepticism until the intellect had analyzed the situation and observed the facts in the cool light of reason.

Consider the opposite situation. You are waiting in an airport. Your gaze is met by an attractive person. Destiny puts you into adjoining seats. During the journey the stranger unfolds a tale of woe that requires fifty dollars for its resolution. Something in you is touched by the other, and even though the person is a stranger, you find yourself completely sympathetic to the situation, resolving against all logic to be of service. All acts of will require such a basic soul mood of sympathy. In acts of revenge, passion, or fear, the sympathy is directed toward oneself, while in acts of altruism it is directed toward others.

Both antipathy and sympathy are hallmarks of the level of inner experience which Rudolf Steiner calls *sentient soul,* in which the individual experiences his inner life as surges of psychic force. The force of the polarization between antipathy and sympathy gives the sen-

11

tient soul proof of its own existence. This proof most often consists of the rich mental images of personal fantasy which are produced in the tensions that arise in the sentient soul between its strong likes and dislikes.

If the sentient soul favors antipathy as its primary mode of perception, then the soul life is in danger of being seized by rigid thought forms and fixed ideas. The mental images become hard in outline and fixed in their relationships. Each time the soul tries to use the power of the intellect to objectify facts and perceptions, the hardening force of the overbearing antipathy brings rejection, criticism, and rigidity into the inner life. By contrast, a sentient soul addicted to overbearing sympathy seeks activities which will cause sensational reactions in itself and in others. Co-dependency and enmeshed families are the results of an addiction to feelings of sympathy in the sentient soul. A soul in this state may radically change its thought content merely to experience the feelings engendered by the change. Such a shift of viewpoint would be inconceivable to those who entertain fixed ideas.

The mental images produced by imbalanced polarities in the sentient soul are far from being objective and are often sources of anxiety and confusion. It is necessary both to stabilize extreme fluctuations of sympathy with the force of antipathy, and to warm frozen, fixed ideas into dynamic motion by developing feelings of sympathy. When these two lower soul forces are woven into each other through concentration and a disciplined practice of art or science, then the polarities enhance one another, resulting in a higher soul faculty which Rudolf Steiner calls *transcendence*. Transcendence allows the soul to resonate with higher energies and to comprehend new levels of meaning in the world.

Once sympathy and antipathy are transcended, the lower soul forces are led away from identification with personal sympathies and antipathies into more universal concerns. Through using the intellect or mind in the forming of the mental image, the soul develops an objective ability to observe concepts. This new level of dynamic stability in the soul is known as *intellectual soul*. While the soul is seeking its objective existence in the limitless, universal realm of concept, concepts are simultaneously drawn toward individual existence through that soul's activity. This is the central characteristic of modern intellectual life and is a reflection of the higher self in human beings.

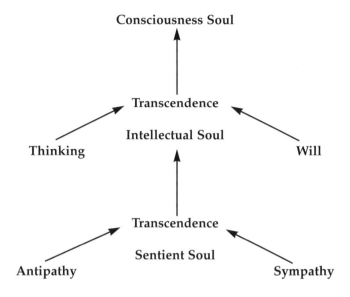

The ability of the intellectual soul to transcend personal sentiment transforms the chaotic perception of mental images in the sentient soul into the ordered perception of concepts.  Likewise, the antipathetic force is further transformed from the ability of the intellect to distinguish between the mental image and its corresponding physical manifestation, into the ability to discriminate between concepts.  The capacity in the sentient soul for discrimination and analysis is thus energized by rectified feelings of sympathy and emerges as a capacity for recognizing truth in the realm of concepts.  In a soul which has raised antipathy into factual, discursive analysis and which has lifted sympathy into a heightened pondering of the subtle differences among the things of the world, sympathy can be transformed into empathy.  While sympathy in the sentient soul has a subjective coloration, empathy in the mind soul is objective and universal, more focused, and freer from personal likes and preferences.  The *mind soul* can be thought of as the soul's experience of its own relationship to the eternal mind or the consciousness of the cosmos.  Thus, another term given by Rudolf Steiner for mind soul is *consciousness soul.  Heart soul* is yet a third descriptive term for this state of consciousness.  The consciousness of the human being comes into contact with the universal mind and from this contact has a change of heart.

The sympathetic and antipathetic forces still present in scientific abstraction and religious fundamentalism are transcended in the consciousness soul into spiritual forces of cosmic memory in which the human mind finds its root. This experience of transcendence engenders awe and humility in the heart, and feelings of cognitive knowing replace calculation and self-will. For a thinker with a developed intellectual soul, the laws of science or art become direct perceptions. Concepts reveal the paradox of the archetype in that they are always the same and yet they undergo continuous change. The concept of the triangle, for instance, is always the same in the requirement that there be three angles and three sides, yet the many types of triangles reveal the limitless, changing possibilities of the concept, for there can be right, scalene, obtuse, equilateral, and metamorphic triangles of infinite variety. The concept "triangle" is thus simultaneously fixed and fluid. This flowing paradoxical nature of living concepts is comprehended by the will force that exists in perception and guides the mind in distinguishing truth from error.

This capacity for the comprehension of truth is the force of Intuition, found to a greater or lesser degree at all levels of the soul. It is Intuition, for instance, which functions in the sentient soul as the capacity to distinguish between a mental image and its physical manifestation. A soul caught in the throes of passion for or against a cause is incapable of listening to the small, still voice of Intuition. Only when the lower soul currents are harmonized and clarified can the mental image be distinguished from the facts. Then, as the mental image is compared to the facts, the truth concerning the manifestation is gradually revealed to the Intuition, and the mental image is corrected in accordance with objective truth. This dynamic stabilization of the mental image produces an inner life which can participate in the objective existence of the world of concepts. The truth of modern science rests upon the soul's ability to objectify and correct its own images. This process is a kind of breathing, as the soul reaches out to find the proper objective concept to describe its inner experience.

The intellect is a tool for ordering the world. By distinguishing one concept from another, it aids the Intuition in the pursuit of truth. This grasping quality of intellect, however, is only one part of the cognitive process, for in order to experience Intuition, the ordered concepts formed and grasped by the intellect must then be released. A soul working toward understanding must develop and interweave capacities of both grasping and releasing in order to approach the next level of transcendence.

At this point it may be useful to distinguish between intuition and Intuition. Intuition (small i) is the force of transcendence in the soul which is always present as the capacity in the soul to transform an error into a correct cognition. This capacity is present as a primary force in the more undeveloped sentient soul states. It allows people of immoderate habits to correct the direction of their lives. It is also present in the sentient soul and intellectual soul as the hunches and intimations of what is commonly called intuition. As such it is a dim image of Intuition, different in degree but not in substance. In the developed soul the force of Intuition or transformation to the good or true becomes the dominant soul characteristic. For this essay, all mention of Intuition will refer to this latter form and not to intuitional hunches.

Modern technical science rests upon the cornerstone that through thinking, the mind can intuit the archetypal truths which stand behind every manifestation in the material natural world. The Intuition working through the intellectual soul comprehends the lawfulness of the manifest world, and the discursive powers of antipathy in the intellect then order and reveal the inmost essences of physical reality. Through discursive intellectual thinking, it is thus possible for the laws governing interactions on the physical plane to be rendered completely transparent to the thinker.

The ordering of phenomena by the intellect is not without its limitations. One pitfall is that the thinking becomes so immersed in juggling concepts that the actual phenomena cease to be perceived. This can be so extreme in modern science that, for instance, pharmacologists can devote years to studying the effects of a plant that they have never seen. When this happens, a subtle veil is drawn between the mind and the external world. Continued emphasis upon the formation of concepts disinclines the senses to be active in the world. Parallel metaphysical universes are constructed which reflect the behavior of ever smaller units of physical matter until at last the scientist becomes a metaphysician observing supersensible realities and recasting them in metaphors that suggest physical properties. Such concepts as atoms and molecules or Darwin's tree of descent describe supersensible connections that the intellect cannot clearly comprehend, and so it constructs convenient fables which can sometimes be proven physically but leave a great deal to be desired spiritually.

The tendency toward metaphysics is a product of the materialistic bias that was adopted in the sixteenth century with the rise of empirical science. In accordance with this materialistic bias many scientific discoveries which were originally experienced in supersensible worlds have been clothed in the noun-rich language of the physical world, but these same discoveries could also have been portrayed in the verb-rich language of the spirit. To illustrate the difference, let us look at Niels Bohr's conceptualization of the movement of an electron across the electron shells of an atom. According to this theory, when a material is heated, the heat radiating from the center of each atomic nucleus causes the innermost electrons to jump from their normal shells to the next outer shell. This pushes electrons from this shell outward to the next shell where they displace electrons which keep jumping out until a balance is reached. A reduction in heat causes the outermost electrons to return to their original positions by jumping back to the next inner shell. As the electrons jump back inward they give off the retained heat of excitation as emissions of visible light. Electrons are thus perceived as particles or particle waves which react mechanically to surges of heat raying outward from the nucleus through the electron shells. The physical, mechanical bias of physics requires physically jumping particles to explain the transmission of heat energy.

In esoteric traditions these same events would be perceived as the activities of beings. The esoteric view allows for the possibility of a morality to be at work in the seemingly amoral mechanics of the universe. Rudolf Steiner characterized a stage of Old Saturn evolution as the Thrones' sacrifice of their warmth substance in the center of Old

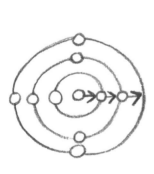

**Niels Bohr**                    **Rudolf Steiner**

Saturn. This love and warmth was rayed out to the periphery of the cosmos where it was perceived in the darkness of primal space by the Exusiai. The Exusiai received the sacrifice of the Thrones as an Inspiration for their own sacrifice, and they in turn rayed the love and warmth back through the blackness of space. As this current was reflected back to the Thrones through the gift of the Exusiai, the heat was transformed into light, and the space of the Universe was revealed. Is it coincidence that both Niels Bohr and Rudolf Steiner saw a strikingly similar Imagination? The physicist chose to clothe the vision in a metaphor taken from the physical world. The esotericist clothed the vision in the language of sacrifice and moral deeds. The perception of moral deeds of will behind the manifestations of the physical world is a further level of transcendence of the mind soul.

The power to form concepts in the mind soul springs out of the antipathy in the intellect, and it brings the mind against the limits of knowledge expressed in Kantian philosophy; living concepts lead the mind to a realm of thought in which the ordering of physical facts has no comparative experience. A kind of wall exists beyond which the lamp of the intellect is overshadowed by the powerful light of intelligence issuing from higher creative realms. Through rigorous mental work, many scientists are led to the wall of light where our knowing is overshadowed by a higher source of knowing. It is here that the intellect must humbly yield to transcendent cognition. Here we can trace the path of Intuition, present in the sentient soul as the ability to distinguish between mental images and physical reality. In the intellectual soul Intuition is transformed into the capacity to distinguish truth from error in the realm of concepts. In the mind soul Intuition becomes at last the force of transcendence which allows the thinker to be present and aware while thoughts are transformed into pure thoughtless thinking at the wall of light.

Usually the scientist working near the wall of light assembles facts into a hypothesis which is tested and proven or disproven upon the basis of experiment. The researcher often experiences the hypothesis as an idea received from beyond the wall of light, a spiritual realm beyond waking consciousness. We say, "The idea came to me." It might be reasonable to ask where it came *from*, but scientists and artists rarely wish to look a gift horse in the mouth. They rather take the hypothesis or insight that is given and then turn their backs on the wall of light in order to make a work of art or perform an experiment, and the inspired touch of a higher consciousness is lost in the working out of the insight in the world. In the researcher, this attitude eventually forms a subjective or possessive attitude toward one's "own" ideas. The gift of the insight is taken into the hypothesis and fixed into the proof of the experiment in hopes of patenting its concepts.

Goethe spoke of the intellect's ability to comprehend a concept and its inability to comprehend the Idea, the archetype or living concept that is the source of the being of each concept. It is at this juncture that the methods of spiritual science differ from the methods of empirical science. Through meditative efforts the spiritual scientist seeks to return the hypothesis back into the spiritual world by *forgetting* the concepts that built the hypothesis, thereby transforming the intellect into the capacity for reason. To transmute intellect into reason, intellect must be woven into the pole of sympathy by developing empathy for the creative being who permeates the forces and the forms in the manifest world. Without empathy for supersensible being, the world of concepts is a chilling abstraction filled with entropic, random forces. Abstract theorists expend tremendous energy mainly to gain an advantage over this system of forces. In an abstract world of computational forces the struggle for species domination becomes the central motif of existence, and the mind soul experiences alienation from the Godhead as the existential proof of its own primacy. The most logical course to take in such a situation is to turn away from the numbing force of the wall of light, deny any being beyond one's individual personality, and base human dignity upon property rights and the production of work units. The logic of this abstract utopia is compelling but denies the basic fact that even states of consciousness evolve for humanity as a whole out of states of being beyond our intellectual comprehension.

The experimental method, which leads the thinker up to the wall of light but no further, supports and fosters abstract systems of thought that depend upon memory and personal knowledge. The force of the personality is present in the subtly subjective choice of experiment once a hypothesis is experienced, and the experiment is designed to prove the validity of one line of reasoning as it is revealed by the experience of the hypothesis. By contrast, in supersensible perception each hypothesis is a gift of grace that is given by a being who stands behind the concepts which the intellect arranges. The intellect forms a vessel into which the archetypal being pours the wine of insight, and once the Inspiration has been received by the consciousness, the spiritual scientist works meditatively to return the insight back into the spiritual world. To conceive of an experiment at this time is the spiritual equivalent of drawing a conclusion before all of the data is collected in natural science.

From a supersensible point of view, there is a subjective bias in drawing a premature conclusion through the design of an experiment, a bias evident in the protective postures that many researchers adopt when defending a hypothesis. The investment of personal psychic energy in what should be an objective thought form is the basic symptom of the onset of apocalypse. The confusion between the higher individuality which is objective and the personality which invades the realm of thought, the mistaking of a personal disclosure for a prophecy, is a movement from objective psychic energies to personal psychic energies and is the hallmark of an apocalyptic age. The lure of abstraction is that the personality wishes to find a perfect system above any challenge, a system which is flawless and universal and undeniably the product of a unique individual whose logic is so deep and correct that the world must bend before it. This hubris is yet another sign of apocalypse, for in it we can see personal motives and a lust for power, the subjective rationales and desires of the thinkers who entertain them.

To escape the terror and alienation of apocalypse it is necessary to weave the rigor of abstract questioning into a moral questioning that involves the heart as well as the head. This is developed when in humility the human intellect addresses a higher being than itself. In meditative states the currents of the intellect are turned away from the construction of theories and into the reception of experiences. The mode of communication is transformed from speaking to listening. One uses shoes to walk to the wall but then leaves the shoes at the door to enter the house. The intellect becomes the witness. The witness observes intently but forms no conclusions, building images out of concepts but then forgetting both in order simply to be present coherently on the other side of the wall of light.

On the other side of the wall the witness feels the touch of the beings standing behind all creation, experiencing the Ruling Will which creates all forms. Through meditation, a certain *thixcipience,* a receptivity to spiritual touch, is developed in the intellectual soul. This receptivity transforms the abstractions of the intellect into questions of reason which can then approach numinous Idea experiences. The transcendence of the mind soul through the thixcipience of the witness transforms the intellect into higher consciousness, and the highest soul member, the consciousness soul, is developed. The consciousness soul is then oriented toward higher experiences of the supersensible world. Abstract questioning is transformed into moral Imagination. Then the goal is not to develop an airtight theory but to expand the consciousness to be able to receive the diversity of touch experience available above the level of waking consciousness. This entails the development of humility when the thinker beholds the long road toward union with the Godhead, toward apotheosis. Humanity as a whole is approaching the transcendent threshold between the intellectual soul and the consciousness soul. The abstract thinking that has led humanity to the luminous wall must be overcome, for unmitigated, it prevents the thinker from perceiving objectively the essence of the multitudes of spiritual beings who wish to help human beings attain apotheosis and who send forces toward humanity from the other side of the wall of light.

# 3

# THE ABSTRACT PREDICAMENT

The technique of abstraction is central to the understanding of the role that higher Imagination plays in the human soul's journey to apotheosis. Along with the rise of abstraction as a cognitive technique in the arts, a peculiar prejudice against beauty became popular among artistic thinkers in the 19th century. As a result, artists working early in this century embraced analysis rather than sensual experience. There is a rich tradition of polar attitudes arising out of the tension between truth and beauty. Such attitudes occupied the minds of Ancient Greek philosophers, were central to the debates between the realists and the nominalists during the Middle Ages, and after the European Renaissance they could be found in the tensions that existed between the classicists and the romantics. In our own age the works of the abstractionists and the expressionists are variations on the same theme of truth or beauty. It is misleading, however, to view the evolution of consciousness as simply a cyclic return of prior conditions.

A subtle shift in values which has occurred since the classicists and romantics battled in the 1850s can be seen by comparing the words of two artists who were active in the late nineteenth century, William Bouguereau and Théodore Rousseau. In the 1880s, Bouguereau, a French academic painter, expressed his concern for truth in art in the following way:

> I fear the mental fatigue that this innovation [of a course in art history] will cause [in the Ecole des Beaux Arts]. I hold that theory should not enter into an artist's elementary education. . . . There is no such thing as symbolic art, social art, religious art, or monumental art; there is only the art of the representation of nature by an artist whose sole aim is to express its truth. (*Artists on Art*, 287–8)

In the view of the French academy of the 1850s, a scientific training in drawing from nature and accurate observation were the primary tools for an aspiring artist. It was felt that theories of art only served to cloud the issues of skill and fidelity to the appearances of nature. Proponents of this view held that in reproducing the appearance of the natural world an artist could approach the   summit of artistic achievement.

Against this academic bias toward verisimilitude in drawing and painting stood the romantic rebellion whose members sought a different model of excellence. Rousseau, a painter and member of the Barbizon landscape painters' group, writing to Charles Blanc, founder of the academic *Gazette des Beaux Arts,* gives the following comparison of Ingres and Delacroix:

> With the works of Ingres [classicist], one could create a museum analogous to the Museum of Natural History; everything there is respectable. Endowed with the considerable talent that must be granted him and which no one ever questions, one cannot help doing good work; but great work is something different. The gift of personal creation seems to me to have been denied Ingres completely. . . . Need I tell you that I prefer Delacroix with his exaggerations, his mistakes, his visible failures, because he belongs only to himself, because he represents the spirit, the form, the language of his time. . . . That is why I prefer Delacroix to Ingres, and I am talking here only of the moral aspect of the man, and not his technique. Ingres, for me, represents in a feeble degree no more than the beautiful art of the past that we have lost. (*Artists on Art,* 289–90)

There are several points here that are worth considering more deeply. Rousseau refers to the lost art of the past as beautiful. He prefers the truth of personal exaggeration. It is interesting to note that both the academic realist and the romantic naturalist hold truth in art to be a primary value. A few hundred years earlier in Europe, matters were quite different. Consider Albrecht Dürer (1471–1528):

> For from many beautiful things something good may be gathered, even as honey is gathered from many flowers. There is

a right mean between too much and too little; strive to hit upon this in all your works.  (*Artists on Art*, 82)

For Dürer then, truth *and* beauty are necessary considerations.  In reading the written works of artists during and just prior to the Renaissance the concern for beauty is mentioned as often as a sense of truth.  Naturally there are many and diverse points of view, but the basic concern for the beautiful is present in many artistic thinkers.

In the centuries between the Renaissance and the modern period a shift of values occurred, spearheaded by the scientific researches of the great masters of the quattrocento.  No longer content with the otherworldliness of medieval models, the artist/scientist of the Renaissance felt that the most praiseworthy goal was to represent the subject of the painting as naturalistically as possible.  The laws of painting that evolved out of scientific studies in space, optics, biology, and human anatomy revolutionized western art in the direction of the material world analyzed through the capacities of the intellect, but by the time Rousseau comments on the lost beauty of past art these laws had become dogmas in the minds of the academics.  It is interesting to note that Rousseau does not appear to lament the demise of beauty but instead expects his art to reveal the truth.  For Dürer, truth and beauty were one, but for many who followed after his creative explorations, beauty faded and truth became the objective of art.  Similarly, while for Cennino Cennini in the 1300s all art was connected to the beautiful through the Holy Mother of Christ, to Delacroix in 1847 the idea of beauty in the arts is laughable.  He equates beauty with purity and says that if Rembrandt or Rubens had sought the beautiful in art, they would have lost their power.

Delacroix was a champion of personal vision, the unifying cause of the romantic rebellion.  This rallying point is symptomatic of the flowering of the mind soul in esoteric development.  In daily life and adolescent experience, the new-born mind soul rejects beauty as a valid concern and values personal vision as the sole criterion for judgement.  Once thinking has been established in the mind soul, the capacity for analysis inherent in the intellect tempers overly subjective values into more objective goals.  What Delacroix and the romantics seem to be seeking in the extreme valuation of personal freedom is the threshold of true egalitarian reform in the arts.  The impressionist painters sought this freedom by shattering the mirror of objective fidelity to nature.  Curiously enough, some of the most beautiful paintings of the nineteenth century were actually formulated to produce scientifically accurate renderings of atmospheric light. In the amazing blend of sensuousness and intellectual rigor that is part of the soul of France, French painters evoked gossamer, fleeting visions that were based on scientifically precise reasoning. Beauty as a serious artistic pursuit was achieved in practice but further dismissed in theory.

The disappearance of beauty as a formal concern in art is economically expressed in the three categories which the French critic Eugène Véron used as criteria for judging an artwork's validity. At Véron's first and lowest level of art is the work which adheres to an established academic method. He viewed this level as uncreative and conventional. At Véron's second level is art which has sought scientific objectivity through copying or recording the phenomena of nature. At this level artists tend to function like cameras or copying machines. At the third and highest level is the art through which the artist has sought to manifest personal impressions. On this level the artist views nature and reflects nature's archetypes in colors that are born out of the artist's individual view. The unique temperament of the artist was thus considered to be the central issue of creative research. In these three categories it is possible to see the evolution from the Middle Ages with inherited canons of beauty, through the scientific/realistic mindsets of the Renaissance, to the deification of the personality so central to the modern movement from the symbolists onward.

It was also the destiny of impressionism to be transcended by a further evolution. The initial scientific/realistic theories of the physicist Chevreul were moved through the abstract, sensual later works of Monet into the the synthetic, symbolic works of Cézanne, Van Gogh, and Gauguin. The impressionists had focused their vision on the activity of perception rather than upon the historical meaning of the subject, thereby breaking from the academic need, for instance, for historically accurate accoutrements on figures. This break was not without its repercussions in the human soul, for artists as they matured intellectually quickly separated traditional ideals of beauty, encrusted as they were by outmoded and suspect academic restraints, ever farther from the artistic pursuit of truth. The art of the symbolists and expressionists was a natural complement to the scientific/realistic concerns of the impressionists, for the symbolists sensed a need to rigorously observe their own consciousness at work.

At this critical juncture there came into being a mental technique that led the human personality into an artistic morass. With the demise of beauty as a valid artistic goal and the rise of the awareness of the temperament of the artist as the vehicle of expression, an intoxicating sense of freedom was injected into the visual arts. With realism passé, academism dead and buried, and beauty no longer a concern, serious art students were left to explore their own personalities and produce ever more eccentric personal works. To counterbalance this extremely sympathetic energy, artists began to cast about into older, more primitive cultures for a model which could satisfy the cognitive side of their consciousness. In place of the logical scientism of realist theory, artists in the 1920s and 1930s searched for thought structures that could support a deeply personal vision. The principle that they discovered and adopted as a technique to balance the eccentric liberated persona was abstraction.

The technique of abstraction is a method unconsciously developed in primitive cultures through the handing down of mythic images from generation to generation of artists. In the process of abstraction each succeeding artist copies and refines the work of his predecessor, leading gradually to an economy of means that stylizes and abstracts through reduction. Images eventually become symbols that convey meanings to those who are literate in the iconography and mythology of the culture. This process, which is largely unconscious in older cultures, was accelerated by Picasso and prompted his radical abstractions of animals and human beings. Picasso's use of abstraction amounted to an instant, one-man historical process in which symbols were forged by a modern, ego-endowed human being into a self-conscious artistic movement cognizant of its place in the history of Western art. In place of the banished criterion of beauty, the lower persona was thereby given access to a personal analytical process that somewhat tempered its self-centered extravagances. The process of abstraction validated the personal fantasy of the artist and gave it the rigor of the intellect.

The use of this ancient technique by modern artists places early modern abstract art at the first level of Véron's critical scale, the level of adherence to earlier methods. Personal abstract reduction suffers from its own inertia and often requires the forces of the collective unconscious to give it meaning, although it can sometimes lead to the second, the scientific/realistic level of development. In the ancient world the process of abstraction through repetition and refinement remained wholesome because the human soul was still embedded in the natural world. Mystical cognition of the spiritual beings standing behind mythic images lifted the artist/seer into higher realms from which icons were created which could speak to other souls in a full and self-evident way. With a modern ego such as Picasso, abstraction through reduction was simply a shortcut devised by the individual-ized intellect to balance the seething feeling life generated by the expanded intellectual awareness of the individual persona. The indi-vidual perceived his divine nature but submerged it in the uncon-scious in order to produce instant myths. In the process of abstraction through reduction, the method or technique becomes the focus of per-ception, and the logical process of the method becomes the actual rea-son for the artistic activity. While in primitive societies the method would be the enactment of the binding ritual, for a modern artist not bound by religious or shamanistic concerns the sacred function of the ritual is taken over by the sacrosanct power of the intellect to order natural phenomena. The technical approach of the modern abstrac-tionist becomes the neo-ritualistic discipline that guides the journeys of the creative soul.

The plethora of "isms" early in this century points to the search for the stability of ritual in a technically obsessed culture. Since the meaning of the work was to come from the persona of the artist rather than from a hierarchical spirit world, the logic of the technique of abstraction lent deductive power and objectivity to the individual's imagery. Scientific realism no longer required that the *outer* world be rendered objectively true by the image but demanded rather that it render objectively the *inner* world of the personality of the artist. This may shed some light on the curious tendency of many surrealists to clothe the most personal fantasies in the most objective treatments of material objects. Shifts of scale, space, and context are enhanced if the images depicted are shown in strict realism.

Many artists also used the deductive logic of the abstract tech-nique to build separate, personally ordered universes that relied upon the power of formal arrangement. For instance, in Kandinsky's and Klee's later periods this movement into pure abstract realms of the point, the line, and the plane produced strongly hermetic works. This tendency was echoed both in the technical rituals of the abstract expressionists, whose works focused on the personality, and in the technical rituals of the more scientific artists of minimalist leanings, who created their own binding ritual out of the logic of pure form.

Whatever their extraction, these abstract techniques share a common ground in that they all are used by artists who wish to establish a deductive, scientific logic capable of balancing their journey of descent into the persona.

The danger of such journeying is the same as that faced by any shaman in the past: If the technical ritual is not performed exactly, the operant may return to find that his soul has been led into madness or that the spirit has been released into the next world and cannot find its way back into the body. The binding ritual used to serve as a silver cord between the traveling soul and the physical body on earth. In abstraction an attempt is made to furnish such a  silver cord through intellectually constructing a technical ritual that will allow the soul to travel into the realm of Intuition.  The ritual must also allow for a return to the body where the soul can reflect these out-of-body experiences into the day consciousness as visual symbols. Psychically, a similar process of travel and return gives rise to dreams, but in art these dreamlike images must be grasped more fully and projected outward into the artwork. The power of the deductive logic found in ritualized technical procedures is meant to be an aid in developing these dream images.

In ancient shamanism it was recognized that the power behind the image came from an objective world of spirit that the shaman gradually began to perceive and work within, a world which connected the shaman to the numinous in nature.  For the shaman, the natural world and the spirit world formed a whole, in which the self of the shaman was embedded.  The ritual was given by the spirit world as a technique by which the shaman could enter more deeply into the spirit without encountering obsession and madness. Through contact between the self and nature the shaman was able to experience the world of spirit.  In abstraction, however, it is the individualized personality rather than nature that is experienced as the creative force in the soul life.  Because artistic perception is focused upon the logic of the technical ritual, the natural world is separated from the self, and the spiritual world which animates nature lies unrecognized.  This inflates the status of the personality and creates situations in which dogmatic allegiance to a particular technique is seen as the only method of approaching the truth.  This split between the self and nature is also keenly felt in the alienating images seen in contemporary galleries and has become so great that a pro-technical, anti-mystical, even amoral stance in art threatens the very survival of culture as a healing force in human lives.

Modern artists cannot and should not return to shamanic or Oceanic roots for creative thoughts. At the same time, the abstractions of the technical realists have moved culture into a blind alley characterized on the one hand by neuroses and despair, and on the other by violent power wielded blindly by critically righteous individuals. This then is the predicament of abstraction: the one-sided search for truth in art, which ignores beauty, coupled with the false identification of the lower self as the source of creative power.

However, the door is open to resolve the predicament. It has always been open, but it is small and narrow and requires us to transcend the deductive logic of abstraction and move to inductive, intuitional reasoning. This movement will allow the search for beauty once again to be a part of the artist's capacities. Beauty is a realm of being which the intellect can merely analyze, and which must ultimately be experienced in the heart. Instead of society simply canonizing masters of technical ritual, the great artist must be able to perceive moral qualities within the inner vision of the heart. The heart must once again be allowed to ponder the imponderables. Art students can be taught to approach wholeness in the natural world with a renewed sense of wonder and mystery. Technical arrogance is as damaging to one's sense of communion with the spiritual in nature and art as is an overinflated personality. Artistic training should involve daily contact with the germinating forces of nature and allow subtle vision to flower in the soul through meditative practice. This heals the thrill-seeking lower levels of the sense life. Such activity harmonizes the human spirit and soul and body into an organism capable of perceiving beauty.

To Delacroix the pure aspect of beauty threatened the creative vitality of an artist like Ingres, for the romantics were rightly suspicious of pure technical mastery as an artistic goal in itself. For moral reasons they favored an art that could make mistakes. Technical perfection was even considered immoral because it did not allow the creative spirit of the human being to shine out from its prison of convention and boredom. In following their hearts to this truth, the romantics were pointing to the third level of abstraction, the vision of the individual.

Both the abstraction produced by tradition and the abstraction of the scientist/realist look to an external, established authority that reveals itself through images and symbols. Through binding ritual and/or drugs and trances, the seer/shaman/artist approached the collective fantasies of the long dead and the unborn, seeking corroboration for the truth of an image. The artist working in a realistic mode sought the corroboration of the empirical, physical world as revealed by conceptual knowledge. Binding ritual was metamorphosed at this level into technical procedure and laws of painting. At the third level of art, however, the technical laws of painting and the mathematical rigor of composition and color harmonies are transformed into a pure soul language that seeks to make the artist not merely a seer or scientist but also a priest and prophet.

In terms of the evolution of consciousness this movement can be seen as a wave in the general movement of humanity toward the New Jerusalem, the consciousness soul. In the language of consciousness soul, people will experience the direct contact of their higher selves, their I-beings, with their individual personalities. This contact leads to the transformation of the feeling life, to *manas,* the leading characteristic of the age of the consciousness soul. The romantic rebellion against the scientific/realistic abstraction of the academics was a true symptom of this transformation. Yet the expansion into the general culture of the consciousness soul or manas culture seems to have fostered a situation which has stifled true creative work in favor of innovative or simulated creative work. It is as if the huge expansion of creative power has brought about a cultural vacuum.

What began in the late 1800s as an advance into manas culture and the accompanying moral responsibility toward action by each individual led instead into a shattering of creative standards in the strong rebellion of scientific/realistic impressionism and shamanistic surrealism. Only post-impressionism stayed in tune with the manas culture. As an answer to the scientism of impressionism, the post-impressionists rightly chose color over form and personal risk over technical achievement. This emphasis on color allowed artists to see into the soul life in a more sensitive way. Leading the consciousness into the contemplation of secondary qualities such as warmth, tone, and light, instead of the primary academic qualities of weight, number, and measure, this use of color was a step toward manas. Similarly, the risk-taking of the personality moves the consciousness in the direction of inductive reasoning rather than the deductions of scientific abstraction.

This sudden expansion in the souls of the post-impressionists into a higher level of perception ultimately proved too much for them personally and for the artistic culture as a whole.  Cubism took a backward turn into scientism and into the modernist shamanism and totemism of the forties and early fifties.  Since then the pendulum has swung between scientism and shamanism, with the personal vision of the individual emerging gradually as a new dominant artistic force. In the 1950s in America the two poles of technical procedure and vision of cultural symbols were forcefully merged by the intensely personal vision of the abstract expressionists.  Since that time the level of innovative personal vision has more and more come to the forefront as the mark of culturally viable art.  By contrast, creative improvisation is the hallmark of the manas culture, for it alone allows the soul to commune with the creative force of the Godhead.  It is around this point of innovation versus improvisation as a methodology that a distinction needs to be considered which has far-reaching implications.

In today's society the idea of innovation carries with it a kind of license to do whatever is needed for the personality to express its own viewpoint.  Since the middle of the 1970s in America, this license to express has been unconsciously connected to an ethos based on production values, that is, a quasi-aesthetic driven by the mass production of a thing—a toaster or an automobile, for instance.  In actuality the innovative values of the production process produce a stylistic homogeneity which devalues individual creativity in the arts in favor of the cult of the "new," of innovation.  With the rise of the technical revolution engendered by computers, a form of technical hubris has emerged based on a thinly disguised Marxist belief in the production values of people.  The computer has ushered in a realm of imagination in which innovative simulation is slowly replacing objective perception.  The creation of an artificial heart and genetically engineered life forms give the human being the illusion of omnipotence, for the simulation of nature's powers by human conceptual life seems to equal the creative acts of the Godhead and fosters the deification of the technical productions of humanity.  Once this divorce from the true source of creativity was operational, the root of improvisation and true creative work became obscured.

In the alienated, simulated world of the 1990s the production values used to define a human being's intrinsic worth emphasize the ever more innovative manipulation of things which already exist,

rather than encouraging the risks involved in new creation or improvisation. Truly new creations often appear awkward and labor inten-
sive, whereas innovative manipulations of old forms are most often
cost effective, sleek, and upbeat.    True creativity becomes subtly
replaced by replicable technical innovation and dazzlingly powerful
displays of virtuosity—all good production values. Much of the reasoning that goes on in such structured innovative work is deductive,
and the individual must cling to deductive languages of abstract logic
or run the risk of cultural ostracism. The personality, when forced to
capitulate to the alienating demands of logical deductive production
values in art, seeks relief in art forms which stimulate personal feelings of expansion. There is no place for the soul to turn except to the
expansive thresholds of the emerging global manas culture.
However, since the deductive neo-language requires integration with
machine values and processes, the resulting personality expansion is
permeated with the technical bias of the neo-language. As a result, a
whole world-view based upon technical production values applied to
the inner life of the human being is the chilling vision of post-mod-
ernist art. Those artists who resist the lure of personality amplification through scientism, i.e., mechanical technology, often choose to
amplify the personality through shamanism, drugs, or ritualistic procedures. The vacuum of the late 1800s when the romantics pushed
into manas culture has today vastly intensified in scope and emptiness.

In this predicament is there any value beyond personal innovation by which future artistic striving can be experienced and understood? If we look back to the romantic rebellion as the first flush of
emerging manas culture we can ask, What made the romantic reaction
a manas experience? The answer would be that the emergence of the
I-being or true eternal self in the individual personality endowed the
personality with objective moral forces. Manas culture, the culture of
the consciousness soul, the New Jerusalem, the Sophia revelation,
these are all epithets for the experience of the universal, objective,
transpersonal I-being, known esoterically as the I Am or True Self,
which flashed into earth existence and is continually giving awareness of the reality of spirit existence to the personality. This high, pure
moral note is what sounded in the romantics, the post-impressionists,
the abstract expressionists, and in painters such as Mark Rothko.

Rothko heard the call of the New Jerusalem. He began as a fer-
vent shaman and ritualistic symbolist, yet he gave up his seership for

a scientific but soul-imbued conversation with the higher self through the pure language of color.   The eccentricity of his early symbolist/shamanistic works was translated into hermetic, somber color fields that spoke of melancholic rapture.  Unfortunately his rise coincided with the peak of the anti-natural technical arrogance that was to sweep the eighties into a deadly proliferation of simulated profundities.  The manas revelation transported Rothko into a position in which the lower self that was experiencing the expansive creativity of the higher self was unable to ground these experiences in a broad enough technical language.   Rothko, like so many others, slowly became divorced from nature.  Unable to tolerate this estrangement, he suffered the fate of all astral travellers who journey to the realm of the True Self with neither a binding ritual to tether them to nature nor a hut, slowly constructed from this side of the threshold, to live in on the other side.  This courageous artist had forsaken his hermetic symbols and his scientism of color and set off into the wilderness of the self without the witness, the true guide to manas experience.  This was not a fault in Mark Rothko, but rather his destiny.  He successfully skirted the technical arrogance and the overblown polemics of personality in order to have an experience of the True Self.  He yearned like Ulysses to hear the siren song, but the lashings of his mind came unbound and he drowned in the power of the Word.

A bleak picture, to be sure, but does this mean that experiencing the age of the consciousness soul will naturally lead to madness and schizophrenia?  Some authors seem to suggest so.  But for every Rothko there is a Blake, for every Van Gogh a Turner.  The secret of the Sophia revelation of the emergence of manas culture is that these stages of artistic relationship to the world are present in each individual as well as in the motion and evolution of the culture as a whole.  Most artists begin with an unconscious shamanistic understanding of the world left over from the shining, luminous fields of childhood.  The emergence of the intellect and its questioning in the intellectual soul is then often met in the arts with an ordering apprenticeship through drawing and formal study of nature.

These stages can clearly be seen in the life of Turner and even in Titian, Rubens, Monet, and Rembrandt.  Each of them was a supremely fluid master who went through a scientist/realist phase early in life in which forms were delineated, effects studied and rendered, and compositions carefully evolved.  In the case of Rembrandt this period included numerous studies of the human face and hands.   The shamanistic stage can be seen in Rembrandt's work in his fascination for the grotesque, the picturesque, and the fantastical or oriental. The exotic headdresses, ornaments, and other baroque flourishes and fetishes served to spark the imaginative fire in the young painter. As he grew and his craft progressed, the exotic was transformed into the alchemical in a lifelong involvement with the waxes and resins, oils and acids of etching. The alchemical work is done on the inner self as well as the outer planes; the door from scientific realism through to personal vision is reached by induction and a preference for holistic views of natural order over inorganic, abstract laws.

During Rembrandt's early and middle years there was an almost prosaic attention to details of dress and the lustre of pearls and lace. When Rembrandt matured into his full power and his imaginative life began to give him a glimpse of the coming age of the New Jerusalem, he abandoned these commonplace details. He took a leap of faith and instead of painting burghers and patrons, he painted inner perceptions of saints based on outer models of those around him. As a result of this change, he underwent severe trials economically. His commissions failed, yet still he pursued the inner vision. But the inner vision of Rembrandt does not fall into the personality-ridden vision of many since his time. We do not find empty innovation or barren technical production—in Rembrandt's work we find warmth and color and the physical world suffused with an atmosphere of spiritual bliss. The physical is revealed in spiritual terms, the spiritual is reflected in the physical. When these two spheres meet and are held together by the work and prayer of a human being, the great forces of the Godhead can find a place to work and ray out to others. Ritual techniques, technical expertise, conceptual knowledge, personal ambition, even regular production must all be given over to the willingness to stand empty-handed in the face of powers of creation much greater than though of the same cloth as our own.

The perception of beauty in nature is the grounding agent that allows the life of creativity pouring from the Godhead to reach our souls. This perception must be distilled, however, like a precious substance whose presence as a fragrance signals its own evaporation. The perception of beauty in nature, when undertaken in a meditative way, can help the soul to release the lower senses so that they may be transformed into the higher senses. The release of the senses from their bondage to matter can be undertaken abstractly through perception of inorganic laws; this path leads to cognitive states and to ideation, but does not help to establish the perception of the witness. But the release of the senses from their bondage to matter can also be undertaken through warm and intimate perception of the life and phenomena of nature. In this case, thinking is connected to Intuition and to the perception of the ever-unfolding archetype that lies behind the organic world. This path leads not to ideation but to a perception of the higher being who is present in the act of perceiving. This higher self, the witness, is the true guide to the emergence of manas culture, the Sophia revelation. Without the perceptions of the witness, the acts of our most innovative beings will be simulated expressions of temporal anxieties, geared for the production values of a technological age but able neither to unfold magic nor to bestow grace onto the future.

# 4

# THE TRANSFORMATION
# OF SYMPATHY

Hidden within a simple sense experience such as the act of seeing a tree, it is possible to observe many subtle levels of perception. As adults we often have the remembered mental image
"tree" rise up in our consciousness along with the image of the tree as
we are actually seeing it. In this fundamental response lies a profound mystery. The act of seeing the tree unites our consciousness
with the physical tree. We reach out with our eyes and touch the tree,
and through letting our eyes wander attentively along the branches
we become one with the tree. Young children often experience this
mystical soul connection with the most everyday objects. Their rapt
attention on a flower or puddle is a manifestation of the capacity for
the inner life to sympathize and unite with the objects which the
world gives to our senses. Inward sympathy extended toward an outward object is the imitative foundation of the soul in early childhood,
before the distinction between "me" and "not me" develops. Even
during the first three years, however, young children who do not yet
form clear concepts do begin to differentiate between what constitutes
their own bodies and what does not. This capacity to distinguish
between self and non-self involves a subtle acceptance of self and a
subtle rejection of the world. The capacity to hold the world at arm's
length and scrutinize it is the basis for inner life and the representation of the world through images or that which psychology calls mental images.

RESISTANCE/ANTIPATHY                    DESIRE/SYMPATHY

**Image forming**                      **Grasping for and**
**and representing**                    **releasing images**

With the development of the capacity to discriminate between self and object, the growing soul experiences a feeling force which cools and dampens down the sympathetic identification with the world. From early childhood on, then, the soul feels a great tension between the tendencies of sympathy and antipathy. This tension is the source of the ability to form an inner picture drawn from sense experiences. Through living, the child brings sympathy and antipathy into relationship with each other, and the sentient soul arises, the level of soul which is sensitive to and identifies with the tension between the soul's desire for and its resistance to the world. Feelings often are not separate and autonomous but rather are mixed into sense impressions. Into the actual sense activity of seeing a tree, human beings mingle past memories of trees and present feelings about trees. The feelings sometimes stimulate conflicting inner pictures which can further obscure the actual sense data being perceived immediately in the senses.

The activity of cognition dampens still further the immediacy of sensation. As a result, inner pictures of many individual trees can be brought into a higher, clearer consciousness and can collectively be given a name: "tree." The consciousness can then experience "tree" without having to go through the entire sensate process of learning to recognize each new tree. This ability has distinct advantages but is far from direct sense experience. The resistance and antipathy of the thinking dampens, characterizes, and orders the chaos of actual sensual experience. A child does not actually form cognized concepts at this level; there is simply an ordering of the sense data. With naming the tree a young child can recall the mental image of the tree without having to sympathetically and sensually become the tree. The forming of names permeates the sense world with cognitive activity, and in naming, the human being creates a duality between the observed and the observer. The observer is the one who either becomes (sympathizes with) the other or names (separates from) the other. This observer has a special name for itself: "I". The human I has the unique simultaneous ability both to be itself and to separate itself from itself through the act of naming itself. As we have seen, at the level of the sentient soul the I is polluted with surging feelings of sympathy and antipathy. Many psychological difficulties such as anima/animus possession and shadow projection stem from this level of soul life. A soul afflicted with these problems finds it difficult to separate from or perceive its own I, and it identifies instead with

limited patterned personality structures composed of habitual uncognized sense experiences and the instinctual feelings associated with
them. The sentient soul caught in extremes of sympathy and antipathy often reveals the formation of fixed ideas as a leading characteristic.

In the attention of such an unbalanced instinctual soul, the excite-
ment of being caught in the turmoil between sympathy and antipathy
takes the place of cognitive activity, resulting in a personality frag-
ment addicted to experiencing its own heightened emotional states.
By contrast, a healthy soul tries to determine the validity of mental
images and can adjust them by comparing true, objective concepts
perceived through thinking to the experiences of sense-perceptible
physical reality. As we saw earlier, this capacity to think in images is
based upon an inner resistance to the outer world. Through resistance, or antipathy, the soul rejects the world and can then form an
inner image of it that is set apart from the self.

If a child wishes to know something about why its fingers are
burned by a candle that looks so beautiful to the senses, it must resist
the desire to become one with the flame and must encounter the
world of the objective concepts (in this case "hot") that stand behind
physical phenomena. At this level, perception of the sense world no
longer revolves around simple likes and dislikes. Things happen for
objective reasons which can be grasped by logically deducing or
inducing the correct relationships between the parts and the whole of
a phenomenon. Both deduction and induction are thinking processes
produced by resistance to the given world. These forms of thinking
about sense-perceptible phenomena constitute the path of the human
soul engaged in scientific work and have yielded the modern scientific world view. The inorganic sciences require deduction, a type of
thinking which is more computational than induction and which
focuses upon the logical sequence of thoughts. On the other hand,
induction involves the perception of conceptual realities that are not
necessarily sequential but are definitely relative to each other, such as
the relationships between parts and wholes in organic systems. The
difference between these modes of thinking becomes very important
in the next level of the soul, the intellectual soul.

The antipathetic forces present in deduction and induction support a rejection of the sympathy-based mysticism of the ancient
world. This rejection of the earlier mysticism upon the grounds that
it was intellectually weak is correct from an evolutionary point of

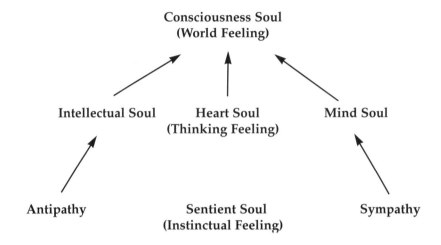

view, for the paradigm of the old mysticism had to give way to the development of the intellectual aspects of the soul. However, humanity must now develop capacities beyond the ideation of the intellectual soul. Indeed, we stand at a new threshold. We must temper and balance the resistance and antipathy toward the given world that is present in abstract thinking, with the forces of sympathy for the cosmos found in the mind soul. In the mind soul the path leads from instinctual image formation to the abyss of the unknowable. There we must learn to abandon the security of fixed intellectual concepts for the insecurity of constantly evolving archetypal ideas. We must forsake the comfort of judgement and opinion for the anxiety of silence. We must weave sure-footed intellectual ideation into our desire to experience greater transcendence in our souls. Here we come into contact with immense vistas of consciousness.

As we have seen, the forces of transcendence become available to the soul when unbalanced sympathy and antipathy are harmonized and integrated through conscious effort. At the level of the sentient soul, this involves the recognition that there is a difference between one's conceptual mental image of reality and one's feeling/willing response to the mental image. Once the power of transcendence begins to operate in the sentient soul, the mental image is lifted into a higher level of being, free of personal instinctual feelings into a higher level of being. At this higher level, the soul's ability to form instinctual mental images is transformed through the power of transcendence into the intellect's capacity to form fixed concepts. At the same time the desire (will) arises in the mind soul to experience broader levels of consciousness. While the intellectual soul finds a source of energy in the antipathetic pole of the soul life, the mind soul relates more to the sympathy and will forces found in the vast ocean of consciousness that is the mother of all existence. The intellect knows the crystal clarity and truth of the laws of the father nature, and the mind knows the acts and processes of the mother nature in their hidden language of creativity.

To attain transcendence, the two poles of intellect and mind that are found in the mind soul need to be harmonized, just as the poles within the sentient soul needed harmonization. An imbalanced mind soul can fall into intellectual abstraction when the antipathetic forces rule the thought life, or it can turn to fanaticism when the sympathetic forces rule the thought life. In the case of fanaticism, the soul ponders and has feelings about the conceptual world without referring back to physical laws. In the case of abstract intellectualism, the thinker bases his conclusions solely upon physical reality, and the world of concepts becomes cold and devoid of healthy feelings. Such a thinker brings concepts and laws into contact with the perceptions of the world by using abstract thinking to perceive inorganic, cause-and-effect relationships and then proving them by means of physical experiment. The result is inorganic science, an objectively true, modern view of the external aspect of the archetype. Difficulties arise, however, when abstract thinking is applied to the organic realm, for the archetypes that create living nature and life processes constantly modify physical reality according to their own ever-changing, unfolding patterns of being.

When abstract thinking is applied to the mobile, ever-fluid inner life of the human soul, a condition of mystical fundamentalism occurs in which moral activity is imposed upon the human being by external laws. The soul of the fundamentalist experiences a grasping sympathy with the ground of all being that exists in the mind. This sympathy is given an intellectual, materialistic coloration by the abstract reasoning of dogmas and moralistic sayings. The polemics and disputes which surround such fundamental abstractions are seen as proof of the effectiveness of dogma in developing moralistic judgement. In actuality, the need for polemical disputations and evangelical correctness is at its root a symptom of materialistic abstraction inharmoniously yoked to the desire for sympathetic Intuitions found in true religious experience.  The materialistic, "scientific" concepts which the intellect develops into religious abstraction gives fundamentalism the view that the human being is inherently prone to corruption and needs strict "God-given" moral codes imposed by higher human authorities in order to perceive and live the Good.  The forces of sympathy at work in the mind soul are not allowed to connect the intellect with the Intuition.  In fact, in the "rational," fundamentalist doctrines of contemporary moralists, spiritual or mystical experiences are suspect.

Such suspicion is not entirely without merit.  Indeed, medieval mysticism, which produced ecstatic visions, often relied upon a suspension of logical thinking.  The mystics favored a heart path in which logic and intellectual discursiveness were rejected in favor of a deep, oceanic feeling life.  The pioneering work of medieval thinkers overcame this tendency, and subsequently, with the rise of modern culture, the age of science required that all human beings begin to analyze and cognize, relying not at all upon personal feelings or the simple sense experiences of daily life as a monitor of truth.  This was an advance in consciousness, and in the culture at large it resulted in a reliance on concepts and abstract thought patterns.  Rudolf Steiner characterized this change as the advent of the intellectual soul age.

But this new attitude produced a split in the soul between the human being as an onlooker who cognizes abstract patterns in the chaos of the natural world, and the human being as ensouled, capable of a rich inner life not dependent upon the sense world.  To the analytical thinker the inner life of sympathy is too permeated with subjective feelings to be trusted, while for the mystic the sympathetic pole in the soul opens a door to a whole world of rich inner experience.  A great leap forward is made if an individual soul can hold both of these views to be true.  Further, the path of transcendence can only be undertaken by those who have first developed the basis for objective thinking, for the dangers of mystical experience demand that the modern mystic be thoroughly grounded in objective science.  Without the thinking capacity, the forces of will in the pole of sympathy can destroy the soul through quasi-creative experience.  The reason for this psychic disruption, a common motif in the arts and sciences, can be sought in the hidden programmed fluctuations of the will.

The pole of sympathy and will endows the soul with capacities for seeking higher truth through Intuition.  The soul can also approach higher truth through logical thinking, but the spiritually adept human being cannot act out of logical thinking alone. The undeveloped soul needs forces of the will in order to grasp the world either physically or psychically. In the sentient soul the will is present as a lower form of intuition, as a hunch. In the act of discriminating between an inner picture and its objective concept the soul through an act of will must focus its forces, reaching a more aware state. Through the will activity in logical thinking, a transcendent relationship can be developed with the ideas that exist behind the world phenomena in the world of concepts. In short, it takes an act of will in thinking to grasp a concept. The concept is then reflected by the physiology into an image that can be perceived by the intellect.

The willed attention that discriminates between a concept and the inner picture of a concept reveals one polarity in the path of sympathy, the capacity of the soul to grasp (discriminate differences). If the grasping capacity takes an upper hand in the soul life then addictive thought tendencies and fixed ideas are experienced. When balanced, however, the lower levels of sympathetic intuition can be grasped and then transcended into creativity and sense-free thought. In order to balance the grasping forces of desire in the pole of sympathy it is necessary for the soul also to develop the ability to consciously release what it has grasped. For a creative thinker, releasing a concept or destroying an already existent thought pattern requires just as much will as grasping a concept or forming a pattern in the first place. Creative problem solving demands the destruction of many erroneous and incomplete hypotheses. Both in the sentient soul and in the intellectual soul the ability to release in the pole of the will is what allows the more resistance-oriented pole of antipathy to approach the will in a gesture of transcendence. By forming an image of the world, the intellect resists and rejects the world. The formed image is then grasped by the sympathies (will) and subsequently invested with emotional power. We have seen where this can be balanced into transcendence through the lower intuition in the sentient soul.

In the intellectual soul, however, the lower intuition faces the danger of abstraction, pitting the intellect against the Kantian limits of knowledge. The lower intuition in the sentient soul is systematically being transcended into Intuition in the intellectual soul. Here Intuition is present as the discursive capacity of the intellect. As the intuition via the intellect weighs concepts, the soul can become aware of a higher region of thought where Intuition is the primary mode of consciousness. At that point the intellect begins to recognize the mind and its infinite levels of consciousness but is not able to experience pure Intuition because the intellect resists the sympathy required to transcend itself. Through contact with the world, however, and through learning to create and release, the intellect allows the life of desire to become tempered and ultimately to transcend into the desire to experience higher states of mind or consciousness. Here we can ponder again Goethe's distinction between intellect and reason.

For Goethe the intellect is the part of the soul which can approach the world of objective concepts. It connects simple concepts to other simple concepts to produce more and richer conceptual relationships. The intellect continues to expand to understand these richer concepts up to the point at which the power of the intellect to understand is benumbed. Goethe thought that at this point the intellect transcends into the capacity of reason. Reason is employed when the intellect releases the concepts it has grasped and can witness in silent states of attention its own act of cognition. With reason it is possible to comprehend the richer living constellations of concepts or mind. For Goethe these richer constellations which were comprehended by reason have the character of archetypal Ideas—spelled with a capital "I" to differentiate them from the lower ideas grasped in the intellectual process of ideation. This distinction can be the cause of misunderstanding, especially today when ideation is such a goal in the arts and sciences. An esoteric name for the constellations of living concepts that might more aptly depict their numinous essence would be *hosts,* for in spiritual reality the transcended concept takes on the character of an active being when perceived spiritually by the witness.

The witness is itself a numinous being which is separate from and yet integrated into the realm of the angelic hosts. It is of the nature of Idea and is produced when the attention of the human consciousness is turned from the sense world and is observant of its own activity. The witness is a living concept which is focused on the spiritual world, which cognizes itself, and which appears when intellect and mind are unified into a transcendent force. Through regular meditative practice the witness is established as a living presence perceptive of its own unique role in integrating the given world with the complex creative hosts in the spiritual world. In both worlds the witness is challenged by a benumbing force within which it exists suspended as a small flame crying in the glory of the sun. As the witness ascends to experience the hosts, their strong yet subtle energies overshadow and benumb the intellect. Since the witness is also composed of universal mind, it can transcend the intellect through the mind soul and develop consciousness soul.

In the consciousness soul the intellect with its discursiveness and the mind with its perceptions of universal consciousness are blended into an Intuition of the true spiritual heart nature of the meditator. Cognitive Intuition, developed in the soul through practicing the awareness of the spiritual nature of human consciousness, enables the thinking to be active with great intent but without any cognitive content, without a subject other than its own activity of cognition. This form of cognitive activity in the witness exists in the soul as a process of knowing in which the goal of the process is not to form concepts through ideation but to form capacities in the soul for its direct perception of higher worlds. In the higher worlds the angelic hosts generate creative deeds which result in the psychic and physical manifestations of the world. The activity of the angelic hosts numbs and overshadows the antipathetic ideation of the intellect in the pursuit of spiritual will in the intellectual soul. In the activity of meditation, the student works with these angelic beings to form inner organs of spiritual cognition.

At the opposite end of the psychic spectrum the activity of spiritual cognition developed in the witness through repeated contact with the angelic hosts sets in motion psychic currents which flow out of the organs of cognition toward the given sense world. These living currents of focused consciousness enhance the capacity for the witness to become aware of the creative processes of becoming which stand behind world phenomena. These psychic currents animate the world of sensation, moving in patterns of elemental forces that are reflected in the laws of nature and finally terminate in the crystallized manifestations of the physical world. The actual source of the forms and substances of the natural world is in a high realm of being. The soul's experience of contact with the fallen or manifest sense world normally numbs and crystallizes the nascent psychic currents of the witness into an illusory perception of the immanent reality of the physical world.

The waxing witness which has initially developed its I consciousness through meditation thus exists as a small flame of awareness suspended in the radiance of an overpowering surging chaos of benumbing creative activity. Rudolf Steiner calls this witness the I, or Ego. In contrast to the everyday ego or experience of self which is connected to the soul's experiences in the body, the Ego (with a capital "E") has the capacities of the witness which allow it to transcend itself and exist as the source of the flame of consciousness. Rudolf Steiner characterizes this transcendence as the experience of the I. The Ego witnesses or cognizes the I as an Inspiration, but when the Ego transcends itself to become one with the I, this state is the state of Intuition, wherein the knower and the known become one. The I is then experienced as its archetype, the I Am.

We have seen then that the path of transcendence has continually involved a blending of the forces of antipathy, thinking, and sense activity with the forces of sympathy and will into a harmonious, dynamic state of consciousness. At all levels of soul life the blending of sympathy and antipathy has used the power of Intuition to support and enhance the act of cognition. In the consciousness soul the intuition has been transcended into Intuition, becoming a soul-spiritual being, the witness that can observe its own cognitive activity. Cognition in the consciousness soul does not make use of abstractions, laws, concepts, or ideation but moves the soul into the realm in which the true I of the human being is in direct contact with the superconscious deeds of the angelic world. Rudolf Steiner tells us that this vast psychic vista is just beginning to unfold for the entire human race. The challenges which this transition into consciousness soul will present to humanity can only be met through conscious meditation upon the relationship between the witness and the higher worlds. This will further yield the possibility of a true seeing of the world of elemental nature forces as well as an experience of the spiritual hierarchies and ultimately of the I Am.

# 5

## The Black Madonna and the Mysteries of Dionysos

E very age has its heroes. Whether they are actual physical beings or mythological beings, each hero is surrounded by circumstances and encounters that are the stuff of dreams. Each hero has to face perilous journeys, accomplish impossible tasks, and ultimately make extreme sacrifices in order to achieve a goal. Recent writers on psychology and human development have given great attention to the role of the hero/heroine. In these works a significant common thread is the relationship that exists between a hero and his mother. I am using the male pronoun in this case because I have a very specific hero in mind: Dionysos. Dionysos had a number of incarnations, according to Rudolf Steiner, and these can be experienced by pondering the image of the madonna and child as depicted by artists through the ages.

One of the early examples of a prehistoric madonna figure is known to art historians as the Venus of Willendorf. This is a figure from middle Europe depicting a buxom pregnant woman, with a headdress of five spherical lumps resembling a raspberry. It is surmised that this image is a fertility totem and that it was used for ceremonial magic. Common sense tells us that no real woman ever looked like the Venus of Willendorf, since the figure is not realistic in its portrayal of the physical proportions of a pregnant woman. One might suppose that the artist either had another idea in mind or was inept at rendering what is seen in physical reality, for ancient artists are commonly pictured as growling, jabbering, ape-like creatures clumsily trying to portray physical reality and failing to do so for lack of intellect. But such a judgement would be an error—as we can see by looking at certain other sculptures of that period which reveal subtle, deeply cognitive minds at work in the fashioning of the objects.

**Venus of Willendorf**

These other sculptures are spherical in overall shape with perfectly spaced smaller spheres set at angles of 72° and arranged in the form of an organic dodeca-hedron. Any attempt to copy one of these spheres fosters a tremen-dous respect for the subtle power of the cognitive abilities of the earliest human artists. The artists who fashioned these objects were no rude daubers who accidental-ly stumbled onto their forms. However, the power of intellect required when one constructs an exact platonic dodecahedron is not engaged in the process of cre-ating those early models. There is a precision and knowledge in the earlier forms, but it is a knowing which seems to seep from deep, dimly accessible springs at the lower levels of the psychic land-scape. This ancient, dark know-ing is not discursive or categorical but is somehow submerged. It is perhaps what Goethe and Schiller characterized as the *total dark idea,* an idea the experience of which stimulates creative tension but which does not emerge into the bright knowing of the intellect. In *Faust,* Part II, Goethe refers to this area of submerged cognition as an experience of the realm of the "Mothers."

Out of this ancient creative chaos of imagination was born a seer who had all of the intuitional capacities and techniques of the adepts. His name was Dionysos Zagreus, or **Dionysos the Elder**. Rudolf Steiner tells us that he was a being who embodied all of the yearnings and will-permeated insights of the natural clairvoyance of the ancient world (Steiner, *Wonders,* 100). According to Greek myth, Dionysos the Elder was born of a union between Zeus, who represented the cosmic astral body of the soul, and Persephone, a goddess closely connected with human beings and innocent, instinctive clairvoyance. This con-nection to humanity and to the earth gave Dionysos the Elder, like his mother, the fate of being a suffering god, for Dionysos suffers death and dismemberment and is buried.

This image of burial is found in many myths in which a corn hero is involved. A corn hero or vegetation hero is killed, usually by being torn apart like an ear of wheat, and is either scattered or buried to be forgotten. Later, out of the power inherent in the total dark idea, each piece of the corn hero is resurrected into a whole being. The cults of Tammuz and Adonis are other examples of corn hero worship.

The central image of the Dionysos myth is that of the soul (a union of Zeus, the cosmic astral body, and Persephone, instinctive clairvoyance) developing a vehicle (Dionysos) which allows it to come into intimate physical contact with life on earth. This birth, however, arouses the anger of the other gods. Hera, in a yearning to be as creative as Zeus, gives birth to deformed sons, the Titans. They are powerful but insensitive beings who wreak havoc on the natural world. They tear apart the body of Dionysos the Elder (ancient clairvoyance) and bury it, but Athena (Zeus' parthenogenic daughter, representing cosmic intelligence) manages to rescue Dionysos' still-beating heart and give it to Zeus, who buries it in his own thigh. Thus the soul takes the heart forces of the old clairvoyance that are rescued by the power of cosmic intelligence and buries them in its own tremendous metabolic will-nature.

Earlier, when we looked at the Venus of Willendorf, we saw that the representation of the ancient gods and goddesses centered around pregnancy. This is an image of the unconscious will-permeated clair-

**organic dodecahedron**

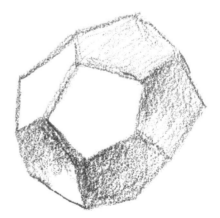

**Platonic dodecahedron**

voyance in which the ancient world was embedded. In the pregnant goddess we see that the corn hero has yet to be born into a true waking consciousness. So he slumbers in his seeing and after seeing returns again to the mother. But what of Dionysos, his beating heart still buried in the thigh (will-nature) of Zeus (the soul)? Naturally, he experienced a new birth. Zeus took the heart and made a love potion out of it, which he then gave to Semele, a mortal woman. Semele had a liaison with Zeus, and the offspring was a second incarnation of Dionysos, **Dionsyos the Younger**.

There are many conflicting images of Dionysos the Younger in mythology. One of the most striking is that of the human sacrifice and drunken orgiastic rites of the Bacchantes—for Bacchus, the god of wine, is another name for Dionysos the Younger. Semele, his mortal mother, was tricked by Hera, the goddess of individuality, into asking her lover Zeus to reveal to her who he truly was. Since he was the total force of the astral realm, Semele could not withstand the powerful light that streamed forth from his true nature, and she was irradiated, killed by the force of this astral vision. The myth goes on to say, however, that the child in Semele's womb was saved by an ivy vine which quickly grew to cover her belly and shield the baby from the astral light. The choice of ivy in the myth is significant, for ivy has long been used as a cure for drunkenness. When put into a drink of alcohol, its bitterness helps the drinker to lose the taste for intoxication. Like Dionysos the Elder, Dionsyos the Younger was also a corn hero, descending into the underworld in search of his mother. During his journey, or burial, the cults of his followers fell out of favor with the ruling powers in Greece, but upon his return he emerged as a resurrected god, cured of his drunkenness.

In the ancient world there was little separation between the gods or goddesses and the human beings who were acting under their inspiration and guidance. We find heroes continually being prodded by gods to form thoughts and take actions, and the gods themselves were incorporated into the heroes and could establish liaisons of every kind with human beings. Gods and goddesses, titans, heroes, centaurs, and fawns all had intimate and significant contact in a real way with humanity. Only more recently has modern consciousness made a discrete separation between human beings and the gods, calling human contact with spiritual realms mythic, and assigning such contact to a dimension far away from the real and present activities of human beings in the workaday world. In ancient times such a division would be unthinkable, almost immoral, and embarrassingly ego-centric. Members of a cult who worshiped a god were considered to be physical embodiments of that god, some to the degree that they took the name of the god. Thus the various incarnations of Dionysos were religious, psychic, mythic, poetic, and physically real all at the same time.

Those who impeded the work of the younger Dionysos were most often stricken with madness. A typical reaction to this madness was for a mother to kill and devour her son. These images of drunkenness, lust, and murder are disturbing in association with a god. It must be recognized, however, that in his work on behalf of humanity, Dionysos the Younger had to struggle with a problem that continues to face humanity in more recent times. He represents the young I-being of the human being which can only be born upon the earth and can only learn the lessons it needs to learn by struggling with the temptations that arise out of the lower astral realms. The elder Dionysos represented the first dim emergence of the ego-being as ancient clairvoyance. This ancient clairvoyance had to give way to a clearer vision of the physical world as seen in the younger Dionysos' teachings of agriculture and science to human beings. The elder Dionysos had to die, but the transformed I-being had to use the cosmic intelligence (Athena) of day consciousness to save the inner heart strivings of the ancient clairvoyance. The transformation of ancient seership into discursive scientific intellect is thus not without its difficulties. Dionysos the Younger straddles the gap between the consciousness of the old world, in which the madonna has not yet given birth, and the emerging cultures of science and intellect which must rise out of orgies and drunkenness into the clear light of reason.

How is this transition to take place? An ear of wheat or corn growing on a stem can either serve as seed for new plants to grow or as nutrition for an animal or a human being. As seed it fulfills the natural evolutionary purpose of sustaining its own species, and the work of God unfolds according to divine plan. When the seed is eaten, however, the animal life which uses it for nourishment has taken it out of its natural order and used it for its own purposes. These different roles of seed in an ear of grain are reflected in aspects of the corn hero which can be traced all the way back to Cain and Abel in the Hebrew tradition. The corn hero who is broken, scattered, and buried only to rise again whole, can be meditated upon as an image of the artistic/religious creative process that involves the releasing of an idea into other levels of consciousness, forgetting and burying it, and letting it resurrect out of the womb of the total dark idea. This image of the corn hero, however, is not useful in describing the challenges of the scientific thinker, a different kind of hero who must keep the problem close at hand and concentrate on mastering each sequential bit of data until the whole has been consumed and assimilated. The scientific thinker can then be identified with the goddess who holds all of the answers. For both types of hero the reunion with the goddess is the goal.

The artistic/religious corn hero tears himself to pieces in a self-destructive tantrum when he realizes that in order for him to be born his mother had to have a union with his father. The remorseful mother goddess gathers the pieces of the corn hero boy child and buries them. Out of the pieces, new beings are born. This type of corn hero could be called the *buried* god. The other corn hero type, the *devoured* god, is either eaten by the god or goddess or causes devouring behavior in devotees when they try to distance themselves from devotion and rituals required by the god. This type of devouring consciousness is indicative of the type of linear, sequential logic that permeates the pursuit of science. In science the thinker devours the data, bit by bit, until the thought structure becomes one with the data. The burial or gestation of the idea is not taken into account; only the devouring is important.

We can see from this that Dionysos the Elder was primarily a religious corn hero. He was torn apart, buried, and resurrected. Dionysos the Younger, however, has both the attributes of the buried corn hero and of the devoured hero. With the younger Dionysos, the unconscious, mystical abandonment of ancient clairvoyance has fallen into a state of decay and drunkenness. The intoxication is imaged in Semele's love potion and her request to have a supersensible experience of the astral plane. The unborn I-being inside her could not stand such a searing vision and was protected by a plant-induced sobriety. This is a picture of the ancient unconscious clairvoyance which needs to be tempered with the intellect so that the unborn I-being can work toward freedom on earth. The task of the emerging I-being is to transform the power of the lower astral realms filled with instincts and unconscious visions, into the higher astral plane of human spirit and knowledge. Dionysos the Younger is connected both to the burial initiation of ancient clairvoyance and to the awakened, devouring initiation of emerging scientific consciousness. His trial of overcoming drunkenness, or gluttony, and his trial of burial in the underworld while looking for his mother show him to be a transitional figure.

The images that arise out of such a figure as Dionysos the Younger are prophetic of a new order of hero. In art, this new hero is depicted in a different relationship to the mother. In the Egyptian figure of Isis suckling Horus, for instance, we can see that the hero is no longer in the womb. He is still dependent on the mother forces but has emerged as a separate being. The hero as a separate being is the most characteristic depiction for madonnas in late Egyptian and Greek times. The cults of Dionysos underwent a metamorphosis from the unconscious shamanistic practices of early Greece through an orgiastic phase that continued into Roman times. Dionysos the Younger had to overcome his tendency to drunken disorderliness and debauchery, and his retinue was also engaged in the trial of overcoming a bestial lower nature. The transformed Dionysos the Younger then used his newly born power of intellect to teach human beings about improved methods of agriculture, viticulture, writing, and other arts. The ancient clairvoyance was thus transformed into sci-

**Isis suckling Horus**

ence based on intellectual knowledge, and in the ancient world the cult of Dionysos the Younger spread throughout eastern and central Europe and Asia Minor.

The image of the transformed Dionysos sitting on the knee of his mother is echoed for the next fourteen centuries as a central image of Christian art. For example, in a ninth century mosaic in St. Sophia we can see the child holding a book and raising his hand in blessing. Later images from the Middle Ages show the child holding a book and a globe of the world like a ball. These symbols are an echo of the initiation deeds of Dionysos the Younger who, by overcoming gluttony and burial, brought balance into his life and transformed the world of ancient channelling into reasoned thinking.

This is not the end of the Dionysos drama, however, for when the Romans introduced their intellectual forms of religion, the tendency toward material excesses made the bacchanalian aspects of Dionysos more popular than the transformed aspects. The rational Romans were already employing the fruits of science in their engineering and judicial activities, and perhaps the mundane aspects of these applications caused ritual practice to lose some of its allure. The cults of Dionysos became linked with places in which mystery schools had been formed. The mystery schools (or simply "the mysteries") sought to preserve religious worship even for the emerging intellect-endowed ego-beings of the participants. The mysteries were actually continuations of far more ancient mysteries that had been taught in all lands to select candidates since the beginning of human evolution. The main difference between the Greco-Roman mysteries and the ancient mysteries was that in the ancient mysteries no recognition of the ego of the individual human being was made.

In the late Greek mysteries, a third incarnation of the Dionysos being came to be experienced and venerated. This being was **Dionysos Jaccus** (also Jaccoes or Iaccus). Legend has it that Jaccus was born out of a liaison between Zeus (cosmic astrality) and Demeter, the suffering earth goddess of fertility. Demeter has similar qualities to those of Isis or Sophia. She is the representative of the all-creative fecund wisdom of God, the companion to God before the birth of the world. Jaccus took the place of Dionysos the Younger when the outward cult of Dionysos became decadent and turned toward the lower instincts, forcing the inner drama of the mystery wisdom to go underground.

Jaccus is a true pre-Christ corn hero. His devotees experienced him not in a shamanic trance, nor in a drunken orgy, but in plays which were chiefly about his birth, passion, death, and rebirth. The plays were staged by the priests of the mysteries for whom Jaccus was the divinity of individual ego-consciousness. The ancient seership had died, was transformed into the first spark of intellectual independence, and ultimately was revealed to waking consciousness through the arts. The important aspect of Jaccus was not his mythological exploits and adventures; it was the fact that his devotees in the mysteries could experience his presence in their own souls as acts of individual cognition. Where the elder Dionysos had enveloped the will in a religious experience, and the younger Dionysos had engaged the intellect in the struggle with the lower nature, Jaccus entered the feeling life of the soul through catharsis, the healing power of the arts.

A look into art history can find Jaccus in madonna settings that are paradoxical, unique, and enigmatic. A Jaccus child is outside its mother, is free of the body, and is not a suckling. He is not cuddly or precocious like a human infant. He is often seen in the act of bestowing a blessing. He is not carried bodily on a shoulder or snuggled in the arms of an adoring mother but floats, suspended by the heart forces issuing from the feeling realm of the madonna. In his expression there is a detached sense of triumph without overbearing severity, and an acknowledgement of the cosmic destiny and origin of his own inner being. Freedom, joy, a sense of floating, serenity, and inner composure are in his demeanor. These attributes describe a being who is cosmic and radiant, yet also dark, warmly detached, romantic, and enigmatic. They are as rare in the art of the madonna as they are in individuals in real life, yet there

**mosaic from St. Sophia**

**Matisse madonna**

are examples of Jaccus Madonnas from the Middle Ages, the Renaissance, and even the modern world.

To begin with, let us look at a modern Jaccus Madonna, an utterly simple and powerful work by the master Henri Matisse. This work was done as the main decoration for a small chapel on the Riviera. It shows a mother who is both supportive and willing to allow her child freedom. The floating child has his arms outstretched in a detached *orante* (praying) gesture of Early Christian art. The gaze of both figures is straight forward. The child appears to glide or fly out of its mother's heart region. The mood is somber, clean, and virtuous, yet cosmic and joyful. Color is given by stained glass windows on the opposite wall, thus leaving the image free to change, grow, and transform. Its austerity gives it richness, and its economy gives it power to bring to mind a feeling of victory over death.

Another Jaccus Madonna comes from the hand of another great master, Leonardo da Vinci. The image is of St. Anne and her son, John the Baptist, seated with Mary and Jesus. Here is a true Jaccus in which the ambiguities abound. He is depicted as a cosmic child floating out of his mother's heart. He gestures in blessing as his aunt continues the gesture of his blessing in an upturned finger pointing toward the Godhead. He is warmly dark but bathed in a suffused, ethereal light. Could the hill behind be prophetic of the place of the Crucifixion? Could the swirling darkness that surrounds the child hint at his trials? And yet the somber children so intent upon their encounter are enveloped and supported by the warm, knowing smiles of the two mothers. Darkness and light, somberness and joy, a floating otherworldliness and monumental form—these enigmatic qualities suffuse this towering masterwork, as echoes of the mysteries of Jaccus resound in the drama of the life of Christ, the image of a god living in a body of flesh.

**Leonardo Madonna**

Finally, the source for the great majority of Jaccus Madonna images can be found in the works of those artists who are inspired by the Black Madonna. The most famous of these Madonnas is Our Lady of Chestachowa (*Chest-ah-hova*), the most revered icon in Poland. During the Middle Ages the church in which the icon was housed was destroyed in flames. The icon was found on the only unburned wall, undamaged except that the ground coral pigment used to paint the features of the mother and child had turned black in the heat of the fire. The miracle of the saving of the Black Madonna has inspired the Polish people for centuries as they have faced the fires of war and oppression. Legend has it that Our Lady of Chestachowa was painted by the evangelist St. Luke, the patron saint of doctors and painters. In the ancient world physicians and artists used the same materials, had similar technical processes, and shared the common goal of healing. This ancient view sits at the very heart of the relationship between Jaccus-Christos and his mother, the Black Madonna. By contrast, science as the pursuit of high technology and art as the pursuit of personal fantasy work in such a way as to deny the common root they have in healing the body and soul.

The vast tradition of the Black Madonna and her son the corn hero, of which Our Lady of Chestachowa is a prime example, repre-

**Our Lady of Chestachowa**

sents a world vision in which nature is not captured, named, and forced into servitude, but rather is understood in a compassionate way whereby the intellect presents its facts but then listens for the answer which the spiritual world provides. This listening perception of nature is symbolized in the ritual burial of the Black Madonna in the darkest recesses of the church. Traditionally, she resides in dim alcoves, shrines, or caverns throughout the late summer, fall, and early winter months. At the winter solstice, the darkest time of the year, she is lifted out of her burial place and carried through the town in a procession. Like Persephone and Dionysos, the Black Madonna endures burial to listen to the silence of the dark earth. The ritual is an exact analog which teaches the creative consciousness to listen in silence to the true voices of nature. In today's world such listening allows the scientifically inclined intellect to fructify its search for truth with Intuitive power. The ability to link clear thinking with Inspiration and Intuitive perception makes the Black Madonna and Jaccus-Christos symbol a powerful meditational image for artists, poets, teachers, and scientists who are striving to allow the spiritual world to enter their work.

Traditionally the Black Madonna is the patron of women about to undergo the dark trial of childbirth. Images of her and her gravity-defying babe were hung in birthing rooms to give strength and comfort in the chaos and insecurity of this deep, mysterious threshold between two worlds. Thinkers wishing to transcend the brain-bound intellect and explore the realms of Intuition are in a similar situation to that of a birthing mother. Inspirations issuing from the realm of the total dark idea are often experienced as painfully confusing riddles or problems that are situated at odd angles to the psychic birth canal of meditation. It is here that the Black Madonna can serve as midwife between the True Self and the soul. She can provide fresh forces to continue the concentration needed for success.

Without the intercession of the Black Madonna, scientific thinking most often produces a stillborn thought—a merely innovative computational sum of ideas without the spark of originality or the forces that promote growth and healing for other human beings. Although ideas such as these initially appear clever, innovative, and progressive, in the long run they devitalize the thinker and the culture into which they are born, bringing sickness and confusion into the cultural life. Linear cause-and-effect "inspirations" by men of "genius" coagulate the experience of earth and its life into an abstract computational landscape. This chills the heart, for it offers only bleak images of impersonal, abstracted forces of nature engaged in relentless combat, with human life caught impotently in their grip. Such alienation from nature is the price that human beings pay for the freedom we have won through developing logical, empirical thinking. The capacity to think in concepts frees human beings from the need to comply unconsciously with the directives of the Godhead. Thus freed, we experience the exhilaration of independent psychic existence and the simultaneous yearning for the union with, succor from, and counsel of a source of wisdom higher than ourselves.

Acting as mediator between the soaring conceptual life of higher reason and the spontaneous creative outpouring of the Godhead who animates and sustains nature, the Black Madonna has guided and facilitated the prayers and meditations of countless devotees. She represents a path whereby the modern human soul caught in the labyrinth of abstract thinking can find its way to a compassionate experience of nature. She enables the transcendent creative forces in the soul to resonate with the transcendent creative forces in the natural world.

To put oneself into contact with the Black Madonna it is necessary first to develop strong powers of concentration through the practice of logical scientific thinking based on an intellectual grasp of the life of concepts. Firmly grounded in the conceptual life, the soul can begin to rise into the realm of supersensible cognition. In this realm thoughts have forms and ideas are palpable realities. The discipline of the sciences serves for the modern human being as the prerequisite grounding in logical thinking so necessary for entrance into higher realms of cognition.    Logic and deduction, however, have limits. Deduction and its inherent weaknesses are overcome and transcended when logical thought is transformed into creative thinking through rhythmic spiritual practice.

Creative thinking recognizes that for every truth experienced through deductive logic there are numerous tangent cognitive planes of experience that can be induced through psychologically and systematically expanding our cognitive view.    To do this the scientific reasoning dependent upon the consumption of data must release, forget, give away, or bury the idea in the womb of the Black Madonna. The thinker must take the will forces of intuition in thinking, which are developed through logic and concentration, and reverse them. The personal will is thereby set free from the lower self and its physical bias and is transformed into Intuition or Cosmic Will.

On this path of reversal, the shift from logical thinking to creative thinking brings ever clearer pictures of the web of desires in which the soul is entangled.    The Black Madonna understands desire and the dark soul yearnings connected with life on earth.    She gives birth to Jaccus—the Logos, the Christ—a suffering God who is able to transcend the abyss, to compassionately observe the dark side of human life, and to sacrifice the freedom of personally willed activity for the higher experience of surrender to supersensible cognition.    The Black Madonna and her black child enable the soul to observe its own darkness in the calm, clear knowledge that transcendent forces are also available to the soul.    Through Jaccus the will can be purified and rectified in its currents.    The purified will can then resonate with higher, finer sources of intelligence.    This allows the soul's organs of cognition to induce creative thoughts much beyond the soul's native capacities.    By meditating on the Black Madonna and her child the purified currents of the will and the stabilized currents of the intellect can be brought together into a fusion in the heart—for it is from the heart that the Black Madonna and her child find their forces of transcendent compassion.    In the human heart the religious impulses of the will and the scientific impulses of the thought life are nurtured into the capacity to surrender what is known in order to be free enough to create beauty, harmony, and healing.    The Black Madonna offers to modern human beings the hope of resolving the predicament of abstraction in the arts and sciences.    She offers a sacred path for those who are left uninspired by layers of ecumenical varnish on the surfaces of world religion.

The late A. B. Giamatti has characterized the coming end of the century and simultaneous end of the millennium as a time in which an *apocalyptic style* will fill the souls of humanity. The apocalyptic style is produced in the soul by a paradox. The paradox is that the things that happen today are simultaneously the newest and the oldest events in the history of the planet. The old quality of modern events is experienced on an unconscious level by the soul as a tremendous sense of failure and fatigue in the face of catastrophically multiplying world problems. On the surface the technological achievements of the postmodern world are hailed as new breakthroughs and advances. Down deep in the darker portions of the soul, however, these achievements are harbingers of dire consequences and catastrophes. The final days of a century or the final days of a millennium are times when, Giamatti has observed, the burden of fatigue and malaise blooms exponentially in each soul.

This collective tendency toward an apocalyptic style is characterized by a fear of culture's irremediable decline, and it engenders a turning away from public obligations into a pathological absorption with the personality. The marketplace urges us to value self-satisfaction as the ultimate goal of existence:  eat, drink, and be merry, for tomorrow we may die. The sciences, the arts, and politics are disconnected from morality because moral judgements take time and we have no time to lose. We are tired and time is short. Drugs are quicker than meditation, channeling is more exciting than meditative discipline, political rhetoric more expeditious than facing hard problems in full consciousness. All of this leads to a style that is redolent with the aroma of apocalypse. Issues are immediately polarized by the media, and overstatement collides with overstatement in a frenzy of pointing fingers, bombast, and coercion. Fear-mongering replaces reasoned passion, and the growing suspicion that nature is about to self-destruct sits behind news desks around the world. The apocalyptic style warns us of the dangers but does not offer solutions. Scientists, artists, clergy, politicians, and educators of the apocalyptic style draw attention to themselves by drawing attention to the problems and then wringing their hands and saying, "But there are no real solutions because the problems are so big."

Amid the clang and clatter of this current Tower of Babel there exists a silent sacred space. In the silent sacred space there is compassion, warmth, and a sense of resolve. There is a feeling that no trial given to humanity is beyond its endurance. In this space there is a feeling that all grievances can be negotiated, all conflicts resolved, and all wounds made whole. The silent sacred space is the source of life for the human heart. Sacred feelings are born in the heart when currents of will and thinking meet in the spontaneous silent perception of the ineffable beauty and wisdom present in the sense world. These feelings are only available to those who have struggled to objectify thinking and who have avoided the cold, apocalyptic visions of self-willed passion.

The Black Madonna and her child speak to the heart in the small, still, silent voice of meditation. In quiet, reflective moments these two suffering deities approach the heart space of the meditating human being to bestow options, ideas, and fresh forces with which to battle against ignorance and greed for power. The Black Madonna teaches the heart to think, and when it thinks, brain-bound cognition ceases and communion fills the void left by its silence. The silent creative thinking heart finds ways to turn technical arrogance into healing insight and self-absorption into the power to recognize the work of the Creator in the world.

Each year at Christmastime as the sun gives its strength to the southern hemisphere, human beings in the darkened northern temperate zones can experience a culminating dread and fatigue. Another year is about to end. We have grown another year older with the sun. Darkness looms in our path as fear of the unknown and the cold of winter fill the heart with anxiety. At this time of deepest darkness it is healing to contemplate artistically the image of the dark Madonna and her eternally blessing child. They have transcended the rigidity of ancient binding ritual, they have suffered burial and rejection, they have devoured the cold light of intellectual abstraction, and in their suffering they have grown to love the human soul.

For these great suffering beings the human soul is the potential seed of a great global process of transformation whereby the work of the Creator can be recognized in its true artistic, compassionate grace. The Black Madonna was there when the Creator summoned up the first dim images of the world. It was she who gave birth to the ancient being of clairvoyance, Dionysos Zagreus. She saw him rent and buried. It was she who gave birth to Dionysos the Younger and saw her mortal reflection, Semele, burn in astral fire. She gave the force to grow the vine and tasted the shame of wantonness and intoxication.

She watched her son suffer and struggle and overcome his animal nature. She saw him triumph over the grave only to fall before jealousy and suspicion.

Today the Black Madonna sees her son born again in the hearts and imaginations of human beings who learn her lessons of humility and sacrifice. At Christmas, near the end of the century, near the end of the millennium, she is there watching and listening to the silent thinking of human hearts. Out of these forces she will fashion creativity, healing, and a renewed respect for the natural world. Just as she gives birth out of the primal darkness to life-enhancing forces, so the sun will once again be born out of its womb of darkness in the earth and guide the rising life of earth into a new spring. At Christmas, then, her son is born who brings to darkened human souls the perception that the risen Sun Being dwells within their flesh, the conviction that the eternal presence of God the Father is the source of their thoughts, and the direct experience that the Madonna and Child breathe and float on currents flowing silently in and out of every beating human heart.

# 6

# FROM IMAGE TO VISION

The word for a seer in ancient Persia was *mage* (or *magus)*, a term which has roots in common with the more familiar words *magic* and *image*. To the ancient Persian a mage was a seer with the ability to transform images into symbols in order to develop the power of inner vision, prophecy, or clairvoyance. In the language of traditional mystery wisdom the power to transform image into symbol issues from a great supersensible being called Holy Wisdom, the Primal Wisdom of God, or Sophia.

The Sophia being resides in the ordering power and creative formal motions of the celestial spheres. This primal ordering guides the forms or energetic templates which physical manifestations follow on the way into a material incarnation. In an esoteric sense the physical is not synonymous with life. Life is the supersensible state of existence out of which the physical manifests. In the life realms are found the forms or laws lying behind existence on the manifest level. The forms themselves are not material but can be thought of as somewhat like the forms a sculptor would employ for metal casting—negative spaces into which material is injected. The form in this sense is a living Idea that guides and directs the finished appearance of the material manifestation.

The forms or Ideas found in the supersensible world can also be experienced by reflecting on the concept of biological species. Nowhere is it possible to find the material manifestation of a species. One cannot go out into the world and capture a species. Nonetheless, species live supersensibly. A species exists as a template guiding the manifestations and evolutionary principles that stand behind a group of plants or animals. These Ideas are the archetypes or formal principles which stand behind the biological facts.

In the ancient world Sophia was seen as the source of the wisdom contained in these Ideas. Her name, Holy Wisdom, or the Primal

63

Wisdom of God, reflects her exalted position in the spiritual hierarchies. Sophia was understood to have ordered the manifest earthly world in the image of the celestial starry realms. The ancient mage could approach Sophia by contemplating the forms seen supersensibly through systematic observation of the manifest world. Through the study of astronomy, astrology, geomancy, mathematics, and related fields, the seer cultivated an appreciation of the subtle world hovering just behind the material world. This world is composed of the lawful, mathematically musical modes and intervals governing life and its subsequent physical manifestations. The periodic table of Mendeleev is an example of this harmonic ordering.

Today, the Ideas contained in the Holy Wisdom of Sophia are experienced in human consciousness as personally perceived thoughts. In the ancient world this was not the case. Seers experienced the Sophianic Idea as an inner image which came to overshadow their consciousness, giving them oracular insight or magical power. Those wishing to cross the threshold into the domain of Sophia had a number of tasks to complete which were designed to form an organ of thought in their life bodies. In older traditions the door to the life body was most effectively entered through the feeling realm. Since ancient times, Sophia has been the counselor who stands in the doorway between the feelings and the life forces. In the modern human consciousness the gifts of Sophia have evolved into capacities for logical thinking, while in the ancient world, before logical thought and science had developed, the gift of Sophia was clairvoyance.

To attain this ancient clairvoyance seers had to enter into shamanistic trances to commune with Sophia. In order to prepare the soul for this communion it was necessary to undergo a mystical apprenticeship during which sensitivity to the laws of life and feeling was developed. Central to most traditions of shamanic discipline were two opposite yet complementary tasks: purification and adherence to binding ritual. These two aspects, one outer (ritual) and one inner (purification), were interdependent yet distinct from one another. While often fused and intermingled in practice, at the level of intention they worked polarically in the soul life of the shaman.

One of the first tasks on a novice's path was to systematically purge the desire life of fallen personal feelings. Teachers in the nature religions often used animal totems as a way of effecting this purge. Trainees were required to become so familiar with the life and activities of the totem animal that they could be accepted by the grandfather spirit animating the group soul of the totem animal. At puberty a young person went "crying for a vision," seeking to encounter the totem animal in the form of a mystical vision. Fasting, bathing, and mantras prepared the neophyte for entry into the soul-spiritual realms. Close study of the animal world and skill in tracking and mimicking the animals in the natural world gave the aspiring seer a view into the desire nature of the human soul.

The seeker expected that through such attention to the behavior of animals the purified feelings of the animal's group soul would be revealed. In many respects, this revelation is a validation of the human soul. It was recognized, however, that a tiger that kills a deer is not guilty of murder, for this is not out of the natural order. The natural order, after all, is a reflection of Sophia, the ordering principle of the cosmos. In the cosmos there is direct motion and retrograde motion, acceleration and deceleration, culmination and descent. All of this is without blame until there is a self-aware witness. Since self-awareness is not part of the feeling emanations of the animal world, there is no moral judgement connected to animal behaviors such as acts which in human beings would be called murder, mayhem, and incest.

If an ancient seer were to emulate a totem animal and such acts were part of that animal's path through life, was the shaman expected to murder and rape in order to learn from the brother animal? Quite the contrary was the practice of the progressive ancient mystery paths. By carefully noting the desire life of the totem animal, a neophyte could be shown how an unbalanced, one-sided desire life leads to automatic behavior in an animal—ultimately resulting in its destruction by a smarter, more perceptive enemy.

For most animals the enemy more cunning than any other was the human being. Through totems came the recognition that the human being needed to purify his motives and actions to enable his spirit to communicate with the spirit guides of each animal species. Once a shaman's feeling life was purified and harmonized, it had access to any other group soul in the soul-spiritual world. His spirit could journey there and become each animal in turn. In effect, the purified human soul was equal to the group soul of a species.

In the soul-spiritual world, however, not all beings are benign. There are retarded and fallen beings who produce effects harmful to a seer just as there are predators harmful to prey in the natural world.

These relationships necessitate the development of techniques to protect the astral traveller. Through the forces in tribal bloodlines or through spirit clans, binding rituals were developed based upon insights and experiences gleaned from generations of soul-spiritual research.

While purification had a great deal to do with the development of will and the training of attention for an individual seer, the binding ritual was a purely external set of demands which had to be met under pain of ostracism, madness, or death. Binding rituals had to be followed to the letter with absolutely no room for personal freedom. The purpose was to provide a "silver cord" of safety by which the seer could get back to the physical plane, should the journey prove too dangerous. Binding ritual molded the seer's attention into intention, a coherent force uniting the will and the thinking and lifting the soul to a higher state of functioning at which the seer could do magical deeds in the soul-spiritual realm.

The ritual formation of intention was primarily a willed activity in the unconscious. The external law given to the seer through tradition took the place of what would later become free discursive intellect. The uniting of the will of the seer with universal will was an act so powerful and so fraught with danger and the potential for misuse that the ancient seers categorically prohibited its free use by human beings. The idea of free intellectual creativity as a birthright was anathema to the ancient adepts who recognized that the only safe path through the lands of soul and spirit involved both personal purification and strict adherence to binding ritual. When these demands were met the adept could expand to a perception of the Sophia being, the true Primal Wisdom of God who ordered all creation and allowed human beings to perceive that order, albeit unconsciously. Seers who were capable of meeting the inner and outer demands of seership were developing the seeds of today's natural sciences.

Into this plan, however, there came a drama known to Gnostic esotericism as the rape of Sophia. In this drama the time for the proper development of shamanism was an ancient era when the human soul was a perfect vehicle for revelation from divine beings. As human soul life began to progress, however, the emerging individuality of the human intellect mirrored the prideful intellectuality of the being of Lucifer. By degrees, shamanism became enmeshed in material magic and degenerated into the pursuit of material longevity and the formation of reservoirs of personal psychic power. These developments were the result of a spiritual event in which the primal wisdom of Sophia became increasingly disturbed. Sophia's holy silence, the complete absorption in an inner, meditative stillness, had to evolve into an inner flow of ideas in the human intellect, thereby allowing freedom to develop for human beings. This evolution, though necessary, nevertheless created perturbations in Sophia's life of silence. She lost sight of the Godhead, and the desire that arose in her filled her with longing. This desire did not escape the scrutiny of Lucifer, who was quickened in his desire for the Sophia. He approached her and forced his attentions upon her. In her shame she gathered all of the elements of desire within her being and cast them from herself into the form of another being, Sophia Achamoth. Lucifer then surrounded the Sophia being with a prison known as the belt of lies. Ever since then her image, Sophia Achamoth, has roamed through space as the feeble reflection of the true being of Sophia, now concealed from human perception. This concealment is the source of the illusion that the intellect with its insight into the sense world encompasses the total potential of human understanding.

Purification and binding ritual maintained the purity of seership in ancient mysteries. With the rape of Sophia, the birth of the Achamoth, and the imprisoning of Holy Wisdom in the intellect's belt of lies, the ground of ancient wisdom shifted and its practices fell into decadence. The wisdom of the stars retreated from clairvoyant vision and was replaced by superstition and black magic, i.e., magic for personal power. In most mysteries, purification and ritual were increasingly seen as one event, for purification became simply a means to a desired end—whatever end was being petitioned for by the ritual. For instance, a petitioner might avoid his wife's bed for a few days and offer a token meal in the form of ritual food if he wanted to kill a deer. The Achamoth and her life of desire permeated the seer's life in the spiritual worlds. Similarly, the traditional binding rituals which were passed on through bloodlines or clan lines began to dissolve under the waxing power of personal reasoning. Where once strict obedience was seen as progressive, it then came under question, and the sense world was increasingly experienced as the domain of knowledge and power instead of as an image of the spirit.

In various lectures on Gnosticism Rudolf Steiner gives a clear and detailed picture of the unfolding of these events in the history of human understanding. The purpose here is not to chronicle this evolution, but to ask what influence this transformation has had upon the faculty of Imagination and the unfolding of spiritual vision. Sophia has for long ages been considered the bestower of the power of Imagination; the Imaginations that arise out of the soul-spiritual worlds through Sophia and become incarnate are the spirit substances of her body. These Imaginations were freely given to ancient seers who had undergone ritual and purification training. As personal intellectuality took away the virginal quality of Imagination and replaced it with the obscuring belt of lies, the seeing power in spirit vision was taken over by the intellect and was fettered into the material world. With the loss of the consciousness of Sophianic Imagination, the possibility for freedom in spirit vision was given to the individual human thinker. Cosmic wisdom as an outpouring from Sophia was replaced by the desire for knowledge. Personal intellectual activity came to separate the thinker and the seer. In this separation arises abstraction which focuses the soul on the sense world.

Through intellectual abstraction the material world appears as the source of creation instead of the product of creation. In this activity the desire principle, Sophia Achamoth, becomes mingled with the pure soul-spiritual activity of perception. The perceiving soul uses its sense organs which have fallen into the unconscious physical world, to consume the data of the sense world. That is, we are not conscious of our own perceptive activity in the sensing. The faculty of Imagination becomes merely imaginative—a passive learning device or screen which receives data in the form of mental images projected from the data bank of the memory. These images have no inner vitality and serve simply as grist for the mill of the intellect.

The unconscious reproduction of mental images that lack spiritual validity happens within the human phantom. Rudolf Steiner characterizes this being as the sense activity which remains unconscious. Because the phantom lies outside the awake consciousness, the eyes, ears, and other sense organs do not impinge on the sense impressions coming through them. This virginal, passive quality in the life of the senses enables them to serve human beings in the proper way. On the other hand, with the loss of outpouring Sophianic Imagination no guiding light was left in sense activity to protect it from personal feelings and desires.

The passage in the Bible referring to the opening of the eyes in Adam and Eve as they fell from Paradise points to the problem of the phantom. Rudolf Steiner also describes the phantom as the remnants of the archetypal virginal soul of Adam in the human soul. At the Fall this part of Adam's soul went into seclusion. Since Adam was the progenitor of the human being, however, something of the essence of this soul condition, the virginal soul without karma, was retained in the souls of the human beings who followed. This small sheath of virginal essence, totally open to the world in a selfless way, can be perceived in the human soul as the capacities of the sense organs.

The phantom is living in that it exists as sensitive flows of energies through the "dead" organs. It is not material and it is not pure spirit; it exists in a state that fluctuates between matter and spirit. The phantom's being is as an image moving through space, transmitting sensations and life energies to the soul from the world and vice versa. Soul currents move from the soul through the phantom into the subtle productions of the arts as well as going in the other direction for everyday sense activity.

The phantom is a vehicle that has the potential to be used more or less consciously by the soul. It is formed in the likeness of the soul and has been ordered since ancient times by the patterns implicit in the starry cosmic realm—in other words, by Sophia. The phantom was impoverished by the primeval imprisonment of Sophia that robbed the Sophia being of her capacity to endow human beings with Imagination. As the phantom lost this current of benign protection it became vulnerable to the rigidifying death forces of abstract intellectuality. The currents of Imagination no longer flowed through the phantom, and the image nature of its being was filled with the forces of death, of materialistic thought.

The life nature of the phantom puts it into continual communion with the starry realm, and it is here that, lacking pure Sophianic Imagination, the phantom becomes tainted by the desire nature of the fallen Sophia Achamoth, and the lower imagination becomes attached to images from the sense world. The vulnerability of the phantom in its encounter with death and desire make it susceptible to fear and illusion. The selfless phantom existing as an image in the soul-spiritual realm is thus caught between the death images of the material realm of intellect and the irrational desire life of the personalized feelings of the fallen Sophia Achamoth.

At the present time, then, is it any wonder that the realm of the senses is mistrusted by science and religion? Is the phantom to remain enchanted forever? Is Sophia destined to remain in her prison, and are her life-bestowing currents of Imagination to be withheld from the human soul for all eternity?  To begin even a tentative answer to this we must return once again to the two basic tasks of the ancient seers:  binding ritual and purification.

With the coming of Christ, the binding ritual of old Hebrew law fulfilled its mission.  Christ as the archetype of creative humanity rejected the external binding rituals of the Pharisees in favor of an inner, creative, cosmic ritual which served the same purpose as the older outer ritual.  This inner ritual is none other than the process of willed creative thinking which is the Sophia-imbued capacity of human beings to move their thinking in harmony with cosmic law. Christ gave the phantom the ability to return to the currents of Imagination, for the soul forces inherent in imaginative thinking were brought to earth once again by the virginal soul of Adam in the form of Jesus of Nazareth.  By uniting these soul forces with the cosmic star-initiated thinking forces of ancient initiates, Christ Jesus showed the way of redemption for the human phantom.  Through rigorous, cosmic, creative thinking the phantom and its sense life can be irradiated with cognition and understanding, and the soul can once more approach the Imagination of Sophia.

For this to happen the thinker must first control and organize sensations into the reasoned perceptions of natural science.  Such a process can have the same effect as the old binding ritual except that the thinking springs from the effort of each individual and is not imposed from outside.  There is a danger, however, that the death forces inherent in the material world may overwhelm the soul and create the illusion that all of existence is devoid of creativity except in the field of technical innovation.  Learning then takes on the form of memorizing laws and "correct" views and applying them in the proper ways at the proper times.  The binding force of the old mysteries thus replaces creativity with innovation, and abstraction destroys the soul's capacity to improvise.  The phantom is reduced to a screen upon which images are projected in order to corroborate facts and data from the technical world, ordering them according to abstract laws that are outside the soul's realm of influence.  This creates a mood of soul in which images are valued only on the level of information and are seen as unrelated to concepts.  In truth, however, the image is the link between a sense impression, which may change according to the perception of the thinker, and the eternal truth of a living concept.  In connecting sense impression and concept, an image can serve the thinker as a tool for inner transformation through disciplined perception.  In modern life, sense perception is rejected in favor of the fallacy that abstract thought is the ultimate authority for the thinker who is trying to understand the sense world and its appearances.

For the seer, the new inner ritual of thinking protects the soul in much the same way as the older, external ritual did.  The advantage over the old way is that the thinker, through his individual capacity for thinking, is now free to improvise creatively.  The danger for the thinker is that the exuberance of freedom and creativity only too easily falls prey to the rigid thought forms of a science ruled by logic and causal relations.  This danger becomes even stronger as the amount of data increases and as the soul loses control over the inner activity of the phantom.  Moreover, in modern life the human being is subjected to a vast number of sense impressions which do not issue from human beings in a living way, but are rather penetrated with the forces of death.  This produces a certain numbness in the already unconscious phantom.  Modern use of video displays, computer graphics, and electronic media with their enormous flow of images accelerate the paralysis of the phantom to an alarming degree.

It is this paralysis of the phantom that unleashes in the soul an overwhelming desire to be sensually stimulated from the outside.  The ancient seers practiced fasting and sexual abstinence to control their earthly appetites.  They also controlled the desire for sense experiences through meditation, for meditation, too, is a fasting process in which the soul abstains from outer sense activity.  The senses are turned inward in order to develop a womb of silence in which the soul may begin the slow process of healing—healing itself of the urge to understand everything with the intellect.  As we saw earlier, Goethe saw this as a movement from intellect to reason.

In reason the ability of the soul to form abstract thoughts is turned into the capacity to observe one's own processes of cognitive perception.  In this activity one can experience oneself as a creative source of moral ideas, transforming the chilling force of abstraction in a dynamic experience of the living beings at work behind the veil of human sense perception.  Meditation is an inner path of development in which our transformed relationship to our senses allows us to lift the natural world order into a moral world order.  It enables human beings to have their own moral Imagination in place of what previously flowed to them from Sophia.  For human beings it is useful to develop the perception that moral Imagination flows out from them and that they can create living images which, as Sophianic revelations, will once again inspire the soul and will further human evolution. On this path we travel from outer image to inner vision, finding healing in a world torn into the duality of outer and inner.

Adam and Eve had their eyes opened in the Fall. Esoterically this was the awakening through the sense life into a world that contains many things outside of and separate from the self. In the ancient world, this experience was softened by an inner connection which seers maintained to the spiritual world through trance techniques. In these states the human being was given direction and impetus to behave in certain ways, and cultures arose out of these directions and impulses. This relationship in which the spiritual world gives and the human being receives is the signature of the old clairvoyance. With the fall of the mysteries into rational empiricism, the spiritual world ceased to be the source of guiding Imaginations. Imaginations no longer come through traditions or from the natural world, and it now seems as if each person, through exercising the intellect, can invent inner imaginations independent of the cosmos. In this frame of mind human beings do not simply receive indications from the cosmos; they have power to transform nature on a large scale. Whether or not human beings have the wisdom through Sophia to become transformers for the good of the whole remains to be seen and is the central problem of this book.

In paradise, the fall of Adam and Eve raised this dilemma for all human beings who were to follow. We begin to awaken from the dream in which the sense life has been embedded and to experience a world order pouring through Sophia into the manifold forms of nature. This heals the abyss between the self and the world. We awaken to our role as transformers, given to us in potential by Father Adam and rooted in the very nerves and blood of our sense organs. We restrict the images we allow into our soul or even fast from images entirely. We make a commitment to practice daily inner exercises so that the creative forces seeking human souls will find shining, vital vessels into which to pour their Imaginations. These resolves impregnate our thinking forces with warm, dynamic will. Through such work, human beings grasp and employ their birthright to be co-creators of the universe working humbly as servants of the Divine Word—the Logos—and the eternal Wisdom of God, the Holy Sophia.

# 7

## THE PLACE OF THE NORTH

According to Goethe, "All things corruptible are but a semblance." Goethe was thus describing the fundamentally alchemical point of view that visible reality is a sign or image of a higher, invisible reality. The alchemists knew the visible or corruptible image as the *simulacrum*. The invisible or eternally incorruptible was called the *imponderable,* or *archeus*. In the alchemical view, the archeus has its source in the movements and radiations of the stars, in the enduring reality which is world-creating. While what is created comes into being and dissolves away, the creative is always present as potential in the cosmos, for the created is an image of the creative beings and forces who generate it. From this perspective an image is not causal. It is rather a simulation of a being whose true nature lives in a dynamic invisible state of existence.

There is a way for a simulacrum to be moved closer to its invisible source. This method involves the concentrated attention of a human being who holds the image in the mind's eye for an extended period of time. This practice of concentrated visualization or contemplation of an image transforms the image into a symbol. After a time the symbol can become charged with the willed attention and can initiate causes. Some symbols then can stand for certain states of mind within a mystery school or a culture.

Jeanne Achterberg in "The Shaman: Master Healer in the Imaginary Realm" (Nicholson, *Shamanism,* 103–124) gives four qualities of shamanic symbols which can be found in most shamanic cultures. The first is that the symbol is the reality in the non-ordinary state of consciousness. This we have just described. The second is that most symbols used in shamanism are culturally determined. This allows the shaman to draw upon a wealth of sympathetic psychic forces from the community in order to effect a healing. Through usage some colloquial symbols gain universal importance or are found to express universal qualities. Third, similar symbols found all over the world suggest a level of symbol that is an aspect of a collective unconsciousness. And finally, in shamanic cultures the symbol is only a tool endowed with power by the esotericist. "It is not the tools and rituals that heal, it is the power endowed in them by the imagination" (Nicholson, *Shamanism*, 112). This last quality suggested by Achterberg can be seen to be at odds with the first idea that the symbol lives a life as a real being in the spirit world.

In western esotericism the conscious work to perform a marriage between the symbol and the mind is considered the source of imaginative power. This is the alchemical marriage of spirit and matter, with the symbol being a guide for the soul of the esotericist as it enters the upper world. Viewing the symbol as a tool for power is the perspective needed to enter the lower world. The difference here is a significant one, for in the work of Rudolf Steiner the distinction is made between imagination with a small "i" as the capacity in the soul to generate fantasy and inner visions, and Imagination with a capital "I" as the capacity in the soul of an initiated seer to see cognitively into the higher worlds. As the poet and seer Novalis says, "Imagination is the shadow of the soul's intelligence." This points to the structure of the soul with its connections both to the lower elemental worlds and to the world of the spirit. The soul itself is an analog of these two levels in that there is a split between the lower astral realm and the higher astral realm.

The soul's lower astral region is composed of shadow images in which the patterns of activity of the elemental beings find expression. Elemental beings are spirits who are intimately connected to matter. They are the offspring of higher hierarchical beings who live in the higher astral realm. The elementals are images or shadows of these beings. Their activity is what the human consciousness experiences when contemplating the patterns of forces found in the laws of nature. In other words their activities are very wise and lawful but not free. This is an image of the level of instinct in the development of consciousness. Thus the instinctual life among the animals is the very epitome of wisdom.

Human beings, however, have a destiny to be free of the laws which guide the wise but unfree instinctual life of the elemental world. Conflict between what is wise and what is desired is symptomatic of the state of human consciousness which produces illness. This conflict traps and imprisons elemental beings into patterns which are not wise, and as a result human beings are allowed to experience temptations, greed, and a turning away from the sacred, while animals are not. Human consciousness cannot simply forget the destiny of freedom and return to the consciousness of the collective as an ultimate answer to the dilemma of freedom.

The soul, split by the conflict, must develop sacred techniques which are appropriate for the level in which the problem appears. In the shamanic tradition we find a sacred technique perfectly adapted to exploration of the lower astral world with its images and shadows. For this the imagination (small i) is the most useful mode of consciousness, and a body-centered organ journey which leads to the etheric fields that flow among all life forms is most effective. Here battle is done with sub-personality fragments, demons, incubi, succubi, and the host of elemental shadow beings which have been unlawfully imprisoned in physical bodies by human beings through the ages. This is the collective unconscious in its subconscious/unconscious modality. It is a world of illusion and compulsion, of attraction and repulsion, seduction and abandonment. In modern depth psychology this is known as the shadow work.

In the animal consciousness such compulsion and abandonment are not morally corrupt. If a fish eats some of its offspring there is not a moral dimension to its action. It is simply following a higher directive in its instinctual life. A chicken eating a chick is a bit more disturbing. A chimpanzee eating a dead baby chimpanzee seems alarming and strange, but a human being eating a dead baby is morally unthinkable. What has changed here is not the wisdom of the body. That is still intact. What has changed is the relationship between the soul and the astral world and the higher spirit world above that. The fish does not have the possibility for self-sentience. It has a group consciousness. All other animals are also on a continuum between total instinct and moral self-awareness. The human being has the potential for total self-awareness. This makes the inner work of the human being a moral question.

In the Native American tradition this problem of the moral judgement of natural acts is clearly expressed in the great Sun Dance Wheel of the four directions. In each direction there is an animal which varies according to tribe and nation but in general the four directions have similar, corresponding attributes. In the East, the place of the rising sun, is the eagle who can see far and represents the soul attribute of illumination. In the South is the mouse who trusts in life and represents the soul quality of innocence.  In the West is the bear who can look deeply within and represents the soul quality of introspection. In the North is the buffalo who through its death gives away all it has in order to attain wisdom.  The buffalo represents the capacity for forgiveness and self-sacrifice.  Also, each of these animals sits on a smaller wheel in each direction of which is a reflection of the four places of the large wheel.

People who are fundamentally sees-far eagle people, who are clear thinkers or visionaries, will have the eagle as their totem.  Eagle people will have very good capacities for planning and thinking in big pictures but will often struggle with issues of trust or forgiveness. They may also see things so clearly that they fail to check their motives through introspection.  An eagle person, then, would have to do some work to move his wheel and gain control of the totem or power animal.  To do this, he would have to visit the place of the mouse as an eagle and the place of the bear as an eagle and the place of the buffalo as an eagle.  He would have to cook and eat the projections, or shadows, of his compulsive eagleness in order to gain balance.

Cooking and eating the shadow is an alchemical term.  Old alchemical manuscripts contain the image of a naked man holding a lizard impaled on a trident.  The man is using the fire of his thinking will to cook and eat his reptile consciousness.  In modern therapy this is called owning the problem.  Clinically we must realize that these shadows which we project are all ours.  Eagle people, for instance, must realize that others live on the same wheel and that everyone cannot simply "be an eagle," for this is not progressive.  When eagle people visit the other places on the wheel, they often transcend their totems and get a new name or quest to identify with.

In transcending the totem, shadow work is done to move the soul from its instinctual image-forming processes of cognition into a realm of freedom as a human being.  To do this the seeker must work through the physically manifest animal into the group soul of the totem which is not manifest.  The group souls of the animals live in the realm between the lower astral and higher astral.  They are the great reservoirs of the wisdom of the instinctual life, of which the individual animal on earth is an image or shadow.  The numinous power of the totem can teach the human soul, with its destiny for freedom, how to walk where the light does not cast shadows.  It is here that the shamanic consciousness is at home, and it is a significant achievement to be able to work into this realm as a sacred technician. It is not, however, the end of the line for humanity.

The group soul of the animal lives in the zodiac, the animal wheel that encircles the celestial north pole. The north star, or pole star, is seen as a center, a cosmic nail, the world tree with its center in the earth. Those wishing to develop more personal power can work with the forces from the north star, and it is significant that many shamanic techniques involve concentration exercises on the pole star. Such practices place the consciousness of the practitioner in a relative center with the rest of the cosmos "out there." That is, the zodiac becomes the periphery for a north pole focus. Such an orientation places the highest heavens in the zodiac or animal wheel, a location consistent with animism.

Suppose, however, a practitioner were to use the zodiac as a concentration point. The zodiac, containing the whole created cosmos of planets and nature forces, would then be a new center within its own periphery. The new periphery would be all that is outside the cosmos in a realm where space and time are not in linear relationships. This view is founded on synthetic or projective geometry and serves as the basis for the construction of new mystery techniques experienced from the point of view of the spiritually creative hierarchies. Thus, depending upon the viewpoint, the zodiac is either the highest of heavens ("out there") as in animism, or the center of the soul as seen in modern esotericism.

The flavor of this imagination may be more clearly experienced by looking at an abstracted image from Roberto Assagioli's *Psychosynthesis*. Assagioli pictured the layers in the consciousness as a kind of egg. The central section represents the waking consciousness. The star represents the center of the personality. In the undeveloped human consciousness this center lives in the lower levels of the waking consciousness in semi-self-cognitive states. Below the threshold of waking consciousness lies the unconscious subconscious, dominated by fixed or habitual personality fragments or shadows. The unconscious subconscious has a semi-permeable border with the collective unconscious. We could say that the subconscious unconscious is a special case of the general collective unconscious realm in that the unconscious subconscious is connected to a specific personality. This makes any entrance into the subconscious also an entrance into the unconscious. This is the perspective in which we are a center looking out at a periphery in the zodiac. The dreaming subconscious

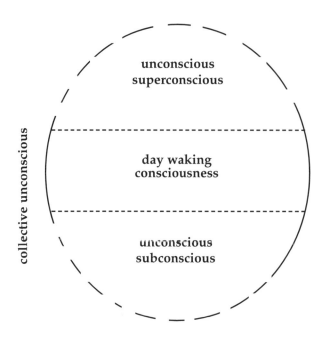

soul experiences the totems of the forces which guide the animals from the zodiac. The boundary between the subconscious unconscious and the day waking consciousness is also perforated, allowing the waking consciousness to be penetrated by the lower state. This lower state is roughly equivalent to shamanically going down the tunnel *(sipapu)* into the underworld, except that in pathological states the lower consciousness dominates the personality in the waking state. This is because there is no will in the personality. In shamanism the practitioner is fighting for control.

Will is formed by mystery training, concentration exercises, rituals, and so forth. These waking exercises strengthen the personality so that it is not overwhelmed by going down below. Through this work the personality of the shaman is purified and begins to rise toward the upper border of the waking consciousness. At this border the seer meets the gods and must learn their lesson from the wisdom beyond the zodiac. If the ascension is more advanced, the seer will learn that the implements and drugs and rituals are simply tools which eventually must be discarded. The seer can further approach the upper border by constellating the ecstatic experience into cognition. At this level the seer is no longer simply a sacred technician, for the binding ritual has become internalized as the intellectual capacity to know. At the higher border, however, the awake, conscious intellect must give way to the capacity to see beyond any totem, that is, to be a creative human spiritual consciousness coherent among other spirit creators in the superconscious realm. It is at this level that journeying into the shadow realms seeking allies in ecstatic states must be transformed into a superconscious unconscious. At this upper border the higher archetypes (gods) begin their existence.

To enter this realm the seer must encounter the composite of all of his own lower shadows. This shadow composite takes the form of a hideous human being which the seer recognizes as his own distorted beingness. This apparition, the double, calls on the seer's personal cognitive memory in order to engage the higher Ego. This double could be thought of as the composite image of the lower ego, with its will engaged in instinctual patterns of hunger and satisfaction in the personality. This being is the source of the great wound of humanity. It can only be transformed when the will at the upper level of the waking personality is reversed from serving the self to serving others. The shaman who cognizes the great wound is at this boundary.

Also at this boundary are the group souls of the plants and minerals who live in the beauty and wisdom of their archetypes. These beings are the stars in the zodiac and beyond. The shaman who takes on the illness of another is learning the will reversal so necessary to confront the double at this higher entrance into the spirit world. At this juncture the bestial in the human being must be renounced and the virginal in the soul-spiritual embraced. This requires an impulse to transcend the space/time cosmos inside the zodiac wheel and become truly human. As Paracelsus put it, "Man is altogether a star." (Paracelsus II 7, note) The star existence requires that the human being meet and transform the bestial elements in the soul. This is taught by the animal group souls at the edge of the cosmos in the "center" of the zodiac.

As the human being approaches this "center," the double, or lower guardian, presents the human being with an image of himself which must be integrated and accepted in order to pass beyond the created cosmos, past the zodiac into the silence of causal spirit being. This passage transforms intellect into the intelligence of the heart. The need for personal power and personal allies dissolves in the clear objective gaze of the causal realm, the higher astral realm. Here the soul can see the world creative spirit face to face without the intervention of flesh or its desires. In short the soul is truly living in freedom, living in non-causal or unconditional states of consciousness, a star living in the starry realms. The great difficulty with this, of course, is that the human being also does live on the earth in a body of flesh, surrounded by illusion and ignorance. It is here that we can finally address the great problem of the simulacrum in the past, in the present, and in the future.

The shaman manipulated a pantheon of images in order to heal himself, balance the tribe, and promote the well-being of nature. In this, shamanism was the perfect response to the human dilemma. The key function of image-maker in a shamanic culture was in the hands of human beings who had regular, disciplined access to archetypal realms where images which were to become cultural icons were divined and then transmitted to the community for the purposes of enculturation. The members of the community, who often had blood ties and who lived a common lifestyle in nature, could readily incorporate the intuited images and convert them into symbols of universal portent. The symbols and their numinous power then could serve theological, aesthetic, and hygienic or integrative functions in the cultural life. No doubt this was a splendid system within the parameters in which it was developed.

Today, by contrast, the bulk of images encountered by contemporary people is not produced by minds and hearts turned to the sacred. Profane, simulated images explode in bewildering profusion from every corner of every space in the contemporary world. The community, which has no blood ties and does not live a common lifestyle, is in no way the traditional, homogenous culture in which animism flourished. For many, contact with nature is limited to videos and educational television programs which simulate nature. As a result the images which are encountered have no way of being lifted close to their archetypes by communal sympathy. Consequently the term "symbol," which to an alchemist is a living supersensible being of great power and majesty, has been reduced to the level of an abstract sign giving information by "standing for" something not quite cognizable. This has resulted in a rampant hunger for symbolic images which have true meaning and has led in modern life to the consumption of image after image, with no hope of satisfaction or inner development in the soul life.

Such a situation results in a technical society desperately in search of a culture. Instead of soul nourishment the souls of the technical society are given a simulated culture, a simulacrum, a corrupted image of a higher reality in which to unfold their destinies. The outcome of this estrangement from nature and impoverishment of the soul is an epidemic of mistrust and disbelief. Trust and belief were the cornerstones of the old shamanic practice. Without the trust of the community, no healer could work. Without the belief that the healing power came from a higher source, the shaman ran the risk of madness and death. The difficulty here is not a personal failing but the unavoidable evolution of the human soul into a universal perception of each soul's own separate individuality.

Many old traditions warned against the development of the ego which would assert its individual existence against all of creation. The death forces which have issued from the development of the ego have indeed withered every indigenous culture they have touched. The answer, however, is not to move back toward tribal existence and trance consciousness as we look for symbols. Rather, the answer lies in returning to nature, for the transcended intellect and the superconscious state are the vantage point of the new earth healer. We could say that human beings are earth people who have come from the stars and are in the process of purifying themselves and the earth to such a degree that the earth and all her life forms will in the future become a sun. Instead of looking back to techniques for entering shadow world, we should seek to become one with the founder of the Sun Dance, with the Nagual teacher Wohogus, the Light of the World.

Wohogus was a mysterious teacher of peace, known by many peoples on the American continent in ancient times. Called also Dawn Star, Elder Brother, Healer, Light of Life, and Light of the World, he came to the Native American peoples to teach that the old way of counting coup, clan warfare, and retribution had become decadent through intrigue and distrust and were not leading in the proper direction. Wohogus taught that whatever we do to anyone else we do to ourselves and that sacrifice and give-away were the basis for the new mysteries. His message was to spread light and peace by transforming the self and by turning the heart away from anger and revenge. To do this the light of the waking consciousness must be shed down into the teeming shadows present in the underworld of the soul, for the healing light of the Elder Brother first illuminates our weaknesses and dark places of unfree patterns. This is the purifying fire of the Sun placed in the center of each heart. Slowly the heart then begins to see the reality of the spirit. With this force established within the heart, external binding rituals or objects of power are no longer of any use. The light of the heart is the light of the Sun, and the new way of light is brought to earth for the healing of others. Such is the teaching of Wohogus, the Elder Brother, the Light of the World.

Perhaps an example from the Shinto religion of Japan can illustrate this new consciousness of light. In Shinto, much use is made of the trance consciousness in which oracles receive the *kami,* or gods, from above through spirit possession. The oracles have always worked with another shaman who is called the agent, or judge. The oracle and the judge would travel a route up a sacred mountain, and at designated power spots the oracle would kneel in a yoga posture. The judge would begin to perform vigorous hand gestures, mudras which were directed at the chakras of the oracle. Through such a ritual the judge could manipulate the life energies of the oracle until trance consciousness was initiated. At this point the kami would descend and "break the barrel," or drive the waking consciousness out of the oracle. In such a state the oracle could become clairvoyant and give forth prophecy. People from the community could then come and ask questions to which the oracle, now filled with the power of the kami, would give answers. The judge, however, would listen to the oracle from the point of view of the waking consciousness and tell the people which sayings to heed and which to disregard. Through mudra the judge could also "tune" the oracle to get the oracle past his or her own shadow content and truly into the state of inspiration with the kami.

According to a respected shaman and Shinto priest in Tokyo, this technique has had to be modified in the training of new Shinto priests. The reason is that the modern consciousness with its content of self-awareness and discrimination has to be accounted for as a parameter of trance consciousness. When asked how the training would be different today, the priest replied, "Today the oracle and the judge have to be in the same person." This statement shows that an evolution of consciousness is under weigh in order for seership to be effective in the future. There must be a way for the seer to integrate the death forces of the intellect into the practice or else the "left hand" magic of the unrestrained elemental spirits will widen the chasm between the human soul and nature. In the future the seer will find it necessary to approach nature and redeem the fallen souls of human beings by working out of a perspective higher than the intellect. But this can only happen if the awake intellect visits the place of the the North, the place of death, give-away, and wisdom.

In the Sun Dance way of the Native American tradition, a wonderful story is told of Jumping Mouse. Jumping Mouse lives in the place of the South, the place of life and innocence. His favorite pastime is to gather up the interesting things in his environment and store them away. This keeps him busy, and when he is busy he does not have time to think about the spots in the sky which might be eagles. The alleged eagles are his biggest fear, so he makes himself busy being curious about all of the information in his environment. One day Jumping Mouse meets a teacher down by the river, and he is induced to jump higher than he has ever jumped before. When he does this he sees the sacred mountains and also falls into the river of life. He cannot forget his vision but finds that he must leave his treasures and go into the world. This is his first act of give-away. As he meets other teachers he has to learn to trust his inner vision because his give-away consists of giving his eyes to make others whole. He does this out of the goodness of his heart and the trust he has in others. Finally, through give-away he becomes totally blind and must truly trust in beings whom he cannot see. His inner sight alone is his guide. He cannot rely upon information from his environment because he has had to give away the organs of perception for gathering sense information about the manifest world. In his travels from the place of the South he must visit the Buffalo in the place of the North and learn still more about giving away. He then must visit the place of the West and give away to a wolf who also is his teacher. The wolf teaches him to look within for deeper answers. Finally, when he has given away everything, including his curiosity and his fear, he is taken by an eagle, and when he returns to consciousness he can see far. He is given Eagle as his new name. In trusting the spirit world he has been reborn as that which he feared the most. He has transcended information to gain knowledge and the capacity to trust.

In today's world there is a technological analogy for Jumping Mouse, a simulacrum, found everywhere as the door to artificial intelligence. We could call this being Clicking Mouse. Clicking Mouse, too, is curious. He loves to go through mazes of interesting things, gathering up that which touches his curiosity. Clicking Mouse has a great storehouse of curiosities in his burrow. He busies himself running this way and that arranging his information in infinite ways. He delights in his possessions like King Midas. Sadly, Clicking Mouse has teachers who do not teach him to see the sacred mountains. His teachers keep him busy retrieving and storing information. As a result there is no chance for give-away. Clicking Mouse can never learn to trust the spirit world. His need to hold on to what has worked in the past keeps him from visiting the place of the North. Clicking Mouse's teachers have made a simulacrum called virtual reality. The consciousness needed to get to this world is a trance consciousness induced by repetitive movements and sounds from a new shamanic "horse" called "modem."

What Clicking Mouse needs are teachers who have learned to give away spiritual techniques which rely upon shadows. The flickering shadows hypnotize and cripple the gifts of Wohogus the Light of the World who came to teach light and love to all peoples. A new seership on a higher plane than that of old is needed to produce teachers who out of love can teach Clicking Mouse to trust the spiritual world. The twelve initiated disciples who always stood around Wohogus show that the teachers of Clicking Mouse must transcend the zodiac; they themselves become the whole animal wheel of all the grandfathers of the animals and become star people devoted to helping the Earth Mother herself to transcend her shadows and become a sun, a true symbol of the Light of the World.

The new seership must establish a new relationship between the soul and the life of the senses on one hand, and the capacity for intellectual thought on the other. The barrage of images through which the modern soul must wend its way is unprecedented in the traditions of tribal cultures. It is unique to the rise of the modern consciousness of the individual. New techniques and insights are needed to face the new challenges that arise with alarming rapidity. To keep the best of the old mysteries and to move creatively into an uncertain future is the task of the new mystery teachings. Personal power must be given away. Binding ritual must be creatively and lawfully transcended. Tradition must be wed to improvisation in order that free creative deeds which reflect the good of the whole can be accomplished. For this we need a new alchemy of the soul in line with the old ways but already walking the path toward the sunrise, the new dawning of human consciousness.

# 8

# THE WORLD OF IMAGINATION

In his book *Evolution's End,* Joseph Chilton Pearce cites the research of Ernest Hilgard of Stanford University on the hidden observer present behind all states of consciousness. Hilgard found that no matter whether we are asleep, awake, drugged, or hypnotized, there is always an element of consciousness which is an unemotional, detached conscious presence. This hidden observer is the witness of the esoteric tradition. It is an archetypal form of human self-conscious awareness. It differs both from the sensitive or sentient awareness of the animal world and from the self-aware but self-centered lower ego consciousness of the human being. We could call it hyper ego or ego exponent. It is just as powerful and integrated as the sentience of the subtle life body and more aware of the infinite potential of the self than the lower ego. It exists above the intellect and the self-centered lower ego in the realm of the superconscious. Christian esoteric traditions call this consciousness the Logos or Holy Word. It is a consciousness which is focused and attentive yet fluid and without goals or expectations.

In the superconscious state, reality is what is latent, while in the everyday consciousness reality is what is manifest. Gaining the ability to shift between these two centers of reality is the purpose of most esoteric training. It is recognized that the soul has roots both in the manifest physical world and in the potential of the spiritual world. In healing rituals from many cultures the focus is upon harmonizing the misalignments and discrepancies found in souls caught between these two worlds. In shamanic cultures the person who is ill is often thought to house negative thought forms or spirits which have found their way into gaps between these two different worlds or modes of cognition.

A common esoteric picture of the human being is that the body, the soul, and the spirit are living in three different worlds. The body is the source of the consciousness known to shamanism as the under-world and to western esoteric traditions as the elemental world. Here spirit beings who interact with matter find their way into inner dis-continuities in human consciousness. When this happens, the human being becomes driven by instinct.

The second world, or midworld, is the realm of the awake human soul with its capacities for acting both out of instinct and out of cog-nitive impulses. That is, the human being in this level of soul can act either unconsciously or out of a waking consciousness. In western esoteric traditions this is the true realm of the soul, where noble ideas and base drives meet and mingle in a fluctuating capacity for self-aware cognition.

Above this is the upper world, the realm of the Idea. Here reside the gods, devas, or angelic hosts who direct both human beings and nature spirits. The upper world is the source of the various levels of lawfulness in nature. In esoteric traditions the upper world and the lower world are present in human beings as states of consciousness outside of the everyday consciousness or intellect. Even in the philo-sophical traditions of the West, the Kantian distinction between the day intellect and the archetypal intellect points to this esoteric divi-sion.

Another way to view these different forms of consciousness is to make a distinction between brain-bound thinking and sense-free thinking. The first is a way of thinking in which the thinker is depen-dent upon sensation and the mental images arising from sensation. The second is thinking which is free of images that result from sensa-tion. In sense-free thinking we can cognize such concepts as $\pi$ (pi) or $\phi$ (phi). Here the consciousness leaves images of sensations in the lower world behind and concerns itself with the abstract cognitive images which according to neural science may possibly exist not *in* the brain but *around* the brain in neural fields.

Thinking in these neural fields moves away from experiences and images generated by the soul's interactions with objects in space, and moves into imagery which unfolds not in space but only in time. That is, in order to think the sequence of steps needed to solve a problem in geometry, we must think of sequences which are true in the ideal realm but which need not manifest in space. Geometrical theorems exist as realities for the consciousness which intuits them through an effort of will. They remain hidden to the everyday consciousness until the requisite effort is expended to think them. To do this, the mind must entrain the Idea; it must cause the neural fields around the brain to harmonize with the movement of the solution.

The mind is thus guided through the proper sequencing in order to penetrate into the upper world where the Ideas live as creative beings of higher intelligence. In the ancient esoteric schools this was accomplished by enacting rituals whose sequences of actions led living concepts or spirit beings into the substances of the manifest world. These traditions were passed on from teacher to student as binding rituals which maintained their integrity over time, for if done incorrectly, they resulted in the madness or death of the practitioner. These binding rituals of the ancient mystery schools became the source of the flowering of the human intellect and of the intellect's alchemical and scientific capacities.

We can look for traces of the ancient binding rituals in the shamanic practices which generate such intense interest in modern spiritual seekers. As Mircea Eliade says, the shaman is the technician of the sacred ("Shamanism and Cosmology" in Nicholson, *Shamanism*, 17–46). Eliade thus links the shamanic world view with the modern technical world view. We can say that the modern technical ritual of scientific experiment lacks a connection to the sacred. This creates a hunger which the human being seeks to satisfy by again approaching the spiritual through shamanism. The shaman moves toward the numinous and away from ordinary reality by the ritual practice of going into the underworld through the tunnel between the soul and the imaginative world.

In order to put his mind into a state capable of going through the tunnel into the underworld the shaman often uses the repetitive sounds of drums or rattles to focus the consciousness. These sounds (it could also be dancing or drugs) serve as a culturally determined "horse" which the shaman uses to induce a precise state of consciousness. This horse is then ridden on a spiritual quest, perhaps a journey to heal a member of the community, or even to gain personal power.

Michael Harner, a modern shaman, gives a very interesting account of a journey in search of healing in his book, *The Way of the Shaman*. Harner had an experience in South America in which he ingested the vine ayahuasca, inducing a state in which he went into a celestial cavern where a giant reptile sat with waters gushing out of its mouth. He saw a soul boat with many oars moving in rhythmic cadence. He then became aware that the drug had given him the ability to observe certain areas of his brain, such as the higher cortex, the source of his witnessing consciousness, symbolized as a boat full of gods with the heads of blue jays. He also saw that this was distinct from the limbic system which had been rendered dysfunctional by the drug. He saw too that the lower portions of his base brain were the source of what he was experiencing as large, sluggish reptilian creatures below, which had a sinister intent and demeanor. Suspended thus between the gods above and the body with its reptilian instinctual patterns below in the base brain, he panicked. In his distress he sought human help, asking his Indian friends for the antidote to the drug, and saying that he needed a guardian who could defeat dragons, the reptiles in the base brain who were claiming to be the creators of the whole cosmos.

This precise account of the three worlds and their relationship to the functional layers in the brain reveals at once the complete landscape of the imaginal world, its challenges, and the need to rely upon human waking consciousness to defeat the dragons present in the lower instinctual life in the human soul. The key to this work in the soul does not lie in the abstract functions of the neo-cortex where the eternal witness sits living in the upper world of the gods, nor in the sensually reactive instinctual images of the reptile brain (pons and medulla oblongata), nor in the transformation of the limbic system with its reliance on body memory, ecstatic emotion, and instinctual mapping. The true key lies in the midbrain, the link between higher and lower consciousness through sense integration. This area will be explored later. At this time, to build a foundation, let us examine the general categories of neo-cortex, limbic system (old mammal brain), and reptile brain.

The site of the inner activity of an evolving human being migrates from the primitive reptile brain through the midbrain to the limbic or emotional brain, into the right hemisphere of the neo-cortex, and finally into the left hemisphere. The reptile brain presents us with the experiences of the senses, and these sense experiences elicit instinctual responses which are aimed at survival. In the higher centers of the limbic system the instinctual survival patterns are elevated into societal behaviors, emotional responses, symbolic imagery, and the general feeling life of the soul. This is accomplished by the midbrain which integrates lower sense impressions, linking them to the limbic system, which in turn forms symbolic patterns which represent to the soul the integration of the ideas of the upper world with the sense data of the lower world. The limbic system has a direct connection to the right hemisphere, the musical, geometric, intuitive hemisphere of the neocortex. This connection allows for fluid creative thinking but not logical thinking for which it is necessary to enlist the aid of the left hemisphere and its capacity to order ideas and concepts sequentially.

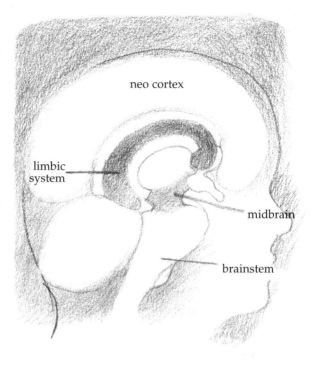

In Michael Harner's account, the dream boat with the jay-headed gods hovering above in the sky is an image of the abstract "bird" consciousness in fairy tales. Harner's connection of these beings to the activities of the cerebral cortex is mythically exact. We can recognize the evolutionary sequence in which the reptile appears to have evolved into the bird. This sequence is also reflected in the metamorphosis of the structure of the brain from the base brain with its reptilian activity center upward through the functionally potent midbrain into the higher cognitive centers. However, modern brain research points to a slightly different evolutionary model with regard to future mental capacities for human beings. Antonio Damasio (*Descartes' Error*, 129) suggests that the cortices in the brain which are formed early on as *sensory input nuclei* are the sites where each sensory experience is formed as a topographical system of nerve points. These points are mapped in the brain soon after the senses have received the various stimuli. The early sensory cortices such as the parietal cortices, the superior colliculi, the thalamus, and the midbrain nuclei are the sites where the formation of images is organized topographically with respect to the organism's movements in the space in which it lives. When a shape is seen, the activity of the neurons in these early sensory cortices maps the image in patterns which conform to that shape. These patterns are not cognized in the awake attention. Indeed, at this level they represent the neural basis for automatic instinctual patterning. Nevertheless, these movement stimuli derived from the sensations are the physiological basis for the inner life of images. This is so pronounced that anatomically there is no way for sensations connected to spatial motion and perception to have access to the cognitive layers in the cerebral cortex and its symbolic mapping of meanings without first going through complex feedback relationships to these early sensory cortices.

These fundamental motions and the sensations which accompany them may be the basis for thought even though they are seldom the actual content of our thoughts. Images, usually lying below the threshold of awake attention, are first integrated into the limbic system for emotional/symbolic mapping, then into the right cortex for geometric, musical, or associative thinking, and finally into the neo-cortex of the left brain for analysis and higher logic patterning. This gives meaning to the sensations to which there must now be a response. For this the brain function has to descend once again through the right lobe of the cortex into the limbic system. The abstract meanings must be integrated into more primitive feeling responses in order for the human being to make sense of the sensation. So once the higher centers have formed conceptual wholes the higher functioning of the brain must once again have

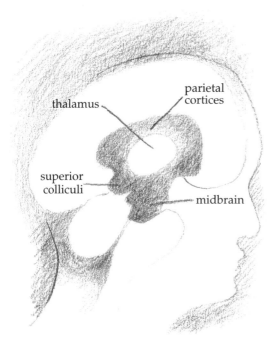

thalamus

parietal cortices

superior colliculi

midbrain

recourse to the "lower" intuitive geometric space patterns found in the right hemisphere.

Further, it is in the still lower limbic brain that the conclusions and concepts which are intuited by the left hemisphere are woven through memories into symbolic forms. The limbic brain includes parts of the hypothalamus (endocrine response) and the cerebellum (limb movements) as well as the olfactory lobe (smell), the hippocampus (emotion), and areas of the neo-cortex. The hypothalmic and cerebellar functions are wide-ranging. They include cognitive input from the neo-cortex as well as space and movement data from the limbs and organs of the body, creating a field consciousness of the space within the body and the kinesthetic placement of limbs around the body in space. Large movements of the body and limbs are integrated into sensory images which give rise to emotions, glandular responses, social impulses, mating rituals, and the maintenance of memory and learning.

Deep within the limbic brain at the top of the brainstem or reptile brain is the midbrain (or mesencephalon). It is a small area an inch or so square, but it is a sort of gate, the focal point for very significant neural pathways concerned with memory, sense integration, and dreaming. The thalamus, the heart of the limbic brain, is directly connected to the midbrain. In this way the midbrain has an intimate link through the median forebrain bundle (MFB) to the geometric/musical right hemisphere. The midbrain sits atop the medulla oblongata and the pons of the reptile brain. It is the area in which the complex thought structures from the neo-cortex and patterned feelings and instincts from the limbic system are integrated into deeper subconscious somatic sense impressions from the brainstem. Directly above the midbrain, the limbic system is linked to the right hemisphere of the neo-cortex. This linkage enables memory to be ordered into learning, and for learning to be heightened into creative vision. The links between the limbic system and the midbrain are considered by some researchers to be the source of inner imagery, the ability to form mental images.

Here we can begin to assess the role of images and the imaginative world in the practice of shamanism. As Michael Harner so clearly stated, he was aware that the second level down in his brain was not active during his shamanic journey. He had a witness (active in the left hemisphere of the neo-cortex) and a reptile brain, but his limbic system and especially his right hemisphere were not functional.

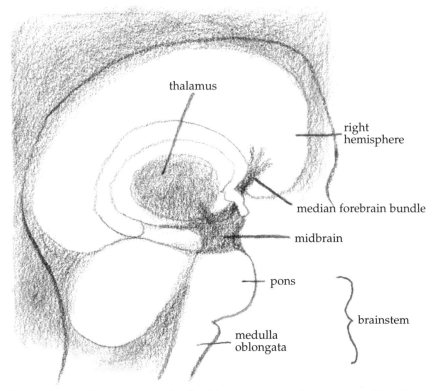

The right hemisphere and the limbic system are the source of instinctual patterns and emotional responses. In these areas optical, olfactory, visceral, and kinesthetic sensations are integrated. Lower down,
the midbrain integrates sense impressions from the oculomotor nerve,
the cochlear nerve, and trigeminal nerves—from seeing, hearing, and
speech.

In the production of shamanic trance states the use of the drum or
a drug deliberately entrains these two areas, the right hemisphere of
the neo-cortex and the limbic system, allowing the shaman easy
access to the earlier brain which he then uses as a *sipapu,* a ritual hole
in the floor of the ritual room. The sipapu is a symbol of the shamanic entry through the earlier or lower brain down the tunnel into the
elemental universe. Here the shaman has access to the beings who
guide the elemental (etheric) life forces of the organs of the human
body. These spirits are also present in rock, water, cloud, plant, and
animal. The seer thus journeys among the beings who animate the

forces of nature, for the journey through one's own body is, at this level, a journey through all bodies.

The seeing on such a journey is imaginative and non-rational. The task of the seer is either to adopt the culturally provided images or to risk madness by gaining access to visions which shatter the ordinary consciousness. Seers who begin to transcend the culturally prescribed images need to develop a code which allows them to integrate non-ordinary reality into symbolic maps and images which can teach other seers. In this way binding ritual and intellectual or rational sequencing provide protection for the journey inward through the various elemental worlds found in the organ systems of the body.

How can we understand the use of the hypnotic state as a tool for achieving higher consciousness? Eva Bányai (referred to in *Shamanism in Eurasia*) found that the state of ecstacy common to the mystic and the shaman was a form of hypnotic consciousness. She characterized this as a *hyper alert,* or *active alert* hypnosis. In traditional hypnosis, a sleep state or relaxed state is induced in the subject, who is then open to suggestion. In the shamanic or mystic active alert hypnotic state, the subject achieves the state through activity rather than passivity, but the state is essentially the same. The significant features of this state are a tremendous openness to suggestion and even auto-suggestion, the ability to rationalize post-hypnotically what was encountered in the hypnotic state, and the enhanced capacity to induce culturally prescribed symbols in order to draw and condense the sympathy of the community. This last quality was present among the shamanic healers. The active alert hypnotic trance state enables the shaman to enter his own body and by virtue of this to enter everyone else's body in a clairvoyant state. He can then form a protocol for future actions based on previous experiences remembered during trance states while simultaneously interacting with members of the community who are in a waking consciousness. These qualities are commonly found in shamanism and in mystical experience in general.

Another positive effect of the active alert hypnotic trance state is the enhanced ability to focus one's attention on the task at hand, also helping the shaman maintain a focus on the binding ritual. However, in the active alert hypnotic consciousness the practitioner loses the ability to will a sequence of ideas or to plan for events in the future. This shows that there is an impairment of the conscious will function in the psyche. And finally, in the active alert hypnotic state the practitioner cannot test reality. This indicates that although there is memory function, the waking consciousness and its ego component in memory are impaired. This is significant for the evolution of consciousness. This may explain the tremendous susceptibility of hypnotic trance subjects to post-hypnotic suggestion, or in the case of the shaman, to auto-suggestion.

The shaman must build a code of behavior out of experiences remembered after non-ordinary events. He must treat his subjective nature as an objective fast and allow the subjective experiences to constellate into a science simply through the integrity of the high level of focused attention. Since shamans enter into the lawful relationships of the elemental world when they go on a journey, the patterns of nature offer healing protocols and therapeutic imaginations for diagnosis and cure. A drawback is that the need for a horse (drum, chant, dance, or drug) to focus such a high degree of attention requires entrainment of brain centers which moves them out of the activity of the free awake consciousness and thus denies conscious access to the potential symbological mapping function of the limbic system and the midbrain. The shaman therefore needs cues and suggestions from the culture in the form of deities, allies, or totems, and he must subscribe to culturally determined, traditional binding ritual for protection. This inhibits the potential for a shaman's individual, creative interaction with the upper world. This lower world is imaginative in that it deals with images in dynamic and effective sacred techniques, but it is categorically not creative in that the images which serve as the guiding force for the attention are culturally prescribed.

Here let me draw attention to distinctions among the terms *imaginary, imaginative,* and *imaginal.* Shamanic experience is profoundly imaginative. It transcends the imaginary or purely subjective entrance into fantasy which is the characteristic of delusion. The healings and deeds of shamans over the millennia are not imaginary. They contain the whole gamut of imaginative experiences, from forming precise mental images of things not perceptible to the senses, to relating ideas and feelings into a pattern, to conceiving real images in sense-free states, whether in unbridled fantasy or in the unspeakable ecstasy of a mystical state. With such a wide area of responses available to trance practitioners the ritual images and binding safeguards are an absolute necessity. By contrast, in the imaginal consciousness the conscious forming of an image inwardly and the cognition of the relationships between the part and the whole in the *awake* state create the first level of achievement for the work.

The term *imaginal* comes from the word *imago,* the form of the adult butterfly which emerges from the pupa or chrysalis spun by a caterpillar or larva. In this sequence it is possible to see the larval form still hanging between the wings of the butterfly. This picture of an image from childhood carried into adulthood is the source of the term imaginal in psychology. Here the imaginal is seen as an unhealthy, even pathological continuation of an image of a parent or loved one carried unchanged into adulthood. There is, however, a magical or esoteric use for the term imaginal when describing different states of consciousness. A person with an imaginal consciousness developed through systematic self-effort has the capacity to follow an image through any number of outward transformations and still recognize the original form in every transformation no matter what the degree of distortion from the original. To do this it is necessary to be able to perceive the whole as it leaves its mark on each part and to simultaneously recognize the specific way in which each part is integrated into the whole. In such a state of awareness one begins to perceive the subtle motions of the archetypal idea as it permeates the field of form in which separate organisms appear and disappear. This form of consciousness could be called original or participatory consciousness which perceives the forces of Ruling Will behind the forms of the world. We can also call it imaginal.

In imaginal consciousness the creative motion behind the phenomenon is perceived inwardly as an exact motion. This movement is visualized (imagined) forward and backward until the creative movement is fully permeated with awakeness and attention. At this point the imaginal will is strong enough to release the image into silence (chaos). Imaginally the consciously represented image is the link between the thing in itself and its incarnating creative motion. To use the butterfly analogy, the larval stage of active imagining and the pupal stage of creative silence allow the attention-saturated imaginal movement to enter the archetypal realm above the level of the elemental world, the realm of the ideal, of the imago. Since the attention is then already tuned to the movements of the ideal, the ideal can approach the mind wrapped in creative silence with Images and Imaginations from the realm of order, from the Logos. In the mind of the adept these Imaginations manifest as numinous experiences of an ordered kind. The harmony between these Imaginations from the ideal realm and the phenomena contemplated by the seeking attentive mind becomes manifest both as insight into the sacred nature of the phenomena and as the potential for the human being to incarnate sacred values into the very substances and process of earth evolution.

The imaginal flash of original recognition between the lower elemental world and the sacred realm of archetypes is a deed of compassion done by a human being for the whole of creation. As a result it is as rare as it is far reaching. This striving for a personally determined imaginal consciousness metamorphosed shamanic/magical tradition in the ancient world into the realm of alchemical practice in the West. Practicing alchemists strove to enter into substances with their focused imaginal attention. Their protocol, which takes the place of cultural binding ritual, involved laborious refining and distillation procedures. In the heightened state of attention brought on by sensory deprivation and fatigue from the work, they would meet spirit beings who gave them insights into the nature of substance. However, like the mystics and shamans who were their contemporaries, the alchemists often gained access in their work only to the fields of elemental forces flowing through their own organs. The movements of these forces stimulated inner experiences which the alchemists described using arcane and often personal images, such as the king and queen in a bath or the serpent eating its tail. These images over time and through use came to represent archetypal forces of a collective unconscious character—they became a tradition.

One such archetypal image is the Ouroboros, the snake biting its tail. This symbol can mean many things to an alchemist, but as an inner perception connected to the activity of a bodily organ we could say that it is an image of the formative forces of the kidney. If we look at a section of the kidney we can see that it is formed by innumerable snakelike tubules and glomeruli. Here we see an image similar to a snake biting its tail. But the analogy is not exhausted simply by the outer image. In the Ouroboros we see a snake obtaining nutriment from its own body or corpus or in the language of alchemy the excrement. In the kidney the tubules excrete large volumes of fluid in the beginning of the process only to take most of the fluid back in in order for the true excretion to take place. The kidney literally consumes its own excreta or corpus. An alchemist who was working on a process of salt purification would continually take the water distilled from the salt solution and feed it back to the salt in the hope of gradually whitening and purifying the salt. This outer salt process of whitening is an analog for the excretion of salts of urea in the kidney. Both are imaged in the Ouroboros. An alchemist who was sensitive to the inner force of the kidney might imagine the Ouroboros during the alchemical process of whitening the salt.

By connecting these insights to repetitive laboratory work, the alchemist would achieve a degree of clairvoyance. The society of the time, however, did not understand the alchemists' imaginative landscape. As a result, the alchemists were hounded into obscurity and, like the mystics and shamans, were accused by later cultures of being psychotic. In the ancient world, some shamans were holy fools, doing outrageous acts in the pursuit of healing forces, but since they were not breaking with tradition and were healers who worked for the good of the community, they found acceptance and recognition. Later on, though, the same skeptical scientific consciousness which persecuted the alchemists would systematically persecute the shamans, and for the same reason.

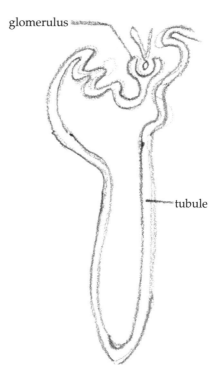

The holy fool consciousness can flourish in a tribal or traditional culture because the great sympathy present in the culture can tolerate personal fantasy as a healing modality. By contrast, non-tribal cultures require that the everyday consciousness be the arbiter of the mores of the culture. To this abstract consciousness, logical thinking is the highest state of consciousness, for in logical thinking the mind must leave the sense world behind and enter into the supersensible world of Ideas.

In the supersensible world of Ideas, however, human beings encounter other beings who are not always beneficent. Carl Jung, in his descriptions of the collective unconscious as the source of super-sensible world archetype, does not make a distinction between the elemental, instinct-driven, subconscious shadow beings of the under-world, and the angelic or hierarchical creative beings of the super-conscious upper world. Since both the subconscious and the super-conscious are states outside of the everyday waking state, they are both states of unconsciousness. To confuse the *sub*conscious uncon-scious and its hypnotic trance states (larva) in which memory can function but no ego is present, with the *super*conscious unconscious in its empty, silent, meditative state (imago) is an error with great impli-cations.

Shamanism has been a great cultural school of mystery wisdom and healing since ancient times. The goal of this school was to devel-op in the human being the ability to maintain equilibrium in extreme states of non-ordinary reality using the silver cord of binding ritual to order ideas in sequence. In mystery training, the work of students and masters develops organs of cognition which will later be found as a legacy among the general population. So it is that today we see the results of ancient shamanic work in the discursive, rational intellect which allows us to order thoughts in the realm of the non-ordinary, the realm of the spirit and soul. The intellect allows new healing rit-uals to be developed and gives teachers the capacity to impart images to their students rather than simply to assign repetitious tasks. The intellect can heal the fear and superstition that arise from mystical clairvoyant experience of the creative imaginations arising from one's own internal organs. It is a rudder on the spirit boat and it is the sil-ver cord which allows the soul of the journeying shaman to return to its everyday consciousness. The intellect was developed from the sil-ver cord of binding ritual to heal the subconscious unconscious and to cast out the demons and shadows living in the soul as patterns of psy-chosis.

In contemporary life, however, the organ of healing has itself become ill, leading to estrangement from the sacred, an increasing existential malaise, and a sense of alienation from ourselves and nature. Can we hope to heal the intellect by using practices similar to those which formed the organ in the first place? Will the answer to rampant technological hypnosis and virtual universes be found in the entrainment techniques contained in drumming for power? Can the old tribal ways transform intellect into intelligence? Can the heart be taught to think by journeying in the underworld? We need rather to give away tradition and seek a global creative consciousness, a consciousness which transcends implements, rituals, trances, and the accumulation of personal power. While respecting the old ways, we need to move beyond them. Above all, we must renounce the need to control the spirit.

Even though alchemy and alchemists most often walked the path into the underworld, the potential to create imaginal consciousness is inherent in its practices. Perhaps now when the old ways are failing and the new are not yet perceived, we can take the best from the old mystery schools and try to see what they can be transformed into. The imaginal butterfly of consciousness must become a precise and inspired metamorphosis of the best from tradition and fly away from its reductionist moorings if esoteric wisdom is to develop a new culture.

# 9

# FROM DOWSING TO DIVINING

In common usage, the act of divining, dowsing, or witching for water goes by any of these names, yet they are different activities, performed at different stages of consciousness. *Witching* refers to the use of a switch or branch, employed by the witcher to lead to a water source. *Dowsing* employs metal rods as well as switches and can be used to find ores and oil and other hidden things such as lost persons or objects. *Divining* uses switches, rods, pendulums, or other specially designed devices to do all of these things. A diviner can also remote-dowse maps, locate missing persons, read auras, locate thought forms, and diagnose medical ailments. To many who dowse, these distinctions may seem to be unnecessarily discriminating. After all, many successful dowsers and water witches can also divine. The point can be made, however, that dowsers do not usually start out divining but work with tangible objects such as water and ores before they can proceed to divining. In divining, the response of the body to the fields of energy being dowsed is extremely subtle, sensitive to the pull of a stressed kidney or adrenal gland, for example, which is far more delicate than the pull from a stream or buried object.

However, at their basic level both dowsing and divining use the body of the dowser to detect the presence of variations in weak fields of energy. In the view of the noted authority on dowsing, Dr. S. W. Tromp:

> As long as the human body is used as a geophysical instrument we are dealing with a new type of geophysical prospecting, but as soon as the body is excluded the instruments [rods and pendulums] are bound to be useless. . . . (*Psychical Physics*, 206)

Dr. Tromp makes this statement in the middle of an exhaustive survey of the physical and psychophysical parameters surrounding the dowsing phenomenon. Throughout his work he again and again returns to the idea of the body as the primary instrument in dowsing. In developing this thought he connects the dowsing consciousness to an auto-hypnotic state often found in animals when the thalamus in the brain is stimulated by fright, sense data, or sexual activity.

The thalamus is an organ in the brain which integrates the impulses from sense impressions into the higher centers in the brain. When the thalamus is stimulated during sex or under conditions of fright, the higher centers of the brain are blocked so that the organism can function more economically in an instinctual consciousness. The blocked impulses are shunted from the higher thalamus to the lower brainstem so that automatic will activities can dominate the consciousness. This state in the brainstem consciousness closely resembles sleep, hence the term *brainstem sleep*. Brainstem sleep in effect induces a hypnotic trance state in the consciousness. The brainstem is the lower brain area of the midbrain, medulla oblongata, and pons. When the brainstem is too strongly activated, the conscious functions of the cerebral cortex are stupefied. When this happens, the brainstem becomes the center for the entire field of sense impressions being

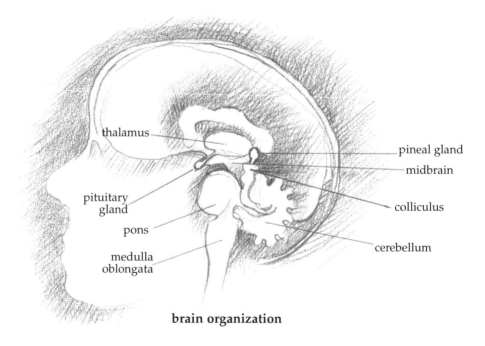

**brain organization**

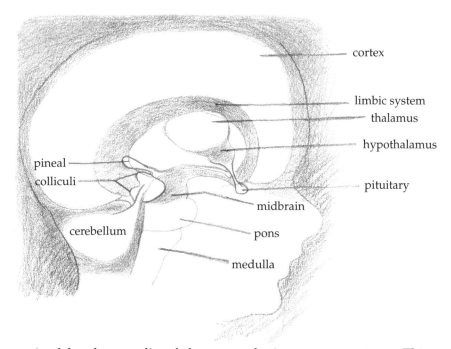

received by the ganglia of the sympathetic nervous system. This greatly increases the receptivity of the organs serviced by the sympathetic nervous system: the viscera, the glands, the blood vessels and glands of the skin, and the skeletal muscles. The thalamus itself is a great sensory ganglion integrating all of these impulses. In effect, it integrates all of the automatic will forces in the body.

Just below the thalamus is another organ of the diencephalon, the hypothalamus. Beneath the hypothalamus is the master gland of the body, the pituitary gland. This gland performs the quintessential synthesis of the endocrine system. The pituitary is connected to the skeleton and to the major glands by extensive ramifications of the sympathetic nervous system. The gland itself is composed of two parts—a neurological posterior lobe which is part of the hypothalamus, and a metabolic anterior lobe connected to the sympathetic nervous system. This division into upper and lower functions is present in the embryo from the very beginning when separate neural and metabolic layers in the embryonic disc are united into the pituitary gland.

As an image we can picture the brain schematically in layers. The outer, higher cognitive layers of the cerebral cortex are where the

higher brain functions lie. Next in toward the center is the diencephalon which includes the thalamus, hypothalamus, and pituitary
gland. The next layer inward is the limbic system which surrounds
the uppermost portion of the brainstem which in turn includes the
corpora quadrigemina, the midbrain, and the nuclei of cranial sensory nerves. The midbrain integrates lower and higher centers in the
brain. The lowest and most slumbering portions of the brain are the
pons and medulla oblongata. These centers are the lower portion of
the brainstem; they regulate instinctual reflexes and automatic movement responses. From this we begin to see a pattern in which the outermost layer, the cerebral cortex, is the site of the most conscious
activity. The diencephalon, limbic system, and midbrain integrate
conscious thinking into instinctual body responses and emotional
states, and the lower portions of the brainstem (pons and medulla
oblongata) function at a still lower instinctual level of consciousness,
that of simply maintaining the organism's primal life functions. The
brainstem includes these lowest regions and also some parts of the
emotional and integrative regions of the midbrain and diencephalon.
The brainstem serves to integrate sensory impulses from the body
and the senses and to transmit the sensations into the higher centers.

In the anterior portion of the midbrain in the thalamus region and
just below the hypothalamus sits the pituitary gland, divided into its
posterior neurological part and anterior metabolic part. In its twofold
division it is a microcosm of the polarity seen in the brain, between
the more cosmic outer layers which are involved in higher thinking
and the lower instinctual, dreaming, and sleeping consciousness in
the lower brainstem.

In form the pituitary gland is like an embryo, with its neurological and metabolic functions separated into two distinct areas by a sensitive membrane. The pituitary receives impulses from a whole series
of organs—the site of higher waking consciousness—within the brain.
The contents of these impulses are channeled into the neurological
upper half of the pituitary. Here these impulses stimulate the lower
metabolic center, which then stimulates the sympathetic nervous system and the other glands of the body, the viscera, the blood vessels,
the skin, the muscles, and the skeleton. These organs are in sympathy
with each other and receive the impulses from the pituitary which
result in proper secretions in response to light changes through the
seasons, the fluctuating hormonal imbalances brought on by pregnancy, or the hormones surrounding flight or fight syndromes. The

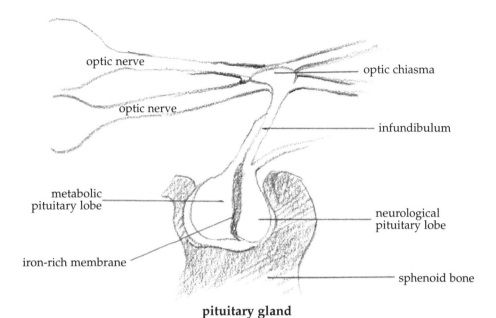

optic nerve

optic chiasma

optic nerve

infundibulum

metabolic
pituitary lobe

neurological
pituitary lobe

iron-rich membrane

sphenoid bone

**pituitary gland**

functions of the pituitary gland's secretions include the production of growth hormones, thyroid hormones, adrenal hormones, reproductive hormones, hormones producing milk in mammals, hormones which stimulate the contraction of smooth muscle tissue in the uterus, and a hormone affecting the function of the kidneys. Broadly, the pituitary is a gland which receives impulses from higher centers and radiates them throughout the body and then listens as these impulses echo back to the gland via the sympathetic nervous system.

In animals the life of instinct governing the directional senses used in migrational navigation, metabolic seasonal cycles, sleeping and waking cycles, and sexual reproduction is centered in the pituitary gland. The physiological placement of the gland in the hollow of the sphenoid bone of the skull also contains a strong image of reproduction. The sphenoid is a bone which is the keystone for the construction of the face. It lies in the base of the skull toward the front part of the cranial cavity. Along the very base of the skull on the inside is a series of bones which look like small lumbar vertebrae. These bones form the base of the brain case. The sphenoid is the last bone in this series. It flares out into strong lateral processes just as the pelvis flares out from the sacrum. There appears in the sphenoid a remarkable echo of the pelvic basket nestled within the base of the

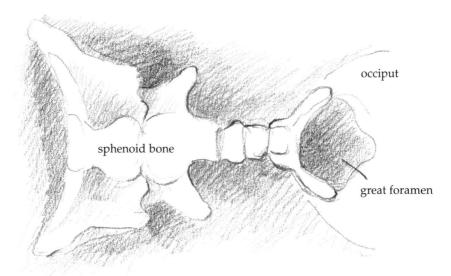

brain case. In the place where the uterus would be found in the pelvis, we find the pituitary gland in the sphenoid. These images point to a common reproductive function in both the uterus and the pituitary. In the uterus, embryos are formed. In the pituitary, images are formed.

The pituitary gland and its surrounding tissues provide a picture of the wall between the upper world of the stars, the source of spiritual existence, and the lower world of the body, its metabolism, growth, and reproduction. Esoterically this polarity between cosmos and earth suggests that the pituitary is a source of mental imagination or inner picture forming. In essence, a mental image is a digested sense impression from earth reproduced and spiritualized in the form of inner light. The transformation of sense impressions taken from the skin, muscles, glands, and visceral organs into a neurologically organized mental image involves a deep coordination between higher neurological organs (cosmos) and metabolic, digestive organs (earth). The pituitary gland is an image of this coordination.

Rudolf Steiner sheds light on these processes of transformation and coordination by describing the absorption of cosmic warmth in the idea-forming capacities of the higher cerebral cortex. This cosmic warmth streams through the cortex into the thalamus of the brain and then into the neurological portion of the pituitary as a stream of imaginative pictures from the cosmos. Below in the metabolic portion of the pituitary this cosmic warmth streams out into the forms of the var-

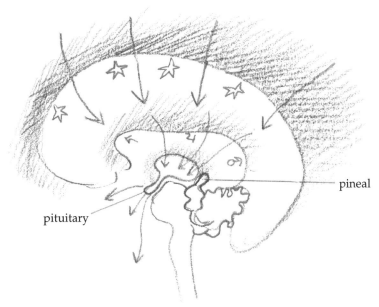

pineal

pituitary

**instreaming cosmic warmth**

ious organs and back again into the gland as the influx of sense impressions from the inner organs, the muscles, glands, and viscera.

Between the posterior neurological section of the pituitary and the anterior metabolic section there is a dividing membrane of melanin-rich tissue. This membrane effectively divides the posterior neurological lobe of the pituitary from the anterior metabolic lobe. The metabolic lobe receives impulses from the body which are transferred to the neurological lobe, the hypothalamus, and the neo cortex. Under intense input from the body, blocking agents in the pituitary and hypothalamus block the brainstem and put the consciousness into a sleep state very similar to trance and hypnosis or shamanic hyper alert states. In such a state the cortex experiences intense electrical fields as a kind of bliss. The form of brainwave found in trance states is also present in the neural profile of dowsers. In activities such as dowsing, the cortex with its connections to the rational consciousness is completely separated from the "damping" day-consciousness-producing influences of the blocked brainstem. It is theorized that the subtle sensations produced in the neuro-endocrine system of the dowser by contact with the magnetic fields surrounding water courses and the like, flood the pituitary/hypothalamus with impressions which induce a form of brainstem "sleep" or mild trance in which various hormonal influences stimulate the tonus of muscles and tissues in the body thereby producing the twitchings and turnings of the rods or pendulums. A good source for these ideas and much else concerning the physiology of dowsing is Tromp's *Psychical Physics*.

Dowsers can train themselves to be aware of these muscle responses and in this way use the viscera, blood, bones, muscles, and major glands as antennae for minute fluctuations in magnetic or electric fields. When dowsing fields surrounding metals or watercourses, there is not a great need for higher brain functions. When dowsing remotely or doing medical dowsing, however, the situation becomes morally complicated. If a dowser hits a dry spring, another well is simply dug, but if a medical dowser is incorrect, his whole diagnostic process could prove to be morally insupportable if it ends in a fatality.

Dowsing at this level needs to be continually supported by knowledge and the capacity of the practitioner to develop clear, integrated thinking in day consciousness. This means that the dowser must strive for the capacity to divine. This development is not without its perils and struggles. The temptation of the dowser is to stay in the instinctual sleeping consciousness of the body with the attitude that "the body knows." This blissful sympathy with all creation is a definite stage on the esoteric path. When, however, the dowser is not content with finding water mains and springs and has the desire to map dowse or dowse a person's aura, this is the signal that another, more rigorous stage of the path is about to begin. The dowser must then choose to strive toward the warmth stream coming down into the pituitary from the cosmos, and to forgo the upsurging brainstem-induced instinctual consciousness of the animal kingdom. When dowsers choose to ignore the demands to rise to a higher consciousness, they are actually opting to exist in the state of bliss in which the instinctual life denies to them the birthright of the human being, namely the gift of freedom. If a dowser decides to take a step toward freedom and approach the divine, the task is to learn the heart-quickening power of sacrifice. Unfortunately, this is only learned the hard way. Fortunately, the powers which have created and ordered the universe have stamped within us all of the necessary potentials needed to attain freedom. The pituitary gland is an actual analog of the human potential to rise above the instinctual, personality-centered consciousness. After all, its very form is a picture of the duality of body and spirit, earth and cosmos.

In alchemy there is an image which illustrates this dual nature. It is the image of Yakim and Boaz, the two pillars which stand at the entrance to the higher world. They represent the great law of polarities which must be assimilated before entrance into the higher world is accomplished. The one pillar is named Yakim, or Joachin, and it represents the concept of Universal Salt. In a salt process the primary condition is one of discrete, separate units, similar to what contemporary physics calls the particle phase. In salt, the manifestation of a discrete substance which is fully under the influence of gravity occurs in the physical plane. Salt arises out of a condition of potential in which the salt is present as an archetypal field of pattern. We could say the mother liquor of a crystal is salt in potential, or that an acidic solution and a basic solution are both saline liquors in potential which when mixed form an actual salt as a precipitate. Both the mother liquor and the crystal precipitate are involved in the process of Universal Salt. Psychically speaking, in the activity of thinking, analytical thought processes based on linear or logical causality are alchemical salt processes. A specific answer exists as a specific potential which the thinker must discover and then manifest in order to "solve" the problem. The answer is precipitated out of the solution. Each solution is specific to a particular manifestation or thought. Analysis finds the most appropriate pattern or logic, and the answer falls out of the solution like a crystal falling out of its matrix.

In the realm of sensation the specific physical properties of physical objects are likewise salt. They exist for the perception in an analogous way to the *a priori* existence of the answer within the solution. Sense percepts are not created by human consciousness but exist as a salt potential in the realm of creative archetypes. The potential or form of the sense object is present in the object as its formal principle. We could call this formal principle a line of emergence, or a morphogenetic field, to use Rupert Sheldrake's term. The morphogenetic form potential is an archetypal matrix of potential form in a vast ocean of unmanifest yet specifically potential archetype.

The pillar opposite to Yakim is Boaz, or Universal Sulfur. In sulfur processes the primary condition is not discrete units but a more intimate unity of all parts. This is similar to what modern physics calls the wave phase. In sulfur, that which is manifest as a discrete substance in the physical plane is led into intimate union with other discrete units until there is no longer any separate existence under the influence of gravity. The manifest units exist in potential or levity-filled states. In sulfur, particles are led from manifestation back into a field of potential. Where base, acid, and crystal form the components of salt processes, the sulfur process is enacted when we lead a substance through combustion and warmth into a condition wherein the physical part of the substance falls out as ash and the energetic part of the substance is liberated as warmth or light.

In the realm of thinking, the analytical salt-thinking which reveals discrete units of data must be transformed into higher states of cognition by meditative will, or soul warmth. When this happens the data or salt appears as an ash and the *process* by which the cognition was built begins to be transparent to the soul. In this sulfur stage of thinking we become more intimate with the process of cognition and less attentive to the data points. In sulfur a solution is always a deed or activity, never an object or thought separate from the thinker. Sulfur as a process transcends the sense world and lies in the realm of the archetypes or Ideas which stand behind the sense world.

In salt perception we can see which archetypes relate to which manifestations. This level of perception is known esoterically as Imagination. When through meditative imaginative exercises we move beyond the formation of the Imaginations, we can as conscious beings experience the archetypal Imaginations directly. To accomplish this we must combust the Imaginations through will in the thinking, or daily practice. The will allows the thoughts to drop their ash content as sense perceptible events and reveal their nature as patterns of light.

When this happens, a deep longing is formed in the soul to become more intimate with the source of the Imaginations. This longing for intimate union with the archetype is sulfur. In salt the soul expects to receive crystals of wisdom from the spiritual matrix. In sulfur the soul yearns to give warmth out to the spiritual matrix. To achieve sulfur all sense-related thinking must cease, and great practice in will is needed to maintain equilibrium in this sense-free state. The characteristic mood in salt is that we will be given the answer. The characteristic mood in sulfur is that the answer is only the image of a being who is asking a question of which we are only dimly aware.

In psycho-physiology the salt pole is the neurological pole in which we have our human waking consciousness. This gives the day consciousness the formative power to create the world around us and to transform it through a technology born out of abstract understanding. The sulfur pole in psycho-physiology is the metabolic digestive pole in which the discrete parts of the world are taken inward and rendered into more intimate union with ourselves. The consciousness of this pole is found in unconscious states and instinctual patterns of behavior.

The division of consciousness above and unconsciousness below is often present in human physiology, as we shall later see. Esoterically, however, this archetypal division is only the pattern which serves as the basis for the third level of development, the level of Intuition. The Intuition is known alchemically as Mercury, or Spirit. It is not an outgrowth of further sulfur forces nor the development of salt. It exists latently in both salt and sulfur as the potential for the two processes to be transformed reciprocally into each other. *Mercury is present in the most basic levels of salt and sulfur and is also the most exalted state to which they can aspire. When the wisdom of the salt pole is transformed into the life in the will of sulfur, love arises as the soul mercury. When the life of the will in sulfur is transformed into the wisdom of the salt, freedom arises as the soul mercury.* These patterns are written into the organs of a human being as well as into psychological patterns of behavior. Where we see neurological patterns and connections above and metabolic patterns below in an organ we

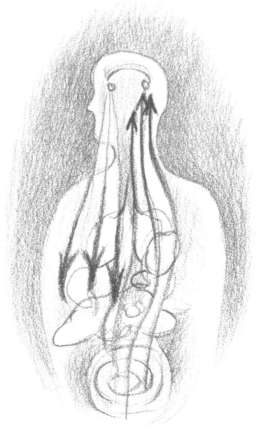

**salt above/sulfur below**

can form a workable imagination of this in the images of salt and sulfur, of Yakim and Boaz.

We saw earlier that the pituitary gland has a neurological section above and a metabolic section below. This division can also clearly be seen in the early formation of the embryonic disc when the neural and gastric layers begin to invaginate into the primal replica of the entire human organism. This early division later becomes the role of the pituitary gland, uniting the nervous system and the metabolic system into a functional rapport. The pituitary gland and its environment also provide an accurate imagination of the whole human being.

There is no such division within the mature pineal gland as there is in the pituitary. In the organs in the immediate environment of the pineal, however, we can see an amazingly primal alchemical/mythic Imagination. This image arises out of the structures of the midbrain and cerebellum. From the drawing of the brain as the garden in Paradise we can see a large structure shaped like a tree under which is standing a little figure. Coming from the base of the tree is a cord which gradually rises, like a cobra with a hood. Above the cobra is a winged figure which has a flamelike structure emerging from it. Viewed overall, this complex of organs seems somehow significant. A tree, a figure, a snake, and an angel. Turning to *Gray's Anatomy*, searching for a clue to this enigmatic image, we find that the early anatomists also noticed the pronounced treelike qualities of the lobes of the cerebellum. This part of the organ is named appropriately the *arbor vitae*, the tree of life. Surprisingly, the small figure below it is called the *choroid plexus* of the *pia mater*, the body of the tender mother. Is the image of Eve standing below the Tree of Life a fantasy, or did the early anatomists have something in mind? But the image unfolds further. The cord is the *vermis*, or worm. Dare we call it the snake? And what of the angel and the flame above? Perhaps we can see a cherub with a flaming sword guarding the gates to Paradise? In this image the flamelike nature of the pineal is a reference to its relationship to light, or Steiner's "cosmic warmth."

In certain reptiles the pineal gland actually serves as a primitive eye. In the human being this gland peers upward through the fontanelle of the fetus, only later migrating into its place in the midbrain of the infant. It remains as a kind of sense organ. It is light-sensitive, functions like an eye, and serves as an integrator for the outer senses. But what is it sensing, being so buried there beneath the brain,

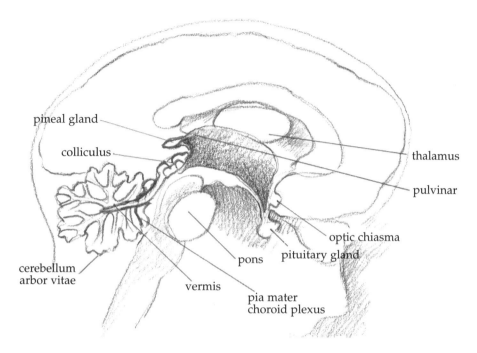

turned around and looking at the back of the skull?  Perhaps another view of the gland and its surroundings can help.

The pineal is so called because of its superficial resemblance to an upsidedown pine cone.  Other researchers, perhaps more spiritually minded, see in its shape a small replica of the human heart.  Modern research (see the work of Joseph Chilton Pearce) has indeed shown chemical connections between the glands and the overall perfor- mance of the heart (for example, the endocrine function of the heart muscle).  If we synthesize the symbols of the inverted heart with the image of the flame, we see an image found in the alchemical writings of the great seer Jacob Boehme.  This inverted flaming heart is a heart which has been purified of worldly desires and is aflame with love for the Creator.  It is devoted to higher vision.  It has become a sense organ for the divine.

Descartes saw the pineal gland as the seat of cognition in the soul. This image is further enhanced when we look at the organ which directly supports the pineal.  This organ, the *corpora quadrigemina* (bodies of the four twins), forms the hood of the snake mentioned ear- lier.  The pineal rests like a jeweled crown on the head of this snake. If one were to draw a diagram of the placement of the four twins and

**the heart of the initiate,
after Jacob Boehme**

compare it with a cross section of the human heart, a striking resonance of form could be observed. Could this organ be the heart of the brain? Could its integrating, circulating function for sense/nerve impulses be linked to the sensing, circulating forces in the heart? If this is so, what is the heart/pineal interlink sensing? And what is the significance of these images for physiology or psychology?

In order to picture this analogy between the pineal gland and the heart we could recall that the heart organ sits in the midst of pulsing currents of blood. It has the primary function of regulating and integrating the two different flows of venous (dark) blood and arterial (light) blood. As it does this, a form of sense life can be cognized in the heart. For instance, an organ within the heart, the sinuatrial node, has the sole function of sensing different qualities in the pulsations of the blood. The heart also senses in the blood the presence or absence of hormones that the glands secrete in response to sense experiences. In the center of the body, the heart is made aware of all that happens in the extremities, and all nourishment or waste products from each organ must also pass in review through the heart. Therefore Rudolf Steiner and other researchers have said that the heart functions as a sense organ. It senses the diurnal rhythms of the organs as the individual goes through the cycles of waking and sleep. These diurnal cycles are the source of the fluctuations in glandular secretions that respond to the changes in temperature and nutritional content of the blood.

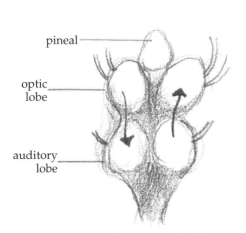

**corpora quadrigemina (colliculus)**

**heart**

By comparison, the pineal gland sits in the midst of nerve impressions sent in from the eyes and ears to be integrated in the nodes of the corpora quadrigemina. While sense impressions from the periphery of the organism are channeled into the area directly around the pineal gland (the optic radiation), the pineal itself senses and integrates the basic experience of diurnal rhythms within the body, the alternation of light and darkness in the alternation of day and night. The fluctuations of length of day and night found in seasonal rhythms are also reflected by the pineal gland's profound role in the treatment of seasonal depression and some manic/depressive forms of mental illness. To summarize, both the heart and the pineal gland sense the alternation of states of light and dark, cold and warmth. They monitor and help regulate sensations which alter moods. They help to integrate and synthesize the influx of sense impressions.

Earlier we introduced the sphenoid bone which lies on the floor of the skull at the end of a sequence of vertebrae-like processes in the base of the brain cavity. On the anterior end of these processes the wings of the sphenoid bone spread out in a gesture highly reminiscent of the pelvic wings, creating in the skull a replica of the lumbar region and the pelvis. Situated in this higher pelvic girdle like a small womb sits the pituitary gland. Like a womb it must separate and integrate substance transformation. An image of the neural and metabolic layers in an embryo, it integrates cerebral function and metabolism, the thinking pole and the will pole.

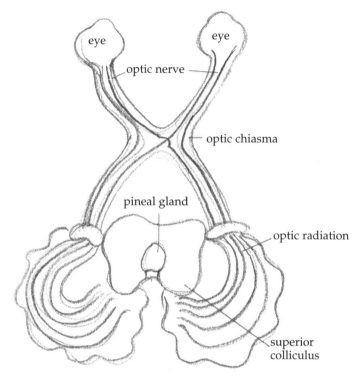

**the optic radiation**

The pituitary gland, the master gland in the body, sits in the center of tremendous activities in which substances and processes pertaining to the integrity of the organism must constantly be exchanged and balanced. The continual balancing between the polarities of nerve and blood, sensation and response, awake consciousness and deep sleep, rest and activity, and assimilation and excretion are functional analogs of the activity of the womb. In the womb neurology meets the blood stream, tissues are differentiated, substances assimilated and excreted, and organs in the fetus respond to sensations in the mother. In no other place in the body does a more heightened balancing of forces occur than in the womb and the pituitary gland. The very formation of the pituitary from two distinct embryonic layers which fuse into one organ is an analog of the myriad anastomosing movements happening daily in a gravid womb.

The pineal gland, on the other hand, lies near the other end of the sphenoid bone at the base of the brain case. It sits surrounded by the

**pituitary forces**

lung-like folds of the diencephalon, bathed in sensory impulses from the forebrain and the corpora quadrigemina. The rhythms of the senses pour into the pineal gland and flow out to the pituitary, the thyroid, and the sexual glands. What pictures arise from a meditative contemplation of this gland? We find an "eye" contemplating the mysteries of light and darkness, and an organ sentient to time and seasonal changes. We see a "heart" listening to the pulses of the eternal movements of forces moving between the periphery and the center, a heart in tune with time, looking into the deepest recesses of the brain, sensing patterns of warmth in movement and subtle fluctuations of patterns describing how space transforms into time. We could say that in the higher womb of the pituitary the spirit (mind) shatters into substance (metabolism). In the higher heart of the pineal gland, the soul divines the original archetypal warmth movements which substance seeks for its forms. With images like these we can touch the edge of the great mystery of Imagination.

If the pineal gland is a sense organ in the manner of the heart, are the heart and the gland somehow connected? Is there a field of resonance between them? If we imagine this possibility of a common field, could we then imagine another field higher than the pineal, yet resonant with both it and the heart, which forms a train of organs linked harmonically and entrained in finer and finer currents? Since the physical heart works in a vortical fashion, we might seek a vortical field around the pineal. Indeed, the four main nerves from the eyes and ears show distinct tendencies to describe the outer arcs of an inward spiralling vortex near the posterior end of the diencephalon. If heart and pineal are resonant elements in a train of vortices, could there not be more vortices, both higher and lower?

What might we observe that would suggest the presence of a higher, supersensible vortex with its center in the brain, spiraling out the crown of the head? Looking at the vortex seen in the hair at the crown of the head, the suggestion that there is a spiral of forces emerging at that spot seems almost humorous. But the form of the midbrain itself is organized in concentric rings, or *crura* (Latin for "legs"), which resemble concentric donuts of nerve tissue surrounding a vortex center in the cerebral aqueduct between the third and fourth ventricles. Directly inside the skull is the cortex of the brain, composed of a number of functional divisions known as *gyri*, or vortices. Seen in dissection, the gyri are cone-shaped radiating wheels of tissues covering the whole outer cortex of the brain. Behind and below this, the neurology of the cerebellar structures shows a pronounced spiral formation. The midbrain region surrounding these structures also shows pronounced spiral neural pathways. Feeding into this area as the vascular supply for these nervous tissues, the carotid artery starts as a spiral rushing upward through the neck into the base of the brain where it then gently spirals out into the brain like a twining shoot of a growing tree.

Taken overall, the movements of nervous tissues and vascular tissues directly below the crown of the head show a pronounced tendency toward the vortexial form. Can we not then imagine spiral forces issuing out of the crown above the head as the possible form for the field of human consciousness when it exists independently of the physical body? Asking such a question implies that the very form of the vortex permeating these structures is in itself harmonic with an ordering principle which exists before the actual manifestation of tissue. The vortex is an organized, sensitive field of forces which through its very structure reveals the cosmic laws of form. In accordance with these laws, organs are formed by patterns of forces. Once an organ is formed, those forces become the function of the organ.

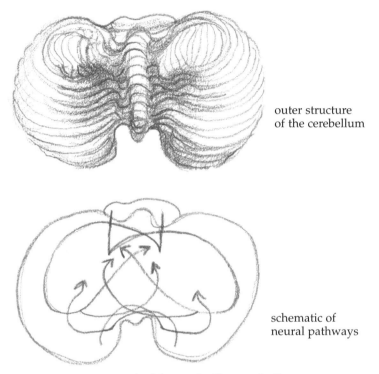

outer structure
of the cerebellum

schematic of
neural pathways

**spiral forces in the cerebellum**

In the region surrounding the pineal gland, vortexial forms are perceptible at all levels of human physiology. Does this vortexial form originate in the tissues, or are the tissues there as a response to the vortex? Are the analogous organs united in a larger field than that which stops at the surface of each organ? If there is any remote harmonic among sensible and supersensible organs, what are these various organs sensing in their environment? Is there something other than electromagnetic waves or various media of transference such as sound and light involved in the transmission and cognition of sense impressions? And finally, if there is something else inherent in sense impressions, and if there are human organs developed to perceive it, can the development of these organs be further enhanced? Is there a systematic approach to the development and enhancement of the higher heart? Is this higher heart an organ which serves as the "brain" of the heart? Could this higher heart also be a sense organ for

an even higher heart which can cognize even more subtle perceptions?

The possibility of giving affirmative answers to these questions
demands a critical review of the traditional methods of practicing
both dowsing and divining. We have seen how the dowser looking
for telluric anomalies cuts off the pituitary gland from higher consciousness by flooding it with sense data from the body. To divine an
aura, however, or to undertake clairvoyant healing disciplines with a
dowsing consciousness puts both the dowser/healer and the client at
risk of inflating the body consciousness into the status of a demigod.
The subconscious patterns in the body, not being in contact with the
higher, creative, potential forces available to the cerebral cortex, reflect
patterns which can be tremendously accurate when telluric or physical energies are being researched, but can lead to feelings of omni-
science when the researcher is exploring the subtle bodies of another
human being. This distinction needs to be brought into sharp relief in
the dowser/diviner's consciousness and in contemporary spiritual
technologies. In general, an impaired ability to check the validity of a
thought or statement being made is symptomatic of trance consciousness. To "read" the deformations of telluric magnetic fields with body
responses also requires no integration of the moral consciousness of
the awake state. To "read" deformities in the fields of another Ego-
endowed being requires clear access to awake states and the accompanying ability to determine the truth or error of a judgement which
is being made.

In the practice of dowsing there is always a physical response to
the supersensible. This stretches the laws of physical research. It is a
grave error, if divining is to be truly held as a pursuit of the divine, to
attribute the source of cognition directly to the body while bypassing
the human capacity for logical thinking. Human consciousness must
seek illumination patiently. Any human consciousness, no matter
how developed, must first put the question to the divine source and
then patiently wait until the answer ripens in the spirit, coming directly out of the movements and the forms which the mind intuits while
it is holding the question. In divining we may not get a ready answer
because the answer may not be ready to leave its source of illumination in the spiritual world. Alternatively, we might not be sufficiently advanced *morally* to hear the answer correctly.

Having to wait in silence for days or perhaps years develops in
the diviner an exquisitely fine organ of cognition for clairvoyant per-

ceptions of the finer forces in the world. In contrast to the dowser, the diviner must be willing to entertain the tension of waiting in silence until the spiritual world is ready to give an answer. More often than not the answer does not come to the diviner directly; it comes through the looks or words of another. Answers come miraculously through loaned books, "chance" comments, "accidents," unforeseen delays, and "coincidental" meetings. These routes ensure that the diviner will not inflate the body consciousness, which has its roots in the subconscious, into an illusory "higher" consciousness capable of consciously cognizing beings, events, and conditions in the spiritual world.

The diviner must use the heart as an organ of cognition. But the physical heart needs to be purified and put into a harmonic contact with the higher thinking heart if the higher eye is to be opened. Once opened, the higher heart/eye must be schooled to divine, in true humility, the healing forces of the Logos which resound through the spiritual world as the great healing Word. This critical distinction is the true basis for the inner work in modern esoteric training.

# 10

# THE DEVELOPMENT OF THE HEART SOUL: A MODERN PATH

In his lectures on occult physiology, Rudolf Steiner suggests that the facts of physiology are rendered more applicable to the healing of soul problems if the anatomy of the human being is viewed from the point of view of mythology. Let us turn again to the stories of Genesis for an image to advance our study of anatomical and physiological relationships a step further. This image does not come directly out of the Bible, but from a Rosicrucian source from the thirteenth century, *The Golden Legend*. This legend, which follows in part, is mentioned numerous times by Rudolf Steiner in his references to the temple legend.

In primeval times there existed the great divine woman, Eva, the sophianic (wisdom) aspect of God. She was approached by one of the Elohim, a world-creating spirit of fire, and had knowledge of him. This union begat Cain, a son of fire. Another of the Elohim, known as Jehova, saw this and created out of himself the son of God, Adam. Adam then took Eva as his wife and they begat Abel from whom come the children of God, those human beings who take the earth as it was given. Out of Cain's line come the children of the earth, the human beings who out of their own vision till the earth, hew stones, build buildings, smelt metal, and work to transform the physical world. Cain made an offering to Jehova of the fruits of his self-initiated labors of earth transformation. Jehova could not recognize Cain's offering because Cain had transformed the earth which Jehova, the creator of the world, had made. Abel, too, made an offering, and his offering was accepted by Jehova because Abel, the shepherd who took life as it was presented by God, did not transform Jehova's creation. Cain, whose offering was not recognized, slew Abel. In these two figures, the one more earthly and analytical (Cain), and the other more cosmic and mystical (Abel), we can see two polarities which can be taken very far in the study of physiology.

Cain represents in a Promethean way the suffering of a godlike nature aflame with an independent initiative to transform matter. This is a picture of will in the thinking pole, the working over of what is given through independent activity. The impulse is to transform and quicken that which is lifeless. Abel, on the other hand, corresponds to the given. Physiologically, what is given is the structure and functioning of the organs of metabolism which lie below the human waking consciousness. This pole puts the thinking in the will. The forces of metabolism impel the human being to satisfy appetites. This is a picture of the instinctual path, of the realm of ancient prescribed inner vision. Prescribed inner experience of the sensations of bodily organs is the root of the religious inspirations coming from the gods in mystical experience.

In the previous essay we saw these two polarities in the structure of the pituitary gland. In the pituitary a glandular/metabolic part is connected to a neurological part, the two parts actually originating from two different layers in the embryo. This is a highly significant fact in embryology. The metabolic Abel function arises out of the ectodermal layer associated with the formation of the primitive mouth. The neurological Cain function arises as a downward-growing, funnel-shaped tube of cells which moves toward the metabolic part of the gland as the embryo is forming the involution which will later become the organs of speech (Rathke's pouch).

As we have seen, the two lobes of the pituitary

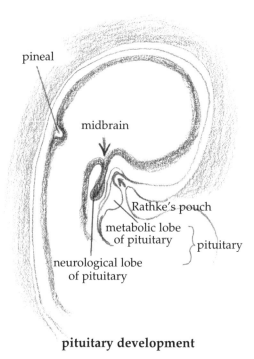

pineal

midbrain

Rathke's pouch

metabolic lobe of pituitary

neurological lobe of pituitary

pituitary

**pituitary development**

gland, the metabolic and the neurological, are separated by a membrane, a septum rich in melanin, hormones, and endorphins. The metabolic part has no nerves but extensive blood vessels. The neurological part does have blood vessels but is also rich in nerve endings to many parts of the brain. Cain is the thinking technologist. His connection to the cerebral cortex enables him to invent, calculate, and organize the things of the sense realm. Abel is the visionary contemplative who shuns the practical life and becomes absorbed in his own inner organic perceptions. Cain desires to bring life into the lifeless world of matter. Abel is aware that the Godhead is present within the microcosmic universe of the body. By listening into the blood as it streams within the body, Abel will have all secrets of existence revealed. He remains in a mode of listening to the word of God. Abel offers his microcosmic perceptions back to a God familiar with their content. He is assured that his offerings will be recognized.

We have seen this picture in the dowser's use of the pituitary gland. The neurological part of the pituitary ceases to function when the consciousness is trained to focus upon the sensations of the inner organs. By contrast, the offerings of Cain are stimulated by the sense impressions from the world. The neurological pituitary lobe, the *neurohypophysis*, is directly connected to the crossing point of the optic nerves, the optic chiasma. This is where the nerves from the right eye and the left eye meet as they journey to the very back of the brain where their impulses are integrated with input from the ears. At the optic chiasma, these signals from the visual sense stimulate endocrine

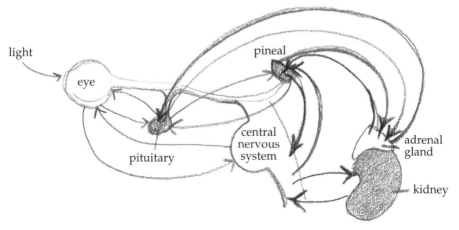

**reciprocal relationships**

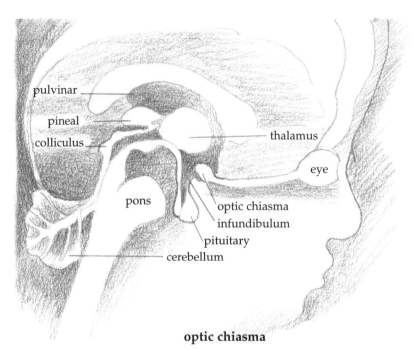

**optic chiasma**

function as the neurological part of the pituitary gland senses the incoming impulses.

A parallel can be drawn here to the structures of the heart where the atrium senses the temperature, velocity, and hormone qualities of the incoming blood. In this analog the heart has strong similarities to the womb. It is the cells in the atrium of the heart (sinuatrial node) that possess an endocrine function. On the other hand, the ventricle, being entirely vascular and muscular, is concerned not so much with sensing, but with proper, lawful distribution. Thus the pituitary itself can be seen as a tiny heart—sensing, integrating, and distributing what is above into what is below—with a septum dividing the functions of its two halves. In the pituitary gland there are no valves between the metabolic and neurological parts, but rather secretions are selectively transmitted from one side to the other as need arises.

But why project the images of a thirteenth century legend onto a scientific physiological study? To begin with, let us consult a diagram which illustrates the intricate relationships within which a gland, or in the case of the pituitary, a portion of gland, must function. The endocrine functions are never simple polarities but are embedded in whole trains of relationships like the plot to a novel. It is these rela-

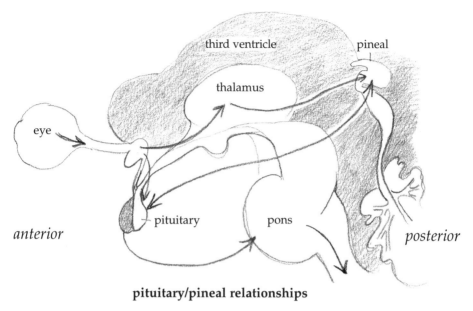

**pituitary/pineal relationships**

tionships which can be revealed by comparing physiology to mythos. In the case of the pituitary, Cain and Abel meet but do not merge, even though they are brothers. The slaying of Abel by Cain can be seen in the Promethean image of the conscious, cerebrally-driven, waking state destroying all that the metabolism has given rise to in the night. Each day the Promethean Cain awakens to his neurologically stimulated struggles at the expense of the metabolic organs. Those who begin to train the thinking through a concentration exercise can experience the first fratricide within themselves. And to be sure, there is a price to pay for this fratricide.

In the Golden Legend, the slaying of Abel calls forth the judgements which result in the great struggles that Cain must endure in his relationship with the forces of nature. The natural world takes on the quality of an adversary, and Cain and his children must invent ever more sophisticated technologies to conquer the elements. Abel, being closer to the ongoing spiritual existence, did not need to overcome nature because he could perceive the working of the spirit within the organs of the body.

A curious detail in the physiology of the neurohypophysis points to this judgement of Cain. Above the neurohypophysis a hollow tube, the infundibulum, descends from the floor of the diencephalon. The superior end of this tube connects to the optic chiasma, the place where the optic nerve from the two eyes cross. This crossing of the optic nerves integrates and weaves the sense data from the right and left eyes into the opposite sides of the brain. Into the recess which houses the optic chiasma runs the nucleus of a nerve bundle known as the superchiasmatic nucleus. This ganglion responds to the impulses which are transmitted through the optic chiasma. The curious aspect of this detail is that the superchiasmatic nucleus is a neural pacemaker whose function is to regulate the rhythms of light and darkness as the optic nerve is stimulated by circadian rhythms in nature. It is a neural pacemaker operating in conjunction with the pineal gland, connecting the neurohypophysis (the neural side of the pituitary) along the optic tract to the pineal gland. This pacemaking function at the root of the neurohypophysis is another reflection of the connection between the heart and the pituitary. Situated between the two atria of the heart is the sinuatrial node, a nerve nucleus which senses, in the way in which an endocrine gland senses, the composition of the blood flowing toward it from the periphery of the body. In like manner in the superchiasmatic nucleus, the neurohypophysis can sense the flowing of impulses of light moving toward it from the periphery of the environment.

The superchiasmatic nucleus regulates sleeping and waking cycles, many subconscious metabolic functions, instinctual adrenal functions, and reproductive cycles—in short, all of those unconscious functions so familiar to the mystical consciousness of Abel. In lower mammals the superchiasmatic nucleus is very large and regulates these functions almost completely. Indeed, the instinctual life based on sensations dominates the soul life of animals. In the human being this organ is so small as to be almost non-existent. The automatic instinctual behavior in human beings must be given over to self-regulated, independently willed impulses and resolves. Cain has slain Abel and now must take on his own shoulders the wisdom that was once given as a gift. The instinctual will impulses must now be penetrated by thinking. Abel can no longer dream the thoughts of the gods and have his sacrifice accepted. Cain must struggle to transform with his own willed thinking the forces of the surging chaos in nature, and he must take in hand and transform the Paradise of instinctual knowledge regulated by the rhythms of light pulsing from the spiritual world. The practical life and the mystical life must be united. It is significant that the withdrawal of insight into the sleeping, dreaming, and waking cycles is God's way of punishing Cain. That Cain no longer has access to dream time means that these cycles must be grasped and transformed consciously as part of Cain's sentence.

In the Golden Legend the deed of Cain has a further implication. After the death of Abel, Adam and Eve conceive another son, Seth. As it always is in fairy tales, the first son, Cain, goes out full of cleverness and ability but falls to passion and arrogance. The second son, Abel, also falls, but into dreaminess, timidity, and the slavish following of the will of others. The third son, Seth, who goes out is innocent and asleep, a simpleton.

In the Golden Legend Seth must go on a journey, for Adam is dying and needs the oil of mercy, or compassion, which can only be found in Paradise. Seth volunteers to go to Paradise where he meets with an angel. From the angel Seth receives the oil of mercy and, according to some versions, a scion cut from the Tree of Life; in other versions, he receives the oil of mercy and three seeds from the fruit of the Tree of Life. The Tree of Life can be compared to the branching of the circulation system, the Tree of Knowledge to the branching of the nerves. Seth returns and plants the scion over Adam's grave after giving him extreme unction with the oil of mercy. In one version, Seth places the three seeds under Adam's tongue as he is buried on Golgotha. So here we see the third son going on a journey to the land on the other side of the bridge of existence between life on earth and Paradise. This image of the bridge, also found in Goethe's fairy tale, is also present in human physiology. In the literature describing the formation of the environment of the pineal gland the word *migratory* comes up again and again. The tissues of the cerebellum exist in a paradisiacal form for a long time, migrating from one layer to another as proliferative, uncommitted germinal matrix cells. Only after their migrational journey do the cells begin to function as cells committed to a purpose.

In human embryology the pontine flexure (*pons* is Latin for "bridge") is the site of a strong curvature of the neural tube. This embryonic bridge is a very conspicuous part of early embryonic development. On the anterior end of the pontine flexure sits the pituitary gland, which we know as Cain and Abel. On the posterior end of the bridge sits the pineal gland, which we will call Seth. The pineal is formed in a hollow of the third ventricle behind the pituitary. In lower animals, especially reptiles, the pineal gland is split like the pituitary, the anterior portion actually forming a third eye, or reptilian parietal eye, while the posterior part is glandular. This third eye is sensitive to light and warmth in some reptiles. In human beings, the parietal eye atrophies, and the posterior, glandular section of the gland takes over the whole structure. Later we will see where this eye-like gesture is highly significant in the crystallization or lens formation stage of the mature pineal gland (or *epiphysis*, the gland which "grows on"). From these biological descriptions we can trace the mythological journey of the third son Seth across the spirit bridge into Paradise.

We have earlier encountered images of Genesis in the forms of the cerebellum and corpora quadrigemina. We saw Eva and the Snake at the foot of the Tree of Life and the cherub guarding the gates of Paradise with a flaming sword, as imaged in the wings of the diencephalon and the pineal gland itself. The pineal sits on the pulvinar fold, which is just behind and above the midbrain at the top of the brainstem. The Roman *pulvinar* was the couch found in the holy of holies in the temple. During rites, the priest would look for the god to descend and sit on the pulvinar in order to have a dialogue with the priest. In our drama Seth, the pineal, has crossed the pons into the paradisiacal world just above the midbrain. Here he must perform a

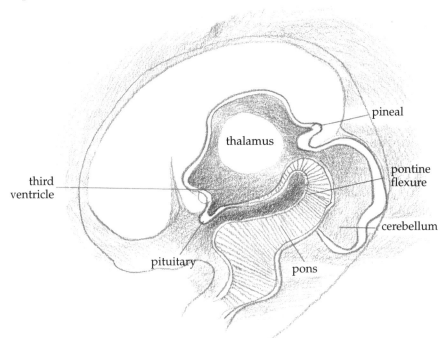

**pontine flexure in the embryonic brain (3 months)**

sacrifice in the holy of holies. In the embryo the pineal begins as a twofold gland like the pituitary. It has an upper neurological portion and a lower metabolic portion. As it develops, however, the pineal rises above the pituitary to become the epiphysis, growing onto the upper portion of the brainstem. At this time the vestigial eye-like nature of the neurological portion of the pineal gland atrophies. The eye-like portion which persists in some reptiles as the gift of the serpent must be given away in order for Seth to stand once again in the door to Paradise and face the cherub guarding the Tree of Life. Unlike Abel, Seth must forsake his inner atavistic clairvoyant vision of the spirit world. A priest in the new mysteries, Seth must face the higher spiritual beings in his waking consciousness. He sacrifices his spiritual vision, his vestigial reptilian eye at the door to the sacred world, whereupon the cherub gives him the gifts of three seeds from the fruit of the Tree of Life, a scion from the Tree of Life, and a vial of the oil of mercy. After receiving these gifts, Seth returns to earth as the prototype of a new human being, a new union of his two brothers, Cain and Abel.

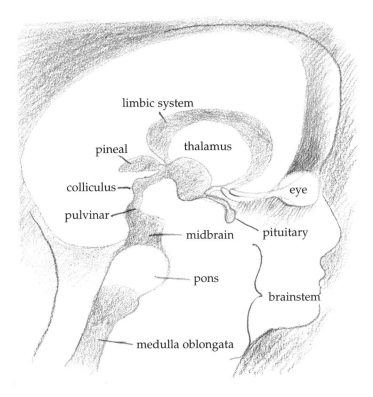

Rudolf Steiner tells us that the tree which Seth planted provided the wood for the cross upon which Christ was crucified. And so one legend weaves into another larger picture. But what physiological basis is there for calling the epiphysis, the pineal gland, Seth? To begin with, there is the migratory nature of the cells surrounding the gland as a picture of Seth's journey. Then there is the position across the bridge of the pons near the Tree of Life, and the drama of the Fall pictured in the cerebellum. Then there is the encounter with the angel of God on the couch of the pulvinar. In an earlier chapter we saw the wings of the diencephalon surrounding the pineal as an image of an angel with a flaming sword. But let us go deeper into this pineal/Seth anatomy and see if the details continue to correspond to the picture developed thus far.

The sources of the pineal gland are very different from those of the pituitary. The union of alimentary tissue and neurological tissue from the diencephalon puts the pituitary gland close to the functioning of a waking consciousness, the neo-cortex being the primary place where thinking and sensation are integrated into the awake state. The stimulant effect of light upon the superchiasmatic nucleus is a reference to this sensate realm of working. By contrast the pineal gland is a gland which only functions when no light is present in the optic tract. It arises embryologically as an interplay between the pia mater, a very fine vascular net of capillaries covering the inner surface of the third ventricle in the brain, and the nerves which come from the superior cervical ganglion, a complex and extensive ganglion of the sympathetic nervous system.

The superior cervical ganglion has nerves which go to many points in the throat and down into the cardiac/aortic complex of the circulatory system. In the pineal gland, however, nerve and blood meet in such a way that there is little nerve contact with the blood supply back to the gland but a great deal of nerve contact from the gland *to* the blood supply. In this way the pineal works in the body mainly to regulate or inhibit; it suppresses the production of hormones in glands such as the thyroid, gonads, adrenals, and pituitary. Between the pituitary and the pineal one can actually envision an endocrine systole and diastole following the circadian and seasonal rhythms of light. Together these two glands can be imagined as the heart of the brain with impulses of neurochemical/electrical activity and currents of cerebrospinal fluid pulsing between them through the ventricles in the brain.

But what of Seth? What are the implications of a genesis from the intricate webs of blood in the pia mater and the sympathetic ganglial innervation from the superior cervical ganglion? These two progenitors, pia mater (vascular/Eva) and the sympathetic nervous system (neurological/Adam), produce a third son who lives much closer to the spiritual world than the first two sons. Seth migrates to Paradise where he obtains the oil of mercy. The pineal is in deep neuronal communion with both the sympathetic and central nervous systems and the vascular system deep within the body. From this we can infer that Seth is able to cross the barrier from this world into the other worlds. He is familiar with the states of consciousness which lie within the inner, "organ knowledge" of Abel and also the outer, conceptual, cerebral knowledge of Cain. Seth's goal, compassion, is the essence of the distillative activity when the sympathetic heart begins to think. It cannot be developed without both inner and outer vision.

In his journey, Seth goes beyond both Abel and Cain. His innocence allows him to travel into states beyond both the sleep of the organs and the upper boundaries of waking consciousness where he can learn great secrets about life from the angels. Endocrinology tells us that the pineal is the main gland concerned with the various levels of sleep. Regular sleep in which long, slow brain waves are produced is the normal sleep state. This is the consciousness of Abel. In what is known as *paradoxical sleep* the brain waves resemble the waking state, but the person is asleep. It is in this

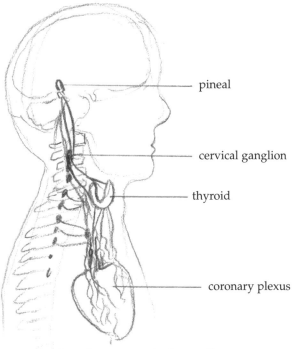

pineal

cervical ganglion

thyroid

coronary plexus

**pineal and supercervical ganglion**

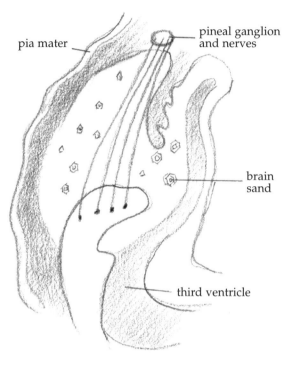

pia mater

pineal ganglion
and nerves

brain
sand

third ventricle

**detail of pineal gland**

state that dreams occur with periods of rapid eye movement as if the optic tract were responding to visual stimuli. In the third state, the cerebral cortex governs the waking consciousness. Various hypnogenic, or sleep generating, zones are spread throughout the brain. These zones are synchronized by secretions of melatonin from the pineal gland and different combinations of these zones result in different levels of consciousness.

Clearly the pineal gland is a guide to the activity of the soul as it moves through different levels of the spiritual world. But how? A look at the anatomy of the pineal reveals a complex neural pattern from the senses. Visual, auditory, and olfactory nuclei move into the area around the pineal gland, as does the pineal nerve from the cervical ganglion which runs the length of the gland as a septum. The choroid plexus of the pia mater sends the blood and cerebral fluids from the entire brain into the region of the pineal through the cerebral aqueduct where it contacts the sense and sympathetic nerves.

According to Rudolf Steiner, the blood is like a tablet upon which the nerves impress their impulses. There are many mysteries embedded in the way in which the nerves meet the blood in the pineal gland. For instance, the body of this gland, which is composed of highly vascular tissue from the pia mater, is the site of a confluence of the major sensory nerves from eyes and ears. Why direct the two major sensory nerves into a small bundle of vascular tissue?

The pineal gland is carried at the upper end of the spinal cord, above the medulla and cerebellum. This position puts it in direct contact with many body nerve impulses from the central nervous system. The nervous organs surrounding it are devoted to the *integration* of tremendous sensory input so that the human being can lead a conscious practical life dealing with the physical realities of earth existence. In this way the pineal, a vascular body, appears to be directly connected to the children of Cain, who are the artists and scientists and builders. They are the ones who must transform everything they meet. To do this, the children of Cain need a thinking process independent of the laws of nature, a consciousness wherein they are free to imagine new concepts and *integrate* sense data in new ways. Esoterically, the effects of the impulses from the sense organs on the blood can be viewed as an image of this autonomous awakening. It is within such influenced and awakened blood that the ego consciousness arises and lives. This is the destiny of the children of Cain, and it is reflected in the pineal gland as the relationship between the pia mater as the body of the gland and the environment of the gland rich in sensory nerve endings from the whole organism.

This direct connection to outer nervous activity would put Seth into the Cain stream. But Seth is also the brother who took the place of Abel. For this he needs to have direct inner contact with the intentions of the Godhead in order to act in compliance with cosmic law. These polarities of inner and outer are the cause of the conflict between Cain and Abel, the anger and resentment which leads to fratricide. Seth must reconcile these differences. He must become capable of very practical and independent outer cognition in the service of others while wandering inwardly in the spiritual world. To be consciously independent within the spiritual world as an act of compassion is the task of the new human being in the new mystery schools.

While the environment of the pineal gland is rich with nerves of the *central* nervous system, the nerve connections of the gland itself comes directly from the *sympathetic* nervous system. We hear from Rudolf Steiner that the function of the sympathetic nervous system is to protect the blood from being directly impacted by sense stimulation from outside, that is, through the eyes, ears, skin, and so forth. The sympathetic nerves, however, do take in impressions which, according to Rudolf Steiner, are from the activities of the inner organs, the perception of which constitutes the mystic path, the path of Abel. For most human beings, this inner world perception is a subconsciou' dreamlike experience. Through esoteric training, however, the impressions being made upon the sympathetic nervous system can be made to enter into ego-consciousness. This leads to a perception that what is enclosed within the inner organs of the human being is directly connected to the movements in the cosmos. Of course, there is a long apprenticeship to making such a connection, but it is through systematic development of conscious perception of the sympathetic nervous system that the mystical path is pursued.

Seth, being in the line of Abel, is treading this path also. To reconcile the differences between his two brothers, he must unite the mystical path and the thinking path. He does this by going on an errand of mercy. There are two images from this journey which are particularly fruitful for meditation: the oil of mercy and the three seeds from the fruit of the Tree of Life. Each of these can be considered from the point of view of the physiology of the pineal gland. From the outset, Seth's journey is a mission of compassion for his dying father, not for his own benefit. He seeks an oil which bestows mercy. In the alchemy of plants, the oil process is the result of an inner distillation which takes place in the plant as finer and finer substances are led into a combustible or nearly combustible state.

In the alchemy of distillation a coarse substance in which essential oils are mixed with water and alcohol is gently heated in a closed container until vapor rises. To an alchemist this vapor is known as the *steam widow*. It is a widow because it is now removed from its union with the other substance. Through controlled and gentle heating (will activity), the most volatile elements in a solution become widowed first. They rise into the upper part of the boiling flask and are quickly led into a condensing chamber with a cold water sleeve around it. The vapors condense into a liquid under the influence of the cold water, but this liquid is now composed only of the most volatile essences which were lifted from the grosser substances.

Distillation is thus a higher form of excretion, the sifting of substances out of a mixed state. The substances lifted in such a way are known as essences or essential oils. Flowers produce their fragrances and essences by a similar organic distillation. Chemical distillation lifts the flower essences up even further and concentrates them into oils. The oil of mercy then is indicative of a distillation process which Seth must undergo in order to lift his consciousness into Paradise where the essences of all things reside. To obtain or distill the oil of mercy, Seth must apply the warmth of his will to undertake an arduous journey for the benefit of someone else. This sacrificed will warms the mixture of dross and subtle elements of the personality and causes the finer essences to evaporate upward and leave the dross elements behind. The sublimated essences must then be condensed into an oil as the cool pole of thinking is applied to the lifted essences. The sublimation/condensation process produces the oil of mercy.

Further condensation of the oil produces the three seeds given to Seth by the angel. In the beginning of distillation the will is applied to the thinking in order to create the concentration of warmth needed to produce the widow of steam. In the later phase of distillation the cool forces of thinking are applied to the motives found in the will. This renders the finer parts of the personality from simply a conglomerate of mixed parts into an organized hierarchy ranging from gross to very fine elements. The oil of mercy then is produced by a distillation/excretion process in the personality. This process allows the personality to perceive that it has a higher and finer, more spiritual existence. This promotes feelings of mercy and forgiveness toward one's own transgressions and those of others.

The physiological image of this excretion/distillation process is the endocrine process in general. An endocrine gland facilitates an excretory/distillation process between the blood and the nerves. The glands are like fruits forming on the branches of the trees of the circulation and the nerves. As fruit-like forms they are the result of distillation processes in the stream of nutrition in which finer and finer substances are deposited after being separated from grosser substances by neural and metabolic processes. In endocrinology whether the nerves create the release of neurotransmitters or the neurotransmitters in the blood cause the nerves to be stimulated depends upon which research is brought forward. The glands in general and the pineal in particular work to modify the interaction of blood and nerve and keep it within reasonable parameters for the health of the organism.

The essence of this reaction and interaction between blood and nerve has been described by Rudolf Steiner as *resistance*. The gland is the site of greatest tension between systems, where the products of one realm must interact with the receptors of another. The gland limits, organizes, inhibits, and generally resists most outer biochemical influences except highly specific ones which are then stored and distilled into essential secretions until they are needed to affect a transition from one energetic state to another. The dross is passed on to be excreted elsewhere.

The pineal is the most inhibitory of all the glands. It must work at the nether boundaries between light and darkness, between good moods and bad, depression and joy, insanity and illumination. The pineal secretes its hormones when the rest of the system is plunged into darkness, a functional rhythm which is connected to the pituitary gland in a reciprocal linkage. Neurons near the optic chiasma are excited by light. This excitation inhibits the neurons of the sympathetic system which form the core of the pineal gland, and the cells of the pineal cease to secrete melatonin. Melatonin is active in the production of sleep states of various degrees. It is also active in the forming of manic-depressive mood swings and some forms of insanity. Thus the pineal gland is at the doorway to other states of consciousness, for when not stimulated by the nerve-sense system, its activities lead the human consciousness into other worlds. This is exactly the task of Seth.

Mediating between the nerves and the blood, a gland is an excretory/metabolic organ similar in function to the liver, gall bladder, or spleen. It absorbs substances from a wide sphere, performs a distillation/excretion process, and stores the finer secretions which it condenses from these processes to be secreted when the nerve/blood polarity is unbalanced due to stimulation. Why could Seth then not just as easily be pictured as a spleen? The spleen is complete in itself, a little king needing no one else in the unfolding of its duties. Seth, on the other hand, puts himself at risk to undertake a perilous journey into alien worlds of spirit. A gland must be open to far wider surroundings than a digestive organ. It must be capable of breathing into the spiritual world and of sensing the beings which live there. This is pictured in Seth's encounter with the angel who gives him the seeds.

In the pineal gland an unusual physiological development can serve as a symbol of this spiritual sensing. This is the process by which the surface of the gland is embedded with calcite crystals known as *brain sand*. (See figure on p. 134.) The crystals emerge as the process of puberty and maturation in the physical body begins. Endocrinologists describe the seeds of the crystals as bits of the cell walls which are dislodged; they slowly migrate to the outer surface of the gland where they are surrounded by concentric layers of calcium in a manner similar to the formation of a pearl within an oyster.

Where a pearl is amorphous, however, brain sand is crystalline in shape.

Karl König (in *Earth and Man*) describes how the crystals emerged in the pineal gland of a four-year-old girl who suffered damage to the gland. As the crystals emerged, the child began to show capacities for difficult mathematics and began to go through puberty. Her capacities for logic and reasoning were likewise accelerated. Esoterically, we could consider that quartz crystal formations in the earth are really like eyes. The forms of the eye and the quartz crystal are very similar in that they are both composed of many layers of siliceous membranes. This multi-layered form is present in physiology as the structure of the lens of the eye. In electronics, the crystal as a sense organ for drawing in signals served as the basic component of early radio sets. Many examples of clear parallels between crystal formation and sensing—both local and remote—could be drawn. The growth of crystals in the surface of a gland which is coincident with inspirative powers for understanding mathematics and geometry is an interesting picture, especially since the same gland in lower animals serves as a rudimentary "eye" for sensing patterns of warmth and movement. This is even more suggestive when we consider that this gland functions only when sense impulses are at a minimum.

These pictures point to the possibility that the pineal is an antenna-like organ, built on the pattern of the compound lens of an insect eye, each crystal of brain sand a facet for receiving subtle patterns of warmth in motion from sources beyond the physical. In many different sources Rudolf Steiner indicates that if humanity is to evolve, it must learn to move consciously past the inherited metabolic patterns of the ether body. This is accomplished by turning the inward-oriented Abel consciousness outward through the visible world into the wisdom behind the will patterns of the spiritual worlds.

Since both the inner realities of the organs and the outer realities of the sense world represent the two limits of knowledge in the human consciousness, it is not to our advantage to seek development either in the atavistic immersion in our own organs or in the technological materialism of sense-perceptible reality. We need to be able to journey into the spiritual world in a compassionate, selfless way and to build a spiritual technology around the supersensible activity of spiritual beings which lies behind the objects of the sense world. When we do so, we meet the angel who gives us seeds for our future development. These seeds will be embedded in our higher heart as organs through which we can sense the creative movements of beings in the spiritual world.

Through a focused attention upon the pituitary and pineal glands, fields of being which act in particular ways become accessible to waking consciousness. This can serve as the basis for an esoteric schooling. Through the pituitary, through the gifts of Cain and Abel, a path is revealed which unites the accomplishments of art and science with a religious veneration for all of creation. Through a meditation upon the pineal, Seth opens a path in which the heart of the soul beats in rhythmic systole and diastole into and out of the spiritual world. Creativity is enhanced when in the space at the center of one's head one can feel the touch of angelic hands, radiating knowledge and love/wisdom into the daily round of thoughts, feelings, and activities. The angel can then plant in the pulsing cerebro-spinal fluid and in the rhythms of the heart of the brain the seeds for a higher existence outside the body. These seeds, after proper preparation and waiting, sprout into the new capacities for Imagination, Inspiration, and Intuition. As these three seeds grow in the third ventricle, a new form of thinking is born in which the oil of mercy, the seeds of higher consciousness, and the shoot from the Tree of Life can germinate, take root, and grow.

The final deed of Seth, the grafting of the scion from the Tree of Life, is the subject of a later chapter, *The Great Tree*. Any orchardist knows that seeds are sown to grow good rootstocks, but it is in the setting of the scion wood that the new may come into being. The grafting of a scion is a very different gesture from the sowing of seeds. Much more "magic" is needed, and the attention required is much more concentrated. Seth, upon his return to the earth, had to perform his duties toward the father in a new way, a picture that the new humanity will have to enter into a very different relationship with nature, agriculture, and the healing arts in the future.

Physiologically, this return of Seth to plant the seeds gathered in the spiritual world can be pictured in the intimate homeostatic oscillations between the pineal and the pituitary involving the seasonal fluctuations of melatonin and the influence of the secretions upon the mental life of a human being. This image is critical in the treatment of anxiety and various forms of mental disorders. In such treatment, melatonin acts as an oil of mercy. From the point of view of mythos, Seth needs to return to the pituitary side of the pons in order that the experiences of the world on the spirit side of the threshold can be brought into waking consciousness.   The conscious ego-controlled process of bringing the contents of divined experiences into the cognitive awareness is a great healing of the fear, anxiety, and alienation of modern souls seemingly condemned to existence in a spiritless universe.

Of course the key here is the control of the process by an awake ego-being waiting at the door to the spiritual world to intuit the truth or falsity of the spiritual experience.  It is here that dowsing and divining give way to the conscious surrender to the guardian angel as a safe step into higher spiritual states.  The traditional conversion of a dowser's body into a sense organ makes it impossible for the spiritual world to approach our capacity for higher Imagination.  By continually flooding the sympathetic nervous system with field data from the physical surroundings, we damp down the higher vibrations and become disinclined to listen into the higher frequencies of Imagination, Inspiration, and Intuition.  For these states to be reached, the content of the senses informing the body needs to be transcended, thus freeing the soul for contact with the angelic world and higher states of consciousness.  To do this, we must forsake pendulums, rods, and muscle testing, in the true or authentic faith that the spiritual world, after the appropriate apprenticeship is fulfilled, will be enthusiastic to aid us in diagnosis and healing insights about ourselves and other human beings in need, and also to help us perceive and heal the life forces of the earth and all of the living creatures so dependent upon her health and spiritual well-being.

# 11

# IMAGINATION:
# THE SACRED DOOR

In thinking about the capacity of the soul to form an inner image there arises the question of the sacred in human life. Since ancient times most cultures have linked the sacred and the imaginative, not bothering with the philosophical question: What is a mental image? Rites and myths simply arose as mental images and made their way into liturgy or the everyday life of the people. Today, however, we must ask the question, "What is the source of the images which arise within me?"

As we saw earlier, *imaginary* is a term used to describe inner images of personal fantasy which are not real. *Imaginative* is defined simply as pertaining to imagination—not much help in expanding our understanding. The common definitions of the word *imagination* cannot take us much farther, for they are too broad to be useful, covering everything from a logical well-constructed inner image to the images which are the source of obsession and delusion. What we need is a word which is an image of a process, since imagination is a process rather than a thing. This word is *imaginal*, from *imago*. We have seen that imago is a biological term for the mature form of an insect which has undergone metamorphosis. The process of going from egg to caterpillar to pupa to imago is the imaginal process, and this entomological term is effective in describing processes in which one image is transformed into another in an accurate way. For example, why does a particular butterfly come out of a particular chrysalis when studies show that when the caterpillar goes into transformation its internal organs are in a complete state of disintegration and chaos? No reference between the caterpillar and butterfly can be drawn, yet through the chaos of transformation an exact relationship is maintained.

As has been mentioned, imago also has a meaning in psychology where it is used to describe an idealized picture of a parent held in the mind of a child through puberty and into adulthood and retained uncorrected in adult life.  Once again, something goes through a chaos and retains an exact relationship to the original.  Using the term imaginal to describe the creative process emphasizes this specific metamorphosis in the evolution of mental images.  In the case of the psychological pathology described above, this constancy of transfer into adulthood is not positive.  Here the idealized mental image does not actually metamorphose.  In the case of the caterpillar, we can still see the worm dangling between the two wings of the butterfly, but because it was a complete metamorphosis, they are harmoniously wedded into the new form.  Indeed, the markings on the wings of a butterfly are often in direct relationship to the places where the wings touched the caterpillar while they were pressed against the skin of the worm in the pupa and stained by its secretions.  In fantasy states of imaginary or imaginative seeing, no such imprinting or relationship to previous forms is evident.  Imaginative fantasies can spring from many pathologies and be, in essence, unrelated to the person except by pure body response or instinct.  An example of this would be endogenous depression, or organ-induced depression.  Such patterns of mental image are highly subjective and are related unconsciously to past traumas.  These unconscious imaginary images arise in automatic reaction to the repressed contents of the traumas and bear a subconscious and therefore fixed relationship to the inner life.

By contrast, in conscious imaginal processes the seer works to form an imagination as exactly as possible.  This is then worked systematically into a condition of dynamic *forgetting,* the technique of *mindfulness* in Buddhist terminology.  In mindfulness the thinking is filled with the potential which it took to concentrate and construct the image, but the image has been released into silence, oblivion, chaos, or original form.  In the silence of this release, the forces present behind the form and which led to its creative unfolding imprint on the "empty" consciousness the new emergent form which is not yet manifest, as in the patterns on the butterfly wing.  When the imago emerges from its chrysalis of silence, it is an image of the previous state but is completely metamorphosed.  It has maintained a spiritually exact relationship to its previous state and yet has totally transcendent capacities.  The process of forming, conscious forgetting, and transcendent remembering are the three stages of the imaginal process.

Philosophically we can compare a mental image of something we have seen, such as a circle, with a concept which is imperceptible by the senses, such as the formula for the circumference of a circle. The circle we have seen somewhere in the outer world. The formula for determining the circumference is somewhere in the inner world, in the realm of Idea. In between we can have the experience of forming an inner image of a circle which is neither outer nor ideally inner but somewhere in the personal world which we call "our" soul. This mental image of a circle is both the image of an actual circle in the world and the image of the concept "circle" in the realm of Idea. The mental image then can be considered the product of a sense impression and an ideal concept. From this experience we can say that the mental image is a merging of two polarities, the sensate and the conceptual.

But where specifically does the mental image arise? Does it come primarily from the stimulus, that is, the circle in the world; or from the medium of transmission, that is, the senses; or does it arise in the thought life? Obviously some element of the mental image is related to the sense object, and there needs to be a medium encoded in some way to transmit the image, and most surely there needs to be a receiver. It seems then that no matter where we look in the sense domain the mental image permeates all levels. Can we say the same for the conceptual side?

Somehow in the thinking of the formula for circumference an intuition of circularity makes its way through our thought processes into our blood and nerves, and an inner image arises which we can then draw on paper. Of course in $C=2\pi r$, the concept $\pi$ never really can come into the sense world in the same way that C and r can. Still, even in order to think this formula there needs to be a receiver that is distinct from the source of the idea. Thus the mental image is like a swinging door in the mind through which the sense and conceptual worlds flow and through which they can be united in the soul of the human being.

Sensation permeates all levels of the sense experience, existing imaginally in the stimulus, the transmitting medium, the sense organ, and the response. The sensation *is*. Seen in this way sensation has more the character of a field than of a specific response. We could say that the whole realm of sensation has life characteristics which make it similar to an organism.  Each step is a recapitulation of the journey of the whole.  The same could be said for the ontogenesis of an idea. It comes into human consciousness imaginally, already having certain movements and, as the poet says, "trailing clouds of glory" as it comes.

For this domain of experience, the ancient world had a fitting analog:  the great tree, or world tree.  The tree is a powerful universal image, for its roots, trunk, and crown are distinct from one another yet are united in one living being, a sensitive link between the heavens and the earth.  The world tree is a symbol for a way of thinking that grasps the inner movements of the mental image, since both the tree and the mental image connect the lower world of sensation to the upper world of Idea.

In shamanism, the crown, roots, and trunk of the tree correspond to the three layers of the world:  the upper world, the lower world, and this world, the middle world—united yet distinct.  The shaman enters the spirit realm by following the roots of the tree into the lower world, for the upper world finds expression in the lower world, with the middle world as the mediator.  The shaman or adept living in this world can thereby shift attentive consciousness to travel between worlds while never fully leaving this middle world.

Physical sensation is analogous to the lower world, the conceptual ideal realm to the upper world, and the mental image is in the middle world where the soul of the adept lives in everyday consciousness.  To ask then where is the place were the mental image arises we must describe not a space or specific organ but an unfolding *process*. Even though root and crown of the world tree exist in separate spaces, as a life form they are united in wholeness.  A visual sensation, for example, is a field of activity which manifests as an object in space, as light waves which interact with the object, as impulses in a transmitting medium, as the lens of the eye, as the retina of the eye, as the optic nerve impulse, as the colliculus of the midbrain, as the central nervous system, and finally as the glands and organs of the body.  At each place if a specialist were to run a test or meter an impulse, the sensation would be present.  The mental image is also present in the whole field of activity as what David Bohm calls a *holomovement* or we could call a *significant motion*.  The significant motion does not quite come into manifestation but the image of it does.

Sensation comes from the sense world through the sense organs into the nerves and then down into the body.  This "downward" stream of forces is the typical path of incarnation. We can see some strong examples of this in the forming of organs in the embryo. In sense perception the head is the most prominent part of the body. The head is also the archetypal organ in the phylogenetic stream. That is, most organisms exist initially as a head to which limbs are later attached. This can clearly be seen in the phylogeny of crustaceans and in the various stages of development in the larvae of the microorganisms which make up the plankton layer. The head is there first, the circulation follows, and finally the nerves, viscera, and limbs unfold.

From this we might imagine the impulses streaming from the partially developed sense organs out into the organism as currents of *form energies.* The forms of the internal organs first exist on the periphery of the organism as impulses of movement and sensation, and only later does a significant form "descend" as an actual organ. Perhaps two examples from human embryology can illustrate this principle of motion as a predecessor of form. In the fourth week of the development of a human embryo the future heart exists as a membranous vesicle, the pericardium. There is no connection to the maternal circulation at this time, but there is a great need for the embryo to develop a pattern of circulation because the yolk sac which has been the nutrition source for the embryo is quickly being exhausted. In the chorion, or the peripheral fetal membrane, blood islands composed of fine reticula of cells form from the periphery of the membrane. The outer part of each spherical blood island organizes into flattened epithelial cells and the inner cells form into primitive blood corpuscles.

The blood islands are the first form of a vascular system and they themselves are found at the periphery of the sheaths of the embryo in the chorion. The peripheral cells eventually form strands which coalesce into general masses of vessels in many separate places on the periphery of the embryonic sheaths. Throughout the course of the chorion along which vessels will originate, capillary networks are first laid down, and later by selection and enlargement definite paths from the periphery begin to stream toward the pericardium in the center. Meanwhile, the mesoderm cleaves into two layers creating an inner cavity inside which the primitive pericardium forms as a slit-like sac. Once again an activity from the periphery creates an inner space through cavitation.

Around the third week two vessels move from the periphery of the chorion at the caudal end of the embryo toward the head and the forming pericardium and invade the tissues of the embryo. Due to a folding of the neural tube in the midbrain, the cranial and caudal ends of the primitive heart reverse their original positions. Simultaneously blood vessels form at the blood islands near the periphery of the embryo. The vessels develop in situ prior to actual circulation, with no connections to the developing heart, and the heart even begins to beat regularly before vessels or a competent valvular mechanism are present.

The human heart itself, as in all vertebrates, is formed by the fusion of two symmetrically developing tubes. The tubes merge to form the inner space of the heart which, however, remains without valves and open except for deposits of cardiac jelly. In essence the heart at this stage is a tube. What gives the heart its forms? *Gray's Anatomy* suggests the following:

> Experimental studies indicate that movements, determination
> of polarity and regional differentiation of the cardiac meso-
> derm are in some way dependent upon the adjacent endo-
> derm, and perhaps also ectoderm. *(Gray's, 207)*

Gray's goes on to say that the motions of the blood influence regional cardiac morphogenesis, that the tissues of the heart receive the impact of changing directions of blood flow, and that these processes contribute to the sculpting of muscles, cords and valves, the forma-

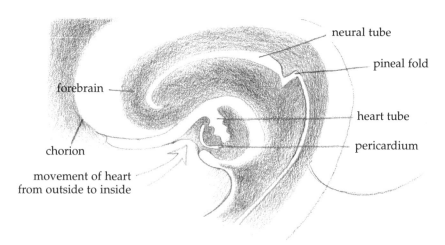

**pericardial formation of the embryo**

tion of the septum in the heart chambers, and the fibrous skeleton of the heart.

All of these forms arise because of motions which the heart *receives.* In none of these images do we find the suggestion that a central pumping mechanism begins pumping and then creates banks in a stream going out from the heart. On the contrary, all organs show a definite genesis on the periphery as if an idea or impression were arising there with the ordering principle moving in toward the organ which is developing.

What then is the source of the formative motions which move the blood to sculpt the heart? Is this not the reverse process from the flow of rivers forming deltas? How can an organized circulation of fluids in polaric motion be sustained without physical vessels and valves? In answer we must be able to see the living idea and its creative movements as present in relationships of forces before material form arises in an organism. This is the concept of the morphogenetic field, developed by Rupert Sheldrake. As Ruskin put it, "form is a diagram of forces," and as Heraclitus put it before him, "Latent structure is master of obvious structure."

A similar pattern emerges when the neurological development of the embryo is considered. In experiments it was found that the tissues of the embryo show a general tendency toward what is known as *embryonic induction.* That is, for a restricted period of time during the development of organs, many regions of "indifferent" ectodermal tissue could transform into highly specialized organs such as kidneys or the lens of the eye if they are experimentally put into an embryo in a place where such organs would eventually arise. The indifferent, or undifferentiated tissue would induce the plan or formal idea of the intended organ, and the cells would metamorphose accordingly. The undifferentiated cells would come under the influence exerted by adjacent tissues. It was also found after repeated experiments that it was impossible "to isolate and identify specific intercellular chemical inducers" (*Gray's,* 107). In the formation of the nervous system in the early life of the embryo at about four weeks, this tendency toward induction as the principle of morphogenesis is of fundamental importance. From the outset the development of the human nervous system is heavily dependent upon the influences of neighboring tissues. Experiment has shown that in its development the nervous system is closely linked to the periphery, that is, to the surrounding non-nervous structure. For instance, there is a reciprocal relationship between the developing eye lens and the nervous tissue of the optic nerve in the forebrain. These relationships determine the invagination of the optic cup out of the ectoderm. No known chemical mechanism has been found for this induction, yet both the periphery and the nerve appear to be following a field of form which is consistent in many organisms. As stated in *Gray's Anatomy:*

> Growing nerve fibers reach and make functional contact with their appropriate end organs . . . during which they often pursue complex courses between the parent cell body and the sites of termination. . . . The earliest nerve fibers are known to cross appreciable distances occupied only by loose general mesenchyme. . . . No imaginable hypothesis is at present adequate to explain the phenomena of the regeneration of the optic nerve. . . . At present the only possible way of regarding the whole question is in terms of a succession of influences which operate in turn upon a growing nerve fiber, from its first emergence to its final link with an end organ." (Grays, 184)

We can now return to the image of the world tree, for what are the circulatory and nervous systems, after all, but "trees" within the physiology of a human being. These trees, however, do not grow by pressure from within. We have seen that forms arise out of a periphery and then gradually move into a center where they become manifest. The origin of the significant form or archetypal form is significant motion. The motion is less manifest than the form, but through induction it is the source of the form's genesis. This concept, as we have seen, evades a materialistic, mechanistic scientific world view. It is found, however, in many places in the ancient world. For example, Paracelsus in his *Archidoxes,* Book I, says:

> The eyes have a material substance, of which they are composed, as it is handed down in the composition of the body. So of the other senses. But vision itself does not proceed from the same source as the [physical] eye; nor the hearing from sound, or from the same source as the ears; nor touch from flesh, nor taste from the tongue, nor smell from the nostrils, any more than reason proceeds from the brain; but these are the bodily instruments, or rather the envelopes in which the

senses are born. . . . For the abovementioned senses have each their own body, imperceptible, impalpable, just as the root of the body, on the other hand exists in tangible form. For man is made up of two portions, that is to say, of a material and a spiritual body. Matter gives the body, the blood, the flesh; but spirit gives hearing, sight, feeling, touch, taste. (Paracelsus, II, 6)

The spiritual potential is at the periphery with its physically manifest form contained within. As Paracelsus further explains in *De Generatione Hominis:*

There is an immortal as well as a corruptible body of man, and it is in this, by the infusion of God's power, that reason, discernment, wisdom, doctrine, art and generally whatsoever is above mortality, do alone inhere. (Paracelsus, II, 6, note)

The realm of the spirit is the upper world on the world tree. In that world the manifest is but an image of eternal Ideas. Access to this upper world is found in the ability of the adept to transcend the forms and mental images of the lower worlds and move to the periphery where significant form transforms into significant motion. Paracelsus saw this very clearly. In the *Archidoxes* and in *De Virtute Imaginativa,* he writes:

Everything that lives has its own motion from Nature. This is sufficiently proved of itself so far as natural motion is concerned. But the motion of which we think may be described as that which springs from the will, as, for example, in lifting the arm one may ask how this is done, when I do not see any instrument by which I influence it; but that takes place which I desire to take place. So one must judge with leaping, walking, running, and other matters which occur in opposition to, or outside of natural motion. They have their origin in this, that intention, a powerful mistress, exists above my notions in the following manner. The intention or imagination kindles the vegetative faculty as a fire kindles wood. (Paracelsus, II, 6–7.)

He who wishes to burn anything needs flint, fire, fuel, brimstone, a candle, etc., and so he obtains fire; but if the sun seeks to burn, it requires none of these things, doing all things together and at once, no one beholding its steel. Such also is the imagination. It tinges and paints its own surface, but no one sees its pencil . . . or pigments; all things take place with it at once [field consciousness]. . . . Let no one, therefore, be surprised that from the imagination corporeal works should proceed, since similar results are manifest with other things. The whole heaven, indeed, is nothing else but an imagination. . . . Man . . . is altogether a star. Even as he imagines himself to be, such he is. (Paracelsus, II, 7, note)

The source of these ideas in Paracelsus can be traced to the philosophical work of the schoolmen, the scholastics of the Middle Ages. They divided creation into four states. The lowest of these, akin to the physical, was the *wrought work,* or *finished work.* A parallel concept in today's world would be *space.* The next higher, more spiritual state was the *ongoing work,* akin to the esoteric ether. A parallel modern concept would be *time.* The next higher state was *revelation,* the esoteric astral plane, a state above time in a condition of simultaneity. A modern word for this state is *causality,* as it is used in quantum mechanics. The final state is *Being.* Being transcends the quantum and its non-linear causes to become the basis for the moral fabric of creation. This level or state is cosmic consciousness, or Christ consciousness.

That which Paracelsus described as imagination or intention is a will substance in the realms of the third and fourth state. Human will can aspire to these higher will states when esoteric inner work is undertaken. Inner work allows the will to become sunlike, like a star. The will then radiates goodness and intent in a transpersonal way. In the ancient image of the world tree, this will conversion is the door to the upper world. In western esotericism the upper world and its pillar of light can be seen as Jacob's ladder.

Jacob's ladder is not the entrance into the lower imaginative but is the journey through the imaginal, upward into Imagination, for while the link in the imaginative world is between the middle world and the lower world, the link in the imaginal world is between the middle world and the upper world. Demons do not climb Jacob's ladder, but climbing up it the seer must encounter angelic consciousness. The four states of finished work, ongoing work, revelation, and Being are also described in western esotericism as steps on Jacob's ladder. The finished work, space, is a resonant image of the higher consciousness of the Spirits of Form, the Exusiai; the ongoing work, time, is resonant with the Dynamis, the Spirits of Motion; the next higher level of revelation, the causal plane, is an image of the Spirits of Wisdom, the Kyriotetes; and the highest level of Being is an image of the Spirits of Will, the Thrones.

In meditating on form, western adepts face the challenge of imaginally transforming their fallen sense impressions of objects in the world, moving them up Jacob's ladder. The adept labors to disenchant form and its identification with matter and to see it as the image of the Spirits of Motion. This alchemical practice transforms matter through the imaginal into Imagination. In this work the intent in the will must be purified so that any shadowlike mental images brought over from the imaginary world and projected into the imaginal world begin to be transformed into world creative forces linked to and harmonic with the workings of the hierarchical creative beings. The point-centered nature of the instinctual mental image can then be transformed to induce the archetype from the periphery of the cosmos. The spiritually embryonic human being then becomes a creative spirit among other creative spirits rather than a manipulator or master of elemental spirits such as is found in traditional shamanic schools.

We have seen where in the very formation of the nerves and heart and blood vessels in the human being the image of a peripherally creative idea is the place of origin. The human consciousness itself now stands at the threshold of the periphery of the spiritual world, on the first rung of Jacob's ladder. All of humanity has emerged from the lower world and has seen the vision of the human sun, the I Am, shining its rays of Imagination and self-awareness through each human soul. The natural world has been threatened to its very core by the misunderstandings this momentous step has engendered. Many wish to return to the consciousness and techniques which have proven effective in the mystery schools of the past. But human beings now stand at a new place. Nature, which has through the millennia been the mother and teacher, is now prepared to give us our freedom. Now more than ever, the human consciousness must be carefully honed and trained to seek exact Imagination, the capacity to have spirit vision.

Rudolf Steiner makes the comment that in modern esoteric training a special part of the nervous system needs to be transformed in a particular way. Seen esoterically, the nerves develop from the periphery according to a plan which exists before any manifestation of the nerves themselves. This plan is then manifest as the form of the nerve. The form of the nerve is like a blueprint, an image of an idea in someone's consciousness. For instance, we would say that the optic nerve and the eye which it serves are nodes in the field of sensation, a field which has at one end the sense world and at the other end all of the processes which unfold in seeing with human bodily organs. All of these components are also images of the unfolding of the archetype.

In the awake state we can sense the forms of the world and their motions in Nature, but in this habitual type of sensing we are not aware of the intent or will of the creative Imagination which is inducing the form. The object remains in space, fixed at the stage of the wrought work, and we merely form mental images which remember the object's particular placement. Through training however we can become aware of the subtle clues which are hidden in the form of a sense object and which reveal the way in which it came into being. The form then begins to reveal its motion of becoming, its *gesture*. Our vision shifts out of space and into time, the stage of the ongoing work. With a time vision we can experience all sense objects as verbs instead of as nouns. Each object *becomes* itself in time. This apparently simple technique has far reaching implications for the inner work in esotericism. With it and its variations we can transform the organs of cognition, the chakras which serve as the doors to the sacred.

To explain this we will once again turn to human physiological evolution to consider an analog for Jacob's ladder. This analog is telencephalization, the process in evolution which underlies the development of the human brain. According to comparative morphological studies with animals, the human brain appears to have evolved by adding organs to increase the brain's capacities. In the lower phylogenetic forms of invertebrates, the whole brain resembles what in a mammalian brain would be a ganglion or relay switch. The impulses which come in from the environment move toward the ganglion and are rerouted to organs which are proper for responding to the stimulus. The stimulus-response inner life which results from this is equivalent to the sleep level in a mammal or a human being.

Animals which live at this level of consciousness develop their ganglion-like neurology by automatically responding to stimuli. Voluntary control of musculature or maintenance of temperature in the body separate from the environment are not possible. In these life forms the most developed neurological organ is the ganglion.

By contrast, among vertebrates even the most primitive members have a neurology which is distinct from the invertebrates. In vertebrates, the central nerve cord is on the dorsal side of the body instead of the ventral side, and the ganglion has become articulated into distinct, specialized organs with distinct capacities. The nerve cord of the vertebrates forms a complex of intricate foldings at the anterior or cephalic pole of the organism. This folded nerve cord forms the basic brain plan of the whole vertebrate group even in the most simple animals. The brain plan of fishes, amphibians, and reptiles shows a brainstem which governs sleeplike responses to external stimuli and a cerebellum which governs posture, coordination, and muscle tone in the body, all of which are below the level of waking consciousness. In addition there is a midbrain, usually with very prominent optic lobes, a diencephalon which governs the ability to exert spontaneous movement, and a primitive cerebrum which is dominated by large olfactory lobes. The inner life of an animal that has such a brain alternates between the sleeping state and the sleep/dream state. Its life and behavior are determined by sensory input from the environment and the resulting instinctual response.

In the brainstem, the heartbeat, blood pressure, and respiration are integrated into bodily responses. The brainstem also governs reflexes such as coughing, vomiting, and eye blinking. In the midbrain and cerebellum more complex tracking data from eyes and ears and body musculature are integrated and relayed back out to the body. The still higher centers of the diencephalon and cerebrum contain many reflex patterns such as urination and defecation and are the source of complexes of memory and association. In reptiles and in animals less developed than reptiles who lack higher centers, the dominant level of consciousness never allows voluntary self-willed responses.

In the more advanced mammals, the brainstem and midbrain/cerebellum levels are very well organized, and the functions which in stimulus/response reptile behavior are the determining factors are much more harmoniously integrated. As a result the higher centers such as the diencephalon and internal capsule (early

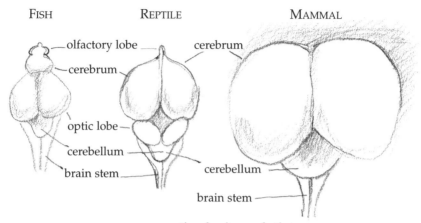

**comparative brain evolution**

sensory cortices) of the brain are more developed.  The internal capsule is an organ in a mammalian brain which is composed of a number of early sensory basal nuclei which integrate into the higher organ of the cerebral cortex.  In lower vertebrates (fish) each hemisphere of the cortex is primarily devoted to olfactory stimuli and to smell and optical sensation.  In the midbrain at the top of the brainstem, masses of grey matter form basal nuclei of the internal capsule in which body movements and optical and olfactory impulses are integrated.  In higher evolution the early basal nuclei are linked at lower levels to the midbrain where visual, olfactory, and auditory inputs are integrated.  In mammals this lower sensory integration frees the organism to develop the "newer" diencephalon into a more complex organ.  This site becomes the limbic system, the chief feature of the mammalian brain.  The cerebral cortex and the limbic system are the organs which govern the dominant consciousness of the mammals.  This consciousness is characterized by complex emotional patterns and a well developed and articulate instinctual response to environmental stimuli.  Complex patterns of seeking prey, courtship, mating, rearing young, and communal behavior are developed in the animals which have neurologically advanced limbic systems and cerebral cortices with integrated sensory centers.

In primates and in human beings, the frontal lobe and neo-cortex appear on the periphery of the limbic system.  Accompanying these developments the higher mammals exhibit a highly evolved sense of space and acute perception of and memory for patterns.  This supports the ability to solve problems beyond the parameters of sensory input. The addition of the newer cerebral cortex to the limbic system allows higher mammals to be relatively autonomous from biological (environmental) necessity. This is evidenced in the use of tools, creative problem solving, and the rudiments of language found, for example, in dolphins.

The ascent in function and form seen in telencephalization is an image of the entrance into the upper world. This is described in the Bible (Genesis 29:12) as Jacob's dream: "And he dreamed and behold a ladder set upon the earth, and the top of it reached to heaven:   and behold the angels of god ascending and descending on it." In lower animals the nervous system is described as ladder-like.   In higher animals the sympathetic trunk is in the form of a ladder on each side and ventral to the central nervous system.   In telencephalization we have an image of a ladder set up on the earth and the top of it reaching to heaven with the angels ascending it.  As we have seen, the development of the cerebral cortex in the higher mammals has made it possible to use tools, think creatively, and form a rudimentary language—all signs of an ascension into heaven.

But in Jacob's dream the angels were also descending the ladder from heaven. Biologically there is no indication of this gesture in the development of new organs of the brain. The primate brain is bio-

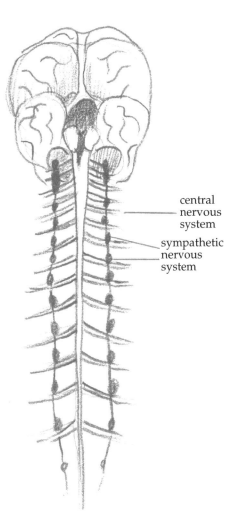

central nervous system

sympathetic nervous system

**the two nervous systems**

logically the same whether it is found in an ape or a human being. This is because the order of primates specializes in the development of the nervous system. We could say the primate brain is at the top of the ladder in regard to brains. What then can account for the difference in consciousness between an ape and a human being?

In problem solving, the highest capacity for abstract thought has been found through experiment to lie in the left hemisphere of the neo-cortex. In *creative* thinking, however, this logical abstract capacity needs to be formed into the language of symbols, for as Joseph Chilton Pearce maintains in *Evolution's End*, creative answers usually come in symbols which must then be translated. This means that the higher abstract functioning must be integrated into the deeper, more primitive layers of the neurology. This is an image of the angels descending Jacob's Ladder.

From this perspective, what apparently separates the consciousness of the ape from the consciousness of the human being is that the human being can experience a lower brain function from the vantage point of a higher brain function. This capacity to go back down the ladder is described in Genesis as the opening of the eyes during the fall from Paradise. To experience the space orientation of the lower right hemisphere from the vantage point of the higher left hemisphere is to discover the sacred in the mundane experience of space. The result is sacred geometry, sacred architecture, and such studies as astronomy. It is also the capacity to intuit meaning in abstractly cognized patterns. From this arises poetry, speech, and myth.

To go deeper down the ladder would be to consciously witness in the limbic system the arising of an emotion, or a habitual response to a stimulus. From this higher perspective, the emotional and instinctual patterns of sensation can be cognized from the higher centers, and laws, codes of ethical behavior, philosophies, and healing modalities can be developed as the basis for moral judgement. Through moral imagination, automatic somatic responses can be overridden by consciously willed behavior. This is the basis of psychotherapy in particular and of the cultural life in general in which the personal emotive response is seen from the perspective of the abstract cognition of the witness who stays in a waking consciousness.

In general this descent back through the layers of the neurology can only be positive when it is truly conscious. Human beings continually act out of lower centers in sleep or dream states which rise up during the day and effectively dim access to higher states. Day

dreams, hallucinations, visions, tantrums, psychotic states, and neuroses of all kinds have their root in such intrusions of lower centers
into the waking state. When this happens the human being behaves
like a reptile or a hyena, depending upon which center is the focus of
the attention. Such brain-bound thinking denies human beings their
true potential. When, however, the human being strives to enter these
lower regions in a waking consciousness, a kind of exponential thinking is developed. The consciousness lifts off of the brain itself and
gains access to the fields of activity which exist as primal, creative
potentials around the physical organs, in the fields of Imagination or
intent, as Paracelsus called them. This quality of thinking which is
field-like is the goal of the teachings in the mystery school traditions.

In true meditative practice trance states are avoided since they are
simply entrainments of lower and higher centers into resonant units.
The meditant seeks to avoid such entrainments so that the function of
the witness can maintain its waking clarity. This capacity could be
characterized as the ability to check inner experience against reality.
As Baba Ram Dass said in the 1960s, "Even in the bliss you should be
able to remember your phone number." The meditative state then is a
return into a lower state with a higher consciousness. Thus we are the
angels descending Jacob's ladder from heaven.

Traditional psychotherapies arise from the penetration of the limbic field by this higher or "second" attention. Carl Jung and his deep
therapeutic insights into the role of the symbol is an example of such
work. It is possible and in today's world most desirable for a conscious esoteric penetration into the field of the midbrain. Out of such
work can arise the consciousness described by Rudolf Steiner as
Imagination and its further development into Inspiration.

We have seen that in the human being the midbrain, linked to the
cerebellum, is the level of the brain at which voluntary control of bodily movements is integrated with higher cortical centers and with
outer sensory input from seeing, hearing, and other senses. In the
embryo near the fourth week a prominent curve develops in the dorsal side which bends the head at a ninety degree angle. This bowing
of the head is coincident with the inversion of the heart and is a significant stage in the life of the embryo.

The bowing of the embryonic head creates a fold in the neural
tube which is the origin of the midbrain. Just below this midbrain
flexure is the pineal gland. From the midbrain, the oculomotor nerve
runs ventrally to the embryonic eye. The trochlear nerve which stim-

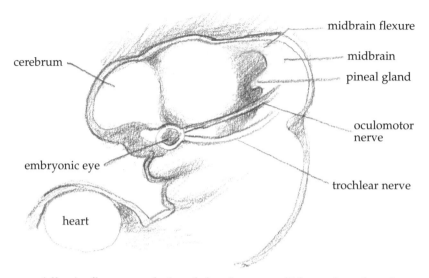

cerebrum

embryonic eye

heart

midbrain flexure

midbrain

pineal gland

oculomotor
nerve

trochlear nerve

**midbrain flexure and pineal development (5th week embryo)**

ulates another motor muscle to the eye runs ventrally from the midbrain to the eye.  There is also a vestigial section of the trochlear nerve
which runs dorsally to the pineal recess.  It is thought that this connection is to oculomotor muscles which in the dim past enabled the
pineal gland to be moved in the fashion of a third eye.  These muscles
are no longer present, but the nerve is left as a vestigial organ.  These
embryonic details become significant when we realize that the midbrain is the area in the brain where higher thoughts, sense impressions, and especially those impulses concerned with voluntary bodily
motion, or will, are integrated and placed into equilibrium.

Further, the innervation of the midbrain also puts it in touch  with
wide inputs from the cerebral cortex.  These impulses from higher
brain centers are directed into a particular area of the midbrain
known as the *substantia nigra,* the black substance.  In the substantia
nigra there is an especially rich deposit of iron-bearing cells arranged
in two convex plates around another iron-rich nucleus, the *substantia
rubra,* or red substance.  These two areas are arranged in such a way
that they give the appearance of the field windings around a transformer.  Into the substantia nigra the neurons of the oculomotor nerve
and the trochlear nerve are imbedded.  This means that whenever the
eyes are moved the substantia nigra is energized.

In the posterior part of the midbrain, which is at most five cen-
timeters wide, the tectum or roof of the midbrain serves as the meet-

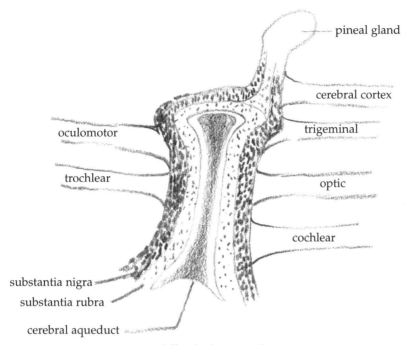

pineal gland

cerebral cortex

oculomotor

trigeminal

trochlear

optic

cochlear

substantia nigra

substantia rubra

cerebral aqueduct

**midbrain innervation**

ing place for the mandibular portion of the trigeminal nerve from the lower jaw, the optic nerve, the cochlear nerve from the ear, and other nerves that connect to the neo-cortex. These are the nerves active in speaking, hearing, seeing, and in the spatial perception involved in turning the head and eyes. At the upper end of the tectum lies the pineal gland which governs reproductive functions and sleep, waking, and dream cycles. Thus a tremendous number of sense impulses come flooding through this very small area in daily life.

Obviously, if one were aware of this while awake, a very unusual state of consciousness would result. In the lower animals who are living in a sleep/dream consciousness, the midbrain functions to allow the animal to sense the space around it and to maintain some sort of equilibrium amid the flood of sense data which results from these sensations.

To a human being who is descending Jacob's ladder, entering the midbrain with the waking consciousness can be a harrowing experience of sensory overload. In essence, the adept who is penetrating the fields produced by the midbrain will have the equivalent of a conscious experience of the rapid eye movement (REM) state of dreaming. We can see the REM connection in a number of ways. For example, the site of entry for the oculomotor nerves is the substantia nigra. Any impulse from REM dream world would tend to stimulate the midbrain, causing eye and body motions as a response.

The substantia nigra is also the most potent source of the substance dopamine in the brain. Dopamine is a neurotransmitter which functions prominently in two polaric pathological mental conditions. One of these is Parkinson's disease. In this condition the voluntary movements of the body are impaired, and the capacity to initiate actions or to control involuntary spasms is diminished. The result is states resembling extreme fatigue and lassitude on one hand and tremors of the hands and limbs on the other. This condition is brought on by a deficiency of dopamine in the substantia nigra.

The other condition is caused by too many dopamine receptors in the caudal nucleus, hypothalamus, midbrain, tectum, pineal gland, and neo-cortex. This group plus the group from the substantia nigra form the mesotelencephalic dopaminergic system, that is, the neurons sensitive to dopamine which connect the midbrain to the neo-cortex. This system, when it contains too many receptors to dopamine, contributes to the condition of schizophrenia. Schizophrenia is disordered thought. Its symptoms include false or delusional beliefs, the inability to test reality, and auditory or visual hallucinations, particularly voices commanding the sufferer to do things.

These symptoms of schizophrenia and the symptoms of Parkinsonism are often described as characteristic of trance states in shamanism. The whole range of auditory and visual phenomena experienced in trance states could be termed schizoid in a person unable to integrate the phenomena into the waking consciousness. In a mystery school of the past, the apparent symptoms of madness then are the predictable outcome of an esoteric training which does not strive to bring waking consciousness into the fields around the midbrain but floods the waking consciousness with subconscious impulses from below.

It is interesting to note that the terms substantia nigra and substantia rubra contain the Latin word *substantia*. In today's world, "substance" refers to matter which is of a fixed nature. To the thinkers of the Middle Ages, however, and to the alchemists who followed their thoughts, substantia did not refer to the finished work, or substance, but to the ongoing work, or motion. To the Chartres masters (AD 1000–1203), substantia was the movement which the hierarchical beings used to create the world. In Paracelsus' distinction between natural motion (finished work) and will or Imagination (ongoing work) we can find a powerful key to unlocking the sacred door to Imagination.

In the neo-cortex the conception of an abstract idea involves no physical motion in the brain. There can be no natural motion in an idea because in the hierarchy of space, time, and causality, the idea lives beyond time in the causal/revelation plane of existence. This is where a thinker must encounter an abstract idea. However in order for a thinker to think the idea it must be brought down out of the causal world of revelation into time. Seen in time, the spiritual or law-ful motion of the idea can be "moved" inwardly. This is the nature of the process any time an idea is contemplated or "rotated" in the mind's eye. We can see its different aspects in time, or we can see its logic in time. We then form a symbol of it in order for it to be brought into the common domain. The sense world, filled with objects, repre-sents such a process wherein cosmic revelation, or causal relation-ships, manifest initially within time as potentials which have become actual events. The events then manifest in space as physical objects. This sequence is the lawful motion of the becoming of the object. As revelation condenses into time, we have the laws of living nature. As time condenses into space, we have the physical world with its phys-ical laws.

To perceive an object in the outer world with the eyes requires that the eyes make natural motions. By contrast, to perceive the Creative Will forces at work in the causal plane of the sense object requires no natural motion of the eyes. Eye muscle movements pro-duce strong changes in the neural fields, especially those fields con-cerned with hearing. When we look at an object in normal sense life the eye must move, but this movement is not part of our awareness. As a result the will forces contained in the movements which come from the Creative Will of the Hierarchies hidden in the form of the object are lost to our consciousness.

If, however, we can train ourselves to look at objects in such a way that we look *with* their forms, we can gradually become aware of how the object has emerged from the causal plane. By moving our inner eyes consciously along the edges of objects and consciously repro-ducing the images of these movements inwardly, we move the will imaginally into the time frame where revelation behind the becoming of the object condenses into time. The object ceases to be fixed but *becomes*, in our mind's eye, according to the lawful motion present in our consciousness.

Through such practice we gradually penetrate the field of the midbrain as it responds to the oculomotor, trochlear, cochlear, and trigeminal inputs. We approach the creative Hierarchies which stand behind nature as waking beings capable of maintaining equilibrium in the surging creative chaos. To do so by using drugs or trance states puts tremendous pressures on the psyche. To do so as a meditative practice allows the soul to move safely down Jacob's ladder and off of the physical brain with the angel.

By using the forms of natural objects such as leaves or flowers or clouds as the focus of meditation, it is possible to form in the fields of the midbrain a precise, imaginal language of form. As the eye moves along the edges and surfaces of a form, the subtle motions of the oculomotor muscles create changes in the neural fields of the midbrain. If we then try to recreate the image inwardly by recalling the movements which were made in our perception, we create an imaginal movement analog of the object. This analog is harmonic with the creative motions of the Hierarchies, present as the line of becoming of the object. The object then lives in us as a time sequence of precise movements. Through repetitions with many different forms we build a conscious, imaginal vocabulary of lawful creative movements into the neural fields around the midbrain.

Once this lawful field of motion is present, any sensation which is not imaginally lawful can quickly be cognized as such when it enters the sense organs. This state is known esoterically as Imagination. It is distinguished from the common imagination, in which personally charged mental images constantly arise, by being imaginally exact and objective rather than personal and fantastic. This level of consciousness allows the meditant to work into nature without violating natural laws. On the other side of the soul, it also allows meditants to explore their own soul forces by allowing the consciousness to experience the arising of mental images connected to feelings and unlawful, fixed thought patterns.

Through this work it is possible to use the faculty of Imagination to accurately explore dream sequences in a manner consistent with waking consciousness. By following form into its motion of becoming we can access imaginally the Idea which stands behind the motion. In this realm Ideas have *reality* and the manifest is seen as temporal. Our dreams are images which are used to clothe the ideational movements which are the true soul experience while dreaming. This work is very useful to the student of meditation in the pursuit of a clear, silent, balanced mental state which signals the entrance into higher worlds.

In today's world where tremendous volumes of throwaway images are given daily to the soul, there is a vital need for people to develop Imagination, to seek spirit vision. The soul life of many is at risk due to the unconscious addiction to unlawful images. Mental instability and tendencies to violence are symptoms of this malaise. The natural world also suffers from this onslaught in that the attentive consciousness of people is taken away from involvement with the spiritual in nature. Where human beings place their attention, things begin to develop. This is our role: to pay attention. Whether we wish to heal the soul or to heal nature, the path is the same—deepen self awareness and learn to control the flow of inner images. When this path is undertaken, the initial stage is experienced in the capacity to actively seek spirit vision by developing a lawful access to the plane of Imagination, the sacred door to the realm of the spirit.

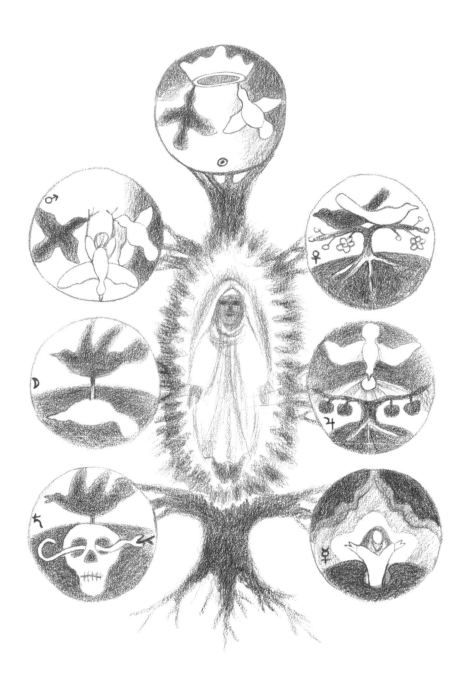

# 12

# THE GREAT TREE

In order to approach the task of soul transformation, it is
useful to take a look at the sequence of processes traditionally given by the alchemists for the transformation of substance. In nature, all substances were considered by the
alchemists to consist of the three qualities of *salt, mercury,* and
*sulfur.* There has been a lot of confusion regarding the exact
nature of these qualities as defined by the alchemists, since the
same names are also applied to elements or compounds of elements which we find in the periodic table. For clarity's sake,
we first need to make a distinction between salt as a substance, or *substantia,* to use the alchemical term, and salt as a
*process.* The activities and qualities which emerge from such a
distinction are very revealing. As a *substantia,* salt tends to
dissolve by absorbing water and going into solution. As a
process, salt arises out of solution into a crystalline form. The
alchemists would say that in solution the crystal of salt is the
*ponderable* part, and that it was united in the solution with an
*imponderable* form, the water, which is more closely related to
the cosmos than to the earth. As a result it was termed imponderable. Salt as a *process* moves toward gravity and a fixed,
crystalline form. Salt as a *substantia,* in its dissolving, moves
into a more expanded imponderable form. This expansion is
enhanced if the solution is warmed, and the salt is aided by
the warmth in moving against gravity. The fixed crystal form
is then dissolved into solution by the relatively mobile or
warm water state.

Thus a movement from ponderable to imponderable is the
salt *substantia,* while movement from imponderable to ponderable is the origin of the salt crystallizing *process.* Curiously,
the movement of the salt *substantia* to a condition of warmth

and levity, away from separate particles and toward a more intimate union, was known to alchemy as *sulfur,* because sulfur as a physical substance is a unity of the ponderable and the imponderable. The inner warmth created by this unity is characterized by the latent heat contained in sulfur. By contrast, combustion is a sulfur *process,* the flame of combustion separating the imponderables (warmth and light) from the ponderables (water and earth). When a lump of sulfur is ignited, the warmth and light rises upward under the influence of levity, and the ash and water vapor fall down under the influence of gravity. To complete the cycle, the ash which falls from the flame is then the source of the physical form of the salt. These relationships between ponderable and imponderable can be seen in the following diagrams:

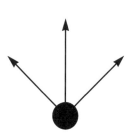

SALT SUBSTANTIA/SOLUTION
Put into water, salt seeks to dissolve and radiate. Salt enters water and moves from ponderable to imponderable.

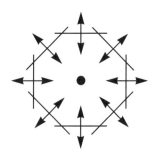

SULFUR SUBSTANTIA/
LATENT WARMTH
Imponderables marry ponderables. Molten sulfur precipitates out of solution. Sulfur contains latent warmth married to physical body.

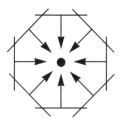

SALT PROCESS/PRECIPITATION
Salt precipitates out of solution as a crystal. It moves from imponderable to ponderable.

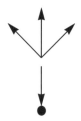

SULFUR PROCESS/COMBUSTION
Imponderable warmth rises, ponderable ash falls.

Thus we can see that there is a fundamental similarity among the substantias and processes of salt and sulfur in that they are all universal activities involving ponderable states and imponderable states. We could call the process and substantia of salt *Universal Salt,* and the process and substantia of sulfur *Universal Sulfur.* The difference, then, between Universal Salt and Universal Sulfur is that in Universal Sulfur the ponderable and imponderable in the substance do not separate out but remain together.

In Universal Salt, the imponderable and the ponderable separate in evaporation. From this, we can see that the evaporation of water which precipitates the formation of salt as a crystal is accomplished by a sulfur-like process in which the water goes into unity with the air and the crystal falls down into manifestation. It is not a true or complete sulfur reaction, though, because no ash is formed. In true sulfur, the fire of the sulfur transforms the form of the manifest object (the "crystallized" physical or mineral body) into an amorphous ash. In true salt processes the crystal moves in and out of form without going through the ash stage. By contrast, the formation of sulfur as a substance is accomplished *first* by an activity whereby the mineral is dissolved by hot water and deposited through a salt-like process in cavities in the ground. From this we can see that where a substantia is transformed it often requires the activity of a process, and where a process reaches its completion, substantia appears. These relationships follow the three laws of polarity that Goethe used in his work:

- **Polarities of the first order**—These are opposite conditions such as gravity and levity, cold and warmth, or contraction and expansion. They are fundamental qualities in nature.

- **Polarities of the second order**—These are complementary qualities such as dry and moist. Cold and warmth as absolutes are polarities of the first order, but dry and moist in nature are always the product of an interaction between cold and warmth. For instance, air takes on water as it warms and gives off water as it cools.

- **Polarities of the third order**—These polarities are truly mercurial or reciprocal in that the cold turns into warmth when it reaches a maximum state and vice versa. These types of reciprocating polarities are present in nature in such formations as convection cells. As warm air rises, it cools and expands. As it cools, it gets heavier and begins to sink. As the cold air sinks, it warms up due to an increase in pressure. Then the warm air once again rises. When it reaches a maximum of warmth, the cycle begins again. In such a reciprocating relationship, a sulfur process would yield a salt substance, or a salt process would yield a sulfur substance. Many medicinal effects originate in such reciprocating relationships.

These images lie at the heart of the alchemical world view. The following concepts of the stages and phases of soul transformation use these qualities of Universal Salt, Universal Sulfur, and Universal Mercury as the foundation from which a systematic soul transformation process can proceed.

# THE SECOND PHASE: CONTEMPLATION

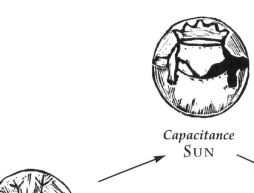

*Capacitance*
SUN

*Resistance*
*Extractum*
*Distillation*
MARS

*Induction*
*Oscillation*
*Imagination*
VENUS

# THE FIRST PHASE:
CONCENTRATION

# THE THIRD PHASE:
MEDITATION

*Reflection*
*Solution*
MOON

*Radiation*
*Inspiration*
JUPITER

*Combustion*
SATURN

*Potentization*
*Intuition*
MERCURY

The Great Tree with its seven stages comprises a complex alchemical imagination which becomes easier to comprehend when the polarities just discussed are sought for in each level of the work. To begin with we can see that the seven stages fall into three phases. The upward motion of Saturn/Moon/Mars on the left is the first phase, that of concentration. The second phase, contemplation, is the horizontal left-to-right movement of Mars/Sun/Venus. Meditation, the third phase, is downward on the right—Venus/Jupiter/Mercury. Transformation from one stage to another or from one phase to another is accomplished by the forces of polarity. At each level the polarities of the first, second, and third order are operating so that the soul can experience the transcendence of its own impurities. The Great Tree is a system which describes the technical transformations of substance as analogs for the esoteric transformation of the soul into the spirit.

In approaching the Great Tree we can see that the first stage is Saturn. In Saturn consciousness, there is a pronounced quality of Universal Sulfur in that the world exists as a given unity of imponderable and ponderable movements. This is the primal consciousness of the not-yet-born. It arises as a warmth state on the periphery. It has a yearning to concentrate, to be. Alchemically this means eventually a corpus will form out of the formless.

From the formless state of warmth an ash is produced, the residue, or *corpse,* of cosmic life which dies out of the great potentiality of the Eternal Idea into the manifest given world. This sulfur process which results in ash is the quality described as Saturn, the first stage of the Great Tree. Cosmologically the sulfur process of Saturn is matter emerging from spiritual existence. Physiologically and psychologically it is also the impact upon the senses of sensations which are as yet unreflected and uncognized. In this Universal Sulfur of Saturn, while the meanings (logos) of the given world of sense impressions return, flamelike, to the imponderable world of the archetypal Idea where human beings have no access to them, the sensations themselves descend to earth as the cosmic ash or corpus which serves as the basis of life on earth. The *meaning* of the sense world is imponderable.

The sensation as a *manifestation* of meaning *is* ponderable. In this relationship the archetype is where meaning and sensation exist together as a marriage of imponderable and ponderable like the warmth in the substance of sulfur. Human beings separate the meaning from the sensation in the activity of having a sense experience. (In the language of quantum mechanics the perception of the experimenter collapses the wave of probability in the experiment.) The ash of sensation is the sense world as it is given to human experience, while the flamelike meaning still lives archetypically in the cosmos.

In Moon consciousness, the second stage, the ash is placed into the water of life. The salt lifts out of the ash, rising away from the earth and dissolving into the water. This dissolving gesture is a movement from the ponderable state of earth to the imponderable state of water. This dissolution of salt substantia is related in kind to the movement of the combustion process of sulfur; it just does not go so far that the ponderables and imponderables separate. Salt substantia goes into the less gravity-laden state of water, but we need only apply a sulfur process of warmth (combustion) to the solution to drive the water into the imponderable state of air, and the salt substantia once again emerges as a fallen image or corpus.

This is a picture of Moon thinking in which our unconscious thought patterns based on uncognized sensations are precipitated out when habitual or instinctual sense impressions are crystallized out of the flow of consciousness. In the Moon stage we place the Saturn corpus or ash of uncognized sensations into the water of life (Moon). Psychologically this means to become aware that our problems and habits result from unconscious patterns of stimulus/response in the life of the senses. We move from unreflected darkness to reflective insight. Still, however, we are living reflexively. In order to live consciously we must proceed to the Mars stage by applying the fire of will to our thinking and sensing. To correct the instinctive, associative Moon thinking, the salt needs to be purified and driven toward the sulfur pole through logical, willed thinking. The salt then moves into the warmth of sulfur and the two find a kinship in moving toward the periphery.

This union of the polarities of salt and sulfur is the Universal Mercury. Mercury is present whenever Universal Salt and Universal Sulfur unite. Universal Mercury always seeks to dampen down an over-exuberant reaction or stimulate a sluggish transformation so that polarities move through complementarity to reciprocation. Mercury is ever fluid and mobile. It is the great transformative force in the cosmos. As such it is the healing force in substances and processes and the source of the rhythm in their interactions. In the Great Tree these three concepts of salt, sulfur, and mercury are the underlying forces of transformation.

In alchemy, scientifically precise processes which are observable in the natural world are transformed into systems of images which allow the natural processes to be perceived on many different levels. Indeed, the entire practice of alchemical meditation is often known as the method of analogy. The following system of images of the Great Tree has its roots in the twelfth century. In this system the image of a tree with its branches spreading into the cosmos is used as an analogy for the path of inner development. The tree has seven branches, each representing a planetary stage along the soul's inner path as well as a process observable in the natural world. These stages and processes are simultaneously psychological and physical. An image system of this sort is only one of the innumerable possibilities inherent in the contemplation of such ideas. Yet such images and ideas have an immense potential for expansion in the consciousness.

The purpose of the great work in alchemy is to expand the consciousness in an orderly, reasoned way so that its own limited, personal viewpoint can become resonant with the multifaceted, fluid creativity of the Logos, the Cosmic World Word. The images presented are poetic and analogical. They take the logic of science and, maintaining its integrity, seek to expand the capacities of the mind from thinking which is causal, mechanical, and bound to the organism, into a thinking which is mobile, warm, and illuminated with the imaginatively pictorial. Thinking of this sort must lift on a current from the soul and, like a newly hatched spider on its single strand attached to its birthing place, launch itself out into the great void. There it hangs suspended, floating in the wind, tethered to what it knows until it reaches a new home where it can release what is known in order to live into the unknown. Such is the mood of the alchemical journey.

The seven planetary stages of the Great Tree are organized into three overlapping groups or phases through which the alchemist ascends and descends. The concentration phase of Saturn, Moon, and Mars is characterized by resistance. The contemplation phase of Mars, Sun, and Venus is characterized by capacitance and oscillation. And the meditation phase of Venus, Jupiter, and Mercury is illuminated by the process of potentization. Each stage of the work is compared to various chemical, electrical, or homeopathic processes to form analogies between work in the world and work in the soul. Together the three phases and seven stages represent a rich poetical/scientific system for thinking about the inner path from instinctual knowledge to the higher stages of knowing found in esoteric literature.

# THE FIRST PHASE: CONCENTRATION

### SATURN
*the first stage*

### THE IMAGE

The image for the Saturn stage is the tomb, or dust, and the polarity between center and periphery. The first stage of the work puts us into contact with the separation of self from the ruling will of the world. It is a stage in which we become dimly aware of the boundaries of the soul. This puts us into the tomb which those boundaries create. It is an image of the unconscious sense activity located at our periphery in organs evolved from skin, that is, in all the sense organs and nerves. In the tomb cosmic creative life turns to dust.

### THE SYMBOL

A skull is buried in the earth with a black bird perched on top, its wings outstretched. A snake moves in and out of the eye sockets of the skull. The bird is symbolic of thinking and represents the capacity of consciousness to freely fly away and land at whatever level, or branch, it chooses. In this symbol the bird is a dark bird. The darkness refers to the unconscious functioning of the senses which transmit the flow of sense data down into the tomb of the skull. The bird flexes its wings but does not fly away. It has a potential to be free but remains stuck to the skull in all its darkness. This bird is the raven, a beginner on the path. It is said that the raven eats the corpses on the battlefield. This is an image of the senses trying to digest the contents of the manifest world. It is also an image of a beginner trying to digest the dead elements of an esoteric system.

The skull as a symbol reveals how the cosmos dies into matter. It is Adam buried in the hill of Golgotha. The snake represents the world and its flowing impressions as they are drawn into the skull through its orifices and cast down as if into a tomb. The skull-like experience of sense data is an image of the basic unreflected, uncognized impulses brought into the skull by the senses. They are buried deep in the earth and serve as the basis for urges arising in the unconscious. The perching raven with outspread wings represents the stage in sense life at which images arise out of the inward-flowing torrent of sense impressions. These images are uncognized and unconscious but are fleetingly perceived as fluctuating mental images. They are the stream of associations which arise spontaneously and serve as the basis for the instinctual habit-life of the soul. They represent the first response of the organism to the inpouring stream of impressions from the world.

## ALCHEMICAL PROCESS:
## SALT FORMATION AND COMBUSTION

In salt processes the spiritual unity of the archetype which resides in the unmanifest begins to manifest as discrete parts. The archetypal or primal unity which lies behind the outer appearances of the sense world flows into the tomb of the skull, and the unity of creation appears as discrete sense objects. The sensations formed in the brain as a result of this process are known alchemically as *dust*. In the dust state the world falls out of the loving guidance of the hierarchies and, losing its primal cohesion, consolidates into matter, becoming discrete bits of sense data which are then reflected as randomly associated but pathologically fixed, fleeting images in the soul life. This loss of primal unity, the consolidation of life into bits, is a process akin to salt formation. We have already seen, though, that this salt precipitation process has its polarity in the salt substantia. Salt substantia enters a levity state in water, and it is from that solution that the salt process produces salt. But what is the source of the salt substantia? For this we must look to the sulfur process of combustion. In the sulfur process the warmth in the body of the sulfur rises and the ash falls down. The imponderable and the ponderable have separated. The ash is a corpse in which a phoenix is hidden. When put into water it reacts as a salt substantia. That is, the salt leaves the ash, dissolves, and enters the relative levity state of the water. The earth or corpus left over falls out and the salt or phoenix rises into solution. From this solution the water can be induced into its next higher levity state of vapor and the salt comes out of solution. It is now not a corpus (dust), for its passage through the fire to form ash (the phoenix) and then through water into solution has refined it into salt, a stage higher than earth but lower than water. The forming of a salt can thus be traced back to a combustion process.

We can imagine this by thinking of wood reduced to dust by sanding. If mixed with water this dust will yield no salt. If we combust the dust in a sulfur process, however, the resulting ash will yield salt. In the world of the senses the heat of combustion which produces ash has an analog in will forces which exist as the patterns of intelligence behind the ordered forms of the sense world. In lower stages of consciousness the archetypal will forces inherent in sense objects stimulate the soul impulses which are centered on fixed instinctual behavior. Sights and smells trigger automatic responses in the obedient subconscious will of the organism. Such responses lie far below the threshold of the light of a thinking consciousness and as a result are dark and full of darkened will forces, hence the alchemical term *nigredo,* which refers to the neophyte esotericist, the beginning stages of a work, or simply the color of ashes which are formless but full of potential for creating salt. The dust of the separate sense impressions and the dark fixed will which lies uncognized behind them act to create soul conditions which support repetitive, patterned, reactive responses. Seen from the level of archetype, the creative will in the archetype combusts into light and warmth spontaneously, and ash falls, the seed of worlds. The holy ash falls into the fluid stream of time and salt emerges out of the seed/ash as the forms of nature. The forms are the salt of the idea in the archetype. These forms then attract matter (dust) which permeates them and makes them appear visibly in space. The human sense organs then perceive them as physical patterns but are not aware of the creative archetypal will forces which contributed to their forming. This will remains dark to human cognition, and physiological responses to stimuli are merely conditioned by the dark will hidden in the sensations. These responses arise in the consciousness as uncognized mental images. The sense impressions themselves as physical energies create salt conditions and patterns in the body in which matter can consolidate, as in the forms of various organs. The will forces inherent in the movements of the archetypes which create the forms produce stimulus/response movements such as are found in endocrine secretions and digestive processes and which serve as the basis for the processes of combustion which lie at the root of digestion. The first phase of the first stage, the nigredo Saturn, is also called the great darkness because of the dark will hidden in the motions which lie behind the forms of physical objects in the world, objects which are experienced through the senses yet remain uncognized.

### INNER EXERCISE

The polarities of the salt process of consolidation and the sulfur process of combustion are absolutely necessary if the human consciousness is to develop from reaction into freedom.  However, the combustion and salting of the sense world into bits of sensory data, or dust, and the constant influx of random images can produce a toxic state of mind. On a psychic level these toxic processes support obsessive unconscious image patterns and instinctual drives. Uncognized, these sensations and the urges which they represent can destroy the integrity of the body and soul. For this reason, it is advantageous to practice becoming aware of the process by which images connected to sense impressions arise in the inner life. A basic exercise to develop this capacity is known as the *pin exercise.* The pin exercise is a classic exercise given by Rudolf Steiner to develop concentration and control of thinking.

> We can think of a pin as having its origin in iron ore in the ground. Then think of it being mined, then shipped, and smelted into pig iron ingots. Then it is processed into steel and extruded into wire. The wire is then made smaller in diameter by a series of drawing techniques. It is then forged, sharpened, plated, and packaged into containers for shipment to stores. Each day we can repeat the exercise, expanding our knowledge through study until we can think an entire complex history of the coming into being of the pin. When this is possible we could continue thinking of all of the uses of the pin or all of the different types of pins and the particular qualities of their manufacture and use. When this seems exhausted, take another subject such as a button, and repeat the exercise.

This seemingly simple exercise is capable of great complexity and finesse and can be modulated in many creative ways. We could, for instance, think only of the different functions for a pin, or of the symbolic significance of a pin. In each case we would still be exploring with our concentrated thinking the concepts directly connected to a pin. This exercise develops the willed attention so necessary for the pursuit of esoteric development.

The pin exercise can also be adapted to the development of the attention connected to the life of the senses. The technique is different, but the goal of concentrated attention is the same.

> Observe a pin or small stone or button. Visualize the pin in your mind's eye. This process is known as representation. Observe the represented inner image carefully. Some people find that the image begins to move or get larger or fade away or change into another image. The exercise consists of stabilizing the image in the mind's eye. Most people find this to be

most easily accomplished if the eyes are closed. Others, however, find that as soon as they close their eyes an inner flood of sensations arises and sweeps away their attention. For these people, it is more effective if they focus with their open eyes upon a blank wall.

The goal of this exercise is to be able to hold the image of a sense object in the consciousness for an extended period of time. Since there is a natural pulsation of the cerebro-spinal fluid in the brain, the ability to keep an image centered in the consciousness oscillates, one sensation seeming to slip away or dissolve into another. By anticipating these rhythmic pulsations, it is possible to watch the body sensations give rise to associative images in the inner life. These images constitute the basis for memory. Esoteric development requires that the sensations and inner images be linked together in the consciousness by a thinking attention. When sensation is linked to the inner image-forming process, we can connect the associations which arise in the soul with their correct sources in the world of sensation. After some practice, the rhythmic ebb and flow of the inner image can be linked into one continuous involvement with its sense form and can be held for extended periods in the mind's eye. This exercise stabilizes the inner eye and makes observation of associated chains of images in the mind possible. With such inner stability, the mind's eye regulates the process of uncognized combustion and the production of toxic urges. The compulsive nigredo patterns of associative fantasy images which accompany such an uncognized combustion process are guided into the more benign condition of solution, *albedo,* or Moon.

# THE FIRST PHASE: CONCENTRATION

## MOON
### *the second stage*

## THE IMAGE

The image for the Moon stage is the retort which draws salt out of ash. In the first stage of Saturn, the dust of death needs to be subjected to the fire of the will. In this process it combusts and an ash is formed. Hermetically hidden in the ash is the salt which carried the life of the plant by attracting water. In the retort the phoenix yields the salt to water as instinct is raised to consciousness.

## THE SYMBOL

Two birds face each other, one below, wingless and buried in the earth, and the other above, facing the earth with extended wings, one blue and one red. The bird with extended wings sits on the earth, a symbol of the as yet unrealized potential of the unconsciousness to rise into the higher spheres of the superconscious. This is an image of the higher capacity of the mind which can look down at the reflected images buried in the earth-like nigredo forces of sense perception. The flightless bird in the earth represents the mental image still in the unconscious, fettered to its object in the world. In this symbol the higher forces of independent thinking in the consciousness witness and cognize the reflective lunar quality of the life force. In the raven, this process happened totally in the unconscious. In this Moon stage, the goose level of initiation, the mental image, rhythmically observed, is now consciously manipulated by the mind of the alchemist. This conscious, organizing force is pictured in the upper, winged bird as it regards the lower, flightless bird. Such a conscious cognizing activity in the mind is Universal Salt. The salt, arising out of the ash produced in combustion, unites with the more levity-filled water element in a solution in which the substantia of the salt exists in a marriage with the higher, imponderable element of water. The thinking of the alchemist is simultaneously fluid and focused.

## ALCHEMICAL PROCESS: SOLUTION

In the solution process, the ashes resulting from combustion are placed in the element of water in order to draw out the salt. This separates out the soluble parts which have a relationship to the fluid nature of water from the insoluble parts, the dregs or corpus, which do not. Alchemically, these insoluble, corpse-like parts are *earth*. The ponderable but soluble salt enters a solution and is lifted into a more fluid and imponderable state. The solution in turn can go into evaporation, in which the fluid nature moves upward out of the solution, and the salt falls out as a ponderable earth. This again is salt's dual activity: as substantia, it arises out of the ash when the ash is put into water, and it unites with the water; as a process, it emerges from a solution as an earth if the water is evaporated.

Viewed as a psychological image the ash which carries the salt is the manifest world of the senses. Hidden in the ash of the sense world are the creative life movements of the hierarchies who willed the forms which stand behind the objects of the sense world. This is the living salt hidden in the ash. The alchemist putting the ash of sensation into a retort filled with water is the equivalent of the work done on oneself in order to address a habit which is bothering us. We must place the patterns of physical sensation (ash) into a condition of higher levity force (a focused attention). The salt or creative will of the hierarchies who created the sense object leaves the ash and lifts into the water of the focused attention. When cognized by the alchemist these creative forces are the source of the healing of the instinctual patterns or wounds in the soul life.

In a normal human being the forces of Ruling Will found in sense experience are divided through an inner digestion or combustion process. Under the influence of sense impressions, the pituitary gland "combusts" the world into two streams, the first of which is the dark warmth of emotional patterns connected to instinct. This warmth rises into the brain as programmed responses of mental images. The actual forces of the sense impressions (not their creative motions) is the other stream, propelled downward as the driving force for the rest of the endocrine system. This force manifests as secretions (matter) which ultimately regulate the forms and functions of the life organs of the body. The cosmic warmth of the creative hierarchies thus combusts into the life of emotions (levity) and the forms and secretions of the glands and organs (ash). In the human being this fine ash, or *sweat*, contains the living salt of Cosmic Imaginations in a fine solution (phoenix) from the back of the head. The solution is salted by the pineal gland while cosmic light in the form of living processes in thinking precipitate the cosmic solutions into the actual living crystalline forms of the substances of the physical organs of the body. Where cosmic warmth was transformed by the pituitary gland, cosmic light is transformed by the pineal.

The pineal inhibits and restricts, giving form to the pituitary responses to outer sense impressions. Here the random, sense-instigated light impulses are ordered and regulated by the attention of a thinking, cognizing human being. Nerves, including the cochlear, oculomotor, and optic nerves, radiate into the area surrounding the pineal gland which, as a gesture of its role in forming patterns, forms crystals within itself as it matures. Esoterically, the pineal gland is the gate for the Ideas pouring down from the crystal heavens, the realm of archetype known to Plato as *entelechy*. Whereas the pituitary combusts the Ruling Will in sense experience into an ash stream and a light stream, the pineal allows human consciousness to consolidate formed thoughts out of a vast light sea of living

Idea. Human thoughts are like crystals falling out of the immense fluid matrix of consciousness. While the pituitary combusts the creative will downward toward the metabolic process which then allows the cosmic elements to flow upward within the organism, the salt activity of the pineal, working in the opposite direction, preserves images from the chaotic flow of sense impressions. Just as salt limits putrefaction and creates a more stable condition, the salt in the psyche allows the soul to organize and stabilize itself within the surging chaos of instinctual will.

In a physical solution, the ponderable salt substantia which is dissolved completely into the more imponderable water crystallizes out of solution again. In the inner life, the stabilization of associative images arising out of the flow of sensation allows the alchemist to consciously control and organize inner states. In the solution process we can first observe the arising mental images as they flow unchecked through the mind. Then we can place specific sensory images in a vessel constructed of a focused attention and begin to move them in specific ways through exercises. This salt capacity in the soul allows images to crystallize, and in this consolidation the ponderables and imponderables are separated, the volatile elements separating from gross elements.

To summarize, the sense world flows into the sense organs as a mixture of Idea, movement, and pattern which all exist in a compound in the sense object. Sensation is a combination of the Idea itself, which remains unmanifest, and its movement, its line of emergence from the archetype. The Idea, which is a cosmic potential, is generally not cognized during the sense experience in the human consciousness, for only the material appearance is commonly sensed. In everyday life the Idea and the movement are the source of energies for the complex yet ordered instinctual responses in the subconscious of animals and human beings. This is the *nigredo*. But with maturity and training, human beings become able to observe the Idea and its movement free of the sense objects to which they are connected. Through such training a person can begin to observe how a mental image arises inwardly as a light/warmth impulse which accompanies each sensation. The flood of mental images is kept well below the awake consciousness in the nigredo stage. Through training, however, the nigredo yields to the *albedo,* the white stage, the stage of the Moon.

In the albedo stage the alchemist separates the movement from the Idea in the sensation by watching the way in which mental images arise in a quiet consciousness or in a consciousness which is trying to order mental images by placing them in a particular sequence. When this capacity begins to develop, a fog or mist of mental images is experienced invading the soul as a kind of waking sleep state. This blizzard of mental images surging in the soul life is the albedo. The lunar signature of albedo is an image of the reflective process by which sense impressions become mental images. The soul still lives in the dream of instinct, but the dream becomes accessible when the flowing movements of the creative will released into the ever-present dream state of mental images is salted by the consciousness of the alchemist. This happens when cosmic Ideas are present to crystallize the movements into meaningful sequences or what we could call *lawful motion.* Sacred geometry, music, rhetoric, and other sciences were used in the old mysteries to accomplish this salting of the flowing mental images.

## Inner Exercise: Moving an Image

In this exercise a mental image is salted from the sense world with its flow of mental images and is moved consciously by the alchemist.

> Visualize two equilateral triangles, one below with its apex pointed upward, and one above with its apex pointed downward. Visualize the triangles moving toward each other until the apex of one touches the apex of the other. Then move the apices into each other until a diamond is formed. Continue the motion until the apex of the lower one touches the base of the upper one and vice versa. Continue the movement until a six-pointed star is formed. Continue moving until a diamond is formed. Reverse the motion until the two stand in their original relationship.

Such a sustained mental imaging creates a benign, preserving "salt" solution in the mind, resulting in a fluid yet concentrated mental condition capable of further alchemical work.

# THE FIRST PHASE: CONCENTRATION

### MARS
*the third stage*

### THE IMAGE
The first Mars image is a hermetic vessel in which the salt of consciousness is raised to a higher essence. The salt has left the dust behind and moved into a higher union with the water. If it is to go to a still higher state, the salt must leave the water and travel through the air. To do this, it must be repeatedly distilled and lifted over the gaseous state to condense in a rarified form known as the *eagle*, or *volatile salt*.

### THE SYMBOL
Two flying birds lift a dead bird into the air. The two birds working together are symbols of the will and the thinking united in lifting the consciousness to a higher level. Here the salted mental image can be moved consciously into contact with the concept or lawfulness which stands behind it. This is accomplished by an act of will, a distillation directed by a thinking consciousness and known to alchemists as *rubedo*. This is the highest stage of salt purification, in which the salt becomes capable of flying over the air as an eagle.

## ALCHEMICAL PROCESS:
## DISTILLATION OF VOLATILE SALTS

The field of attention described in the solution process contains both sense impressions and forces of attention, or willed cognitional forces. These forces are imponderable because they originate in the higher world in which reside the archetypes which form the world. As we saw in solution, the conscious control of the mental image places forces at the disposal of the alchemist which can discriminate between sensations and cognitions. In the solution, however, cognition and sensation are still in a mixed state. What is lacking is a more intense warmth (will) to allow the cognition to be completely separated from any reference to sense experiences. It is necessary to accomplish a separation in which higher forces of attention are consciously and systematically distilled away from sense experiences into a condition of sense-free thinking. In alchemy, this is done physically by placing a salt solution into a boiling flask, applying heat to the solution until its imponderables separate from the ponderables. Through many repeated distillations the salt is led into the air state, and its attraction to the earth is diminished as it is volatized so that its purest parts rise into union with the air and fire elements. This laboriously repeated distillation is very taxing to the patience of the alchemist and takes great will, but results in a volatile, spiritualized salt.

A volatile salt is almost an oxymoron. A typical salt will fall out of solution when the water is driven to a higher levity state. It will just as easily go back into water again and form a solution. This coming into form and going out again and coming back in again to the same form is the essence of the salt process. In the sulfur process, however, once the compound is separated by fire, the cosmic forces go back to the periphery of the cosmos and the earthly substances fall down into a gravity state. This cycle accurately describes the nigredo and albedo stages. However, in order for an alchemist to marry a salt to an alcohol, the salt has to be purified to such a degree of whiteness that it begins to take on a rosy tint. This red stage is very prominent in metal alchemy and not so easily attained in plant alchemy, but the process is similar in both. To marry alcohol, a salt must be able to volatize beyond the water stage, crossing the membrane of the water's surface into the element of air. Since salt falls out of solution when water is evaporated, the volatizing of a salt is a difficult technical feat. The salt is boiled in a flask and the vapors of the salt solution captured in a still. When the salt is almost dry, the solution or *phlegm,* from the boiling is poured back again onto the salt and the process is repeated. For the salt to volatize it is necessary to repeat this "whitening" process many times. The will to do this is the signature of Mars. In higher stages of the alchemy of metals, higher temperatures are used and the most volatile salts pass through the white stage and only after many days at very high temperatures and with repeated whitenings would the rosy hue emerge which was seen as perfection, as rubedo. This red color is also a Mars signature. Such a volatized salt would then follow its solvent out into the air of the still and pass over into the condenser. The

phlegm would slowly be evaporated, and the volatile salt, a fine powder called the eagle, would be left at the bottom of the dish. Only such a purified and lifted salt could marry a spirit like alcohol.

## INNER EXERCISE: EXACT SENSE PERCEPTION

Observe a growing plant. Focus on the lowest leaf. Represent this leaf in your mind's eye as clearly and vividly as possible. When this leaf can be clearly imagined and stabilized (salt solution), observe the next leaf and repeat the solution process. Continue until all of the leaves can be systematically recalled in clear detail, in sequence. Stop your observation when the plant forms the calyx of the flower. If any step cannot be "solved," look back at the plant until it can be clearly represented inwardly. When the whole sequence of leaves can be unfolded, imagine the plant growing in the mind's eye. The next step is to imagine the plant in the exact reverse order until you run out of leaves and are left with an empty consciousness. Pay attention to the quality of the empty consciousness by listening into its silence.

The will thus applied to sense activity boils the solution and releases *vapors* (higher states of consciousness) which are imponderable, akin to the pure nature of sense-free thinking as a spiritual activity. These vapors, alchemically the widow of steam, are widowed from the gross sense impressions when they sublimate and rise up as imponderables out of the top of the boiling flask. Only after many repeated purifications do these vapors carry the salt upward into a rarified eagle condition. Here the steam widow carrying the cognitional volatized salt is subjected to a cold water condenser and condenses back into a ponderable form. Having been repeatedly sublimated from the boiling solution, however, the steam condenses into an essence of the solution. The eagle as a volatile salt then has an affinity for air and fire. Psychically, the forming of this essence is known as sense-free thinking.

This state of consciousness is found when the exact mental image of the plant is rhythmically moved forward and then backward into silent, empty consciousness. This rhythm releases or loosens the *essence* of the salted mental images into the consciously emptied consciousness (widow of steam). Paying close attention to the rhythmically emptied consciousness, we can experience how our sublimated, emptied consciousness appears to densify *of itself* as it comes into contact with a still finer and higher state of consciousness. This causes the expanded consciousness to once again become a consolidated earth-salt—cold and condensed into waking consciousness. Having been subliminated, however, the now-condensing steam consciousness only contains the higher, finer essences of the solution, the living concepts or creative Ideas of the sense impressions, the eagle. The essence is composed of condensed, that is, ponderable, imponderables. This essence represents the soul's capacity to sustain the attention on an unknown or unthinkable conceptual content for an extended period of time—to ponder imponderables.

The higher essence of salt (thinking) is rendered, through this rhythmical activity of distilling sense impressions, into a very dynamic and penetrating salt. Physically, a volatized salt can move easily into tissues and can either fortify tissues or extract toxins. Such a purified salt can be used to draw out still higher principles and preserve them in the form of a potent ferment, or *extract*. In the inner life, the forming of an extract through the application of a purified salt consciousness can be imagined in processes found in abstract thinking. In abstract thinking we draw off concentrated extracts of meaning by means of highly purified, logically simplified concepts. In science this abstract extract renders out knowledge and meaning from the apparent chaos of the sense world. The danger, however, is that the abstract extract will be used as an end unto itself. This is the dilemma of abstraction.

On the alchemical path, the abstraction of an extract is the summation of the first phase of the great work, the phase of concentration. The physical forces of this phase make the sense world reveal its vital essences as knowledge of technology and the world. This first phase of concentration is characterized as a cycle of *resistance* wherein the consciousness systematically learns to overcome the forces and substances of the earth. If pursued as an end in itself, the resistance cycle gives the alchemist a "terrible certainty" about the world of the senses. This terrible certainty of the abstract extract can lead to an inflated arrogance which has sealed the doom of many a magician. The character of the inflated abstract consciousness is symbolized by the peacock, the dark magician preening his tail full of evil eyes, inflated in the hubris of his occult abilities. The Christian alchemist must see the Mars stage of the concentration/resistance phase as the foundation for the great work, not the goal. To achieve higher consciousness, the space of the silence in the widow of steam needs to be amplified and expanded through a heart taught to sacrifice. This theme is the alchemical basis for the next phase, the phase of contemplation and capacitance.

# The Second Phase: Contemplation

### Mars
*the first stage*

## The Image

The image for Mars' contemplation stage is the resistance of a dielectric. As we have seen, the forming process of an inner image is not commonly available to the waking consciousness. In contemplation, however, we must form and sustain exact inner images as part of the development of higher consciousness. The will to do this inner picture forming must resist the unchecked flow of images present in the instinctual consciousness. This resistance is the basis for the waking consciousness which lies at the root of higher vision. Resistance sets the stage for capacities.

## The Symbol

The symbol for this second Mars stage is still the same: a red bird and a blue bird lifting a dead white bird. In contemplation, however, the action is not based upon memory of sense impressions as it was in the concentration phase, but rather upon the forming and placing of inner images willfully before the soul. The lifting birds are now far above the earth, approaching the realm of the sun.

## ALCHEMICAL PROCESS:
## CAPACITANCE THROUGH RESISTANCE

In the previous Mars stage the summation of the resistance/concentration phase of the work was characterized by the production of an abstract extract, the repeated distillation process in which earthly sense matter is overcome by willed thinking. The alchemist must avoid the resulting lure of the power which is gathered by entering a higher phase. Thus, Mars is both the end of the first phase and the beginning of the second phase. Traditional alchemical analogies for this phase were the higher transformation of physical substance in physical ways. In a new alchemical path, however, new references to the higher work are needed to illustrate concepts such as fields which were not approachable in traditional alchemical descriptions of the higher levels of work except through allegories. As beautiful as the traditional alchemical descriptions are, it is useful now to turn to analogies from modern science. In fact, all three stages of the second phase of contemplation are most beautifully and accurately described by an analogy from the science of electricity.

Electromagnetic devices function by consuming power generated by mechanically severing lines of force in a magnetic field. Electricity used in this consumptive way is called derivative. It violates the fundamental law of the biological organism which is to keep energetic membranes intact. As a result, the forces gathered and used in most electrical technology sever etheric membranes in the production of forces which are inimical to life.

By contrast, natural models of electrical forces produce primary, or *electrostatic* forces in which field lines are strengthened. In electrostatic fields, therefore, the power (voltage) is great and the flow (amperage) is non-existent or extremely low. The fields of primary electrostatic phenomena can be amplified tremendously but are useless to electromagnetic technology as we know it because these forces produce no "work." Organisms often show amazingly high electrostatic voltage differential gradients on their surfaces. A 1,000 volt potential gradient on the surface of a woman's arm is not uncommon under certain circumstances. Such high potentials are due to the ability of certain substances such as silica, when formed into thin layers of membranes, such as skin, to resist electricity and maintain a tremendous power potential. This process of a resisting substance, a *dielectric,* building a potential charge is known as *capacitance.* A device or organism so arranged as to have capacitance is called a *condenser.* Condensers build potentials which can later be drawn off in a discharge of current. The greater the resistance to electricity, the more potential there is to build up enough power for a high voltage discharge.

Psychologically, the Mars nature of this first stage of contemplation can be pictured in the force of will needed to construct accurate images in the mind's eye. As the image of a leaf is reproduced or represented to the inner eye, strong forces are developed which expand the human consciousness in an orderly way. Such accurate observations are the foundation of natural science. The difference in contemplation is that the purpose of the visualization is not to understand or even duplicate the leaf, but to build inner forces capable of condensing the mind's resistance to this type of visualization work into a power of concentration able to contemplate that which lies outside the realm of the sense world. By repeated Mars efforts, concentration moves past the pragmatic goals of abstract knowledge and transforms resistance in thinking into a field of power with greater potential for inner work.

## INNER EXERCISE

The contemplation phase requires that a particular quality of focused attention be developed in order for higher consciousness to unfold in the alchemist. This attention must be absolute, yet fluid and unattached to any particular image or result. This seemingly paradoxical state of consciousness is not easy to experience let alone develop. There are some images, however, which can provide analogs for contemplation.

If we consider the relationship between practice and performance in the life of an accomplished musician we can see that without practice no performance would be possible. Yet in performance a player will often transcend his capacities in the practice sessions. We could say that in practice the player is trying to grasp some power in the will by a repetition of the desired activity. In performance the player must release the restrictions of the practices in order to transcend the abilities grasped in practice and enter a spontaneous consciousness of free play in which *abilities* gained through practice are enhanced into *capacities* developed through an intuition of the whole. In abilities we must push; in capacities we are drawn up into a higher realm of functioning. The technique is to work with the rhythmic repetitions during the practice in such a way that enthusiasm for the practice is built. Athletes who are trying to develop strength in a particular muscle group try to avoid strain by always working the muscle in an opposite direction or by developing the opposing muscles as well as the desired muscles. This polar training or cross training prevents strains and keeps the practice full of enthusiasm.

In the development of a meditative practice the daily success of the practice is not the goal. In the beginning there is a natural flush of enthusiasm, but this soon gives way to tedium and discouragement. The inability to achieve a still, open mind or to maintain a train of thought causes discouragement. The force of the will can no longer boil the solution to cause the sublimation into vapor. For example, if we are working with a thinking exercise based on a pin, the willed attention most surely will run out of steam and go dry. At this point moving to a polar exercise, such as working with the sense impression of a pin, can be of great benefit. By bringing the two polarities of thinking and sensation into a reciprocal relationship, our work with the pin can develop a greater force of attention because by moving the will through polarities, a sense of discovery and enthusiasm can infuse the practice. This need for polarity in the practice is seen in the image of the blue bird and the red bird, the nerve pole of thinking and the blood pole of will, which are united in the common effort of lifting the dead mental image into a higher condition. This first stage of contemplation is characterized by oscillation or polarity. Mars, the highest stage of the abstract extract in its distillation stage, now must be induced to resist rhythmically in order that an oscillation between polarities can lift the consciousness off of the body and into the pure spaceless time of the spirit world.

# THE SECOND PHASE: CONTEMPLATION

SUN
*the second stage*

## THE IMAGE

The image for the Sun stage is the Grail. Through working
with resistance in the Mars stage the esoteric student begins to
have direct experience that a large part of daily life in which
the self is involved is composed of resistance to the flowing,
changing forces of life itself. This resistance causes inner
images of life to arise as the content of the consciousness. As
we have seen, these images serve as the automatic, instinctual underpinnings of the lower personality. In the Sun stage of
contemplation, the flow of images is resisted so completely
that the content of the consciousness becomes completely
empty. This emptied consciousness is the Grail. The Grail is
found in the place of the Sun where *my* will is reversed and
emptied to become *thy* will. Here we open to the cosmos and
become aware of how our destiny comes to meet us.

## THE SYMBOL

The two birds of thinking and will, one blue and one red,
carry a crown into the air. In this symbol the burden of the
birds in the Mars stage has been magically transformed into a
crown. There seems to be little effort in the birds' gesture as

the crown floats easily above their heads. The crown is open at the top. In this we see the Grail. The sun forces have ripened the work of the concentration phase. The crown on the head of the king is open to the forces from the cosmos. He receives power, his "divine right," from a field outside his own organism. This field of power and its generation is the mystery of the contemplative life and the underlying activity of the Rosicrucian symbolist who practices alchemy, the Royal Art.

The bird symbol of the Sun stage is the pelican. In olden times it was thought that the pelican tore at its own breast in order to feed its young with blood. This symbol of self-sacrifice is found on altars and vestments in many churches. Biologically, the pelican actually tears out the down on its breast, and the exposed flesh becomes filled with blood vessels so that the bird can keep its eggs warm during brood rearing. Whatever the case, the image is one of *give-away,* of self-sacrifice. This is the lesson of the Grail and as such is the central technique in the Sun stage of the contemplation phase.

### INNER EXERCISE: SACRED SLEEP
The oscillation between the polarities of the waking states and sleeping states in the human life allows the soul to cross inner borders which put it in contact with the periphery of the cosmos. In nature, it is along the membranous borders that lie between one organ, state of being, or condition and another that life forces are generated and condense. Life exists most prolifically in the fringe between the woods and the meadows, or between a cold current in the sea and a warm one. The membrane is where energies are stored and transmitted. As a result, the crossing of a membrane involves an energy transfer. Falling asleep or waking up is such a membrane crossing. If attention is paid to enhancing the quality of this crossing, the capacity of the soul to develop an inner restructuring is enhanced. This can be accomplished through the exercise of sacred sleep.

When falling asleep in the evening, begin in the mind's eye to picture the flow of the day's events in reverse order. Try to review them so that a continuous backward flow is maintained. Avoid spending time on one picture or another, or in judging the pictures in any way. The entire process should ideally not take more than ten minutes. Once the consciousness stands at the door to the sleep world, our angel can be asked to guard our awakening so that we can do a concentration exercise the next morning. Then go to sleep. The angels will often awaken us at 4:00 a.m. to join in the uprising ether forces. If we can get up and do a concentration exercise immediately upon arising, the forces gained in sleep are moved more centrally into the waking consciousness. The practice of such an oscillation at the membrane of the spirit world eventually builds capacities in the mind for inducing higher insight.

The first part of this exercise, the going backward through the day's events, was given by Rudolf Steiner as the practice of the daily review, and it is the keystone for inner development in a Rosicrucian practice. The backward thinking of the daily review is meant to be practiced as fluidly as possible to enable the will forces to lose their attachment to goal-directed thinking. This allows the will to be applied to situations where no goal is perceived. Another benefit of the daily review is the inertial motion of purified will forces which move toward the consciousness we will enter in the spiritual world upon falling asleep. Exploring the sleep/dream consciousness while still awake is the lesson of the old alchemical saying: "When asleep, be awake." Through the daily review we practice purifying the soul from its sense world impressions and habits and enter the dream life as a pure soul/spiritual presence. If we pause at the end of the review and listen intently into the silence, we can literally enter the dream state while still in a waking consciousness. In more advanced work we can place symbols into this silence which will guide us during sleep into proper relationships with spiritual beings. If, upon awakening, we devote some time to concentration exercises, the contents of our dream experiences will arise in us as coherent images and insights composed of feelings of knowing. When the daily review and the morning concentration meet in the silence of the practice, our life becomes a Grail cup which receives cosmic nutrition from our experiences in the world on this side of the spirit.

# THE SECOND PHASE: CONTEMPLATION

## VENUS
### *the third stage*

## THE IMAGE

The first Venus image is the virgin soul, the *nous pathetikos*, the sensitive receptive soul, or suffering soul. The soul of the student who has given up resistance comes into contact with the spiritual world that lies behind sense experience. It begins to be receptive to subtle influences which can eventually lead to creative insight. A soul in this state learns to be awake outside the physical body in the field of activity present in the subtle light body, the etheric sheath. In this state of consciousness the soul experiences the spiritual world as full of potential for meeting spiritual beings and influences which begin to enter into the field of meditative awareness as the daily rhythmical practice allows the spiritual world to gradually approach the awakening soul. The empty Grail of the Sun space now begins to fill with cosmic nourishment. The soul feels virginal, primal, washed, or reborn. The spirit approaches from all sides as new and full of potential. In contemplation the student feels the approach of the beloved and waits in virginal stillness for the oracular touch from the spirit. This state of the virginal soul was known to the ancient Greeks as *nous pathetikos*, the virgin who has hopes to be approached and spiritually touched.

### THE SYMBOL

This symbol of two waiting birds sitting on the bare branches of a tree growing into the earth is an image of inductive reasoning and the need to cultivate what the poet Keats called *negative capability.* This is the capability of maintaining a high level of patient attention upon a problem even when there is no hope of solution. The patient, humble waiting of the birds on the barren tree shows the best attitude toward the spiritual world in all creative pursuits. This can best be expressed in the medieval admonition and mantram for monastic life: *Ora et labora*—pray and work. This attitude and practice renders the soul porous, open to the fields of activity of spiritual beings. A soul porous to these activities can see into the spiritual world.   Anthroposophy knows this phase as Imagination; physics knows it as induction.

### ALCHEMICAL PROCESS

For this stage and the stages that follow in the phase of meditation, the analogical alchemical processes will be given together as one chapter on the preparation for meditation. This is necessary because of the complex weaving needed to accurately describe the higher stages of meditative practice.

### INNER EXERCISE:  BREATHING IMAGES

This exercise is adapted from the seminal indications by Rudolf Steiner known as "The Ancient Yoga Culture and the New Yoga Will." In this work, Steiner lays the roadbed for the establishment of a western esoteric yoga practice. Instead of breathing in the *prana* from the air as eastern yogis do, Steiner indicates that a more effective path for the western soul would be to breathe prana in with the light which comes into the eyes or other senses. For the prana, or ether force, needed by western adepts is, according to Steiner, found in light rather than air. A conscious breathing of light into the eyes in the form of images can be experienced as a delicate process in which the light meets and mingles with a current of will forces from within the human being. To experience the mingling of currents puts the human being at the door to higher worlds. To accomplish this, the following exercise is useful.

Observe a candle flame for a minute. Close your eyes
and observe the after-image. Watch it pulse and ebb
and change colors until no image is perceptible. Pay
attention to the inner state after the image fades away.
Once this becomes familiar, visualize a current of
energy rising up the spine from the kidney area into
the back of the brain, through the optic nerve, and
toward the front of the head. Once this is an experience, combine the first exercise with the second.
Begin by establishing the current from the kidney to
the eyes, then open the eyes and observe a candle
flame. Close your eyes and pay attention to the place
in the head where the after-image meets the kidney
current, where the human will meets the sense
impression.

This exercise is an adaptation of indications given by
Rudolf Steiner in his lecture on the mission of the Archangel
Michael, entitled "The Ancient Yoga Culture and the New
Yoga Will: The Michael Culture of the Future" (Dornach, Nov.
30, 1919). Anatomists may recognize the hypothalamus and
the midbrain or the pineal and the pituitary as an area in
which there is great potential for this type of meeting.

In this exercise an attempt is made to experience the difference between the activity of the life forces and the activity
of the awareness in the act of perception. The first part of the
exercise in which we observe the ebbing of an after-image
comes out of Goethe's color theory. The after-image pulsates,
coming into focus and then dissolving at regular intervals.
This observation, if repeated, can lead to an inner experience
of the role of the life forces in our perception. The second half
of the exercise, in which we experience a current moving from
the kidneys to the head and out of the eyes, puts us in contact
with the current which floods our sympathetic nervous system and lies at the root of our soul's awareness in the astral
body. In the forming of mental images these two currents are
in constant interplay, creating harmonics or disequilibrium in
the soul. Each has its focus in either the pituitary or the pineal
gland as our day consciousness arises through their interaction in the fluids of the third ventricle of the brain. When gen-

tly repeated, this exercise can yield a direct experience of the way in which every sense impression and every thought is accompanied by a subtle mental image which quickly fades and fluctuates into another image—and that the ability to control this is the basis for cognition and the capacity for higher development. This experience serves as the basis for a new yoga of the senses.

# THE THIRD PHASE: MEDITATION

## VENUS
### *the first stage*

## THE IMAGE

As we have seen, the image for Venus as the third stage of the phase of contemplation was the *nous pathetikos,* or passive soul. By contrast, the image for Venus in the first stage of the meditation phase is *nous poietikos,* the married, or productive, soul. This is the state of soul in the student who has established a regular practice of breathing images between the waking consciousness and the spiritual world. As an image is given away into silence the soul gradually becomes aware that the more the Grail can be emptied the more it is nourished and filled from the spirit. The initial virginal expectation of being touched or becoming accomplished at meditation settles into a rhythmic, graceful poise in silence. In this graceful state of neither breathing images in nor breathing images out, images which seem to have no connection to our waking reality arise as if spontaneously in the wakeful, silent soul. If our practice is to think these arising images into silence, then after a period of time we can become aware of just how the images constellate of themselves into lawful patterns. Through sustained rhythmic silence in which we give away all images, profound and lawful images arise and begin to impregnate the soul from spirit worlds. The soul then has the impression that it is seen and recognized and no longer has the anxiety of the virgin wondering expectantly about the nature of the beloved. The impregnated soul is now gravid and productive, not out of its own images and concerns, but out of lawful Imaginations which it receives from the spirit. This lowest stage of the meditation phase is that of Imagination.

## THE SYMBOL

The red and blue birds waiting on a barren tree have let go in the Sun stage and now are sitting at the upper border of the soul listening into the void into which they released their prior activity. They may hear an answer which comes as grace and insight or as a new-found capacity to understand and to do that which was impossible before. This second side of Venus is an ability to sustain a silent conversation. In our alchemical work of meditation, the conversation is with the spiritual world, for the regular practice of contemplation leads to the meditative oscillation between the spirit and the soul known to Anthroposophy as Imagination.

The bird of this Venus stage is the mute swan. It is an image of one who knows but cannot say. In the approach to the Sun in the Mars stage, a goal-oriented consciousness was symbolized as a peacock, a showy bird with a loud voice. The Sun stage gave us the image of the self-sacrificing pelican, living in the burning warmth of a purifying Sun. In the Venus stage the swan has been to the Sun and received an initiation, but now the answer is too grand to express. The peacock did not know but talked a lot. The swan, after purification, knows the answer but is unable to express it. Through our daily practice we can come into contact with beings whose consciousness is so high and so evolved that we lose our ability to describe it. The only way left to pursue, in this instance, is the path of silence and daily practice in patience, offering ourselves to the spirit in humility.

This oscillatory inductive conversation with higher beings is based upon the performance of daily exercises at certain times which overlap and potentize the soul currents and make the human consciousness into a productive womb nourished by the quickening approach of higher conscious beings.

# THE THIRD PHASE: MEDITATION

## JUPITER
### *the second stage*

## THE IMAGE

The Jupiter image is the waking consciousness seen as the membrane between the spirit and the world of the senses— the pearl of clairvoyance.  In this second stage of the third phase of meditation, the student has the experience that the images being presented to the soul in the imaginative consciousness are produced by the activity of distinct spiritual beings.  These spiritual beings have an intention which lies hidden behind the Imaginations which are perceived in the soul as creative movements.  The seemingly abstract nature of such an experience, when cognized by the intellect, is thoroughly transformed into a vibrant sounding interaction in the experience of Inspiration.  It can happen, through exercises such as exact sense perception which are designed to transform perception, that the student experiences a kinship between the meditatively perceived movements in the state of Inspiration and the supersensibly perceived movements which lie behind and sometimes are woven into the forms found in the natural world.  In such a state the movements behind the natural forms and the cognitively perceived movements in the realm of living concepts meet in a harmonic relationship in the meditatively poised and silent mind of the student. This pearl of clairvoyance is actually the transformed waking consciousness which, through meditative practice, has become the true cosmic nourishment pouring from the Grail. Idea and manifestation meet in an undeniable marriage and consummation in the soul of the student. The rough irritation of the uncognized sensation and the transcendent secretive matrix of the virginal Idea meet in the transformed waking state to create a rhythmically formed, luminous, and precious pearl. A gem of transformed irritation evoked from a context of liquid light, the pearl is a perfect image of the rhythmic, patient striving needed to become a vessel capable of receiving the holy grace of Inspiration.

This aspect of Inspiration as the rhythmic transformation of the waking consciousness can be seen in analog in the process of homeopathic dilution or potentization. When a substance is placed in water and shaken rhythmically, the tendency for the substance to "loosen" is enhanced. In potentization, a certain amount of fluid is used as the diluent or medium. After a specified number of shaking or rotating movements, the substance is removed and a specified amount of fluid is retained. This small amount of fluid is added to a specified amount of new medium and shaken or rotated for the same number of times. This operation is repeated in order to further loosen the substance. In most substances the effect of the substance is enhanced as the dilution proceeds until a maximum effect can be observed. This *maximum* usually occurs between the sixth dilution (6D) and the fifteenth dilution (15D). Following quickly on this maximum is a complete collapse of the signature forces of the initial substance. This collapse is known to homeopaths as the first *minimum*. If dilution is continued, then the effect of the substance in its shadow or negative signature are evident in the potentized medium. At this stage there is usually no physical presence of the substance in the medium. However, the medium begins to receive the "radiations" of the substance. This is proven by giving the potentized substance to the patient and observing the response or shadow response to the substance. After continued dilution the stage of 30D is reached when another minimum or collapse of effects is produced. Further dilution past the second minimum once again reveals the signature of the substance, but this time at a very refined level. It is considered by homeopaths that after the second minimum the substance is completely united with the diluent or medium, having been loosened rhythmically by the potentizing process into an infinitely attenuated state. The substance is then considered to be approaching its creative archetype. In the stage of Inspiration, the radiation of the substance into the medium is the basis for the analog. The raw substance of the sense world is radiated into the waking consciousness where its loosened form connects to the archetype. In this stage, the influx of the archetype and the perception of the ruling will behind the phenomenon meet in the rhythmically potentized waking consciousness, in Intuition.

## THE SYMBOL

The Father God, the Creative Spirit of the whole cosmos, is above, looking down from the periphery of the cosmos. The Son, the One who died, is below, united with earth as a tree on whose branches flowers are blooming.

In the old mysteries, the alchemist formed a hermetically sealed vessel and with the fire of the will boiled the sense world and its shadows until the vessel shattered. The vessel, the boiling flask or retort, ruptured the membrane between worlds when it broke. This hole in the membrane allowed the gods to descend and inspire the prophets through dreams, visions, and ecstatic experience. To do this, however, it was necessary that the daytime awareness of the alchemist be obliterated so that the gods could use the vacated instrument to inspire the culture. This was accomplished through binding rituals, fatigue from dancing or physical trials, drugs, magical or sexual practices, or ascetic austerities.

By contrast, in the symbol of the Jupiter phase, a dove flies down from the Father God with the sun in its beak, which sends radiations of light onto the flowering tree. This is an image of the Holy Spirit. The Holy Spirit enables human beings to experience the God in the flesh, Christ, as a direct, waking, cognitive experience, as the force within themselves of the Ego or the cognized I Am. This force, the higher self, the Individuality, is cognized when an alchemist, through the intense potentization of the medium of consciousness (see Mercury stage, following), works past the first minimum of potentization and causes the substance of the sense world to light up in its radiant form within the meditative state. The spiritual, eternal principles behind all sense existence become accessible to the seeking mind as cognitive feelings. The medium of the sensitized consciousness becomes permeated with the spiritual holiness of substance, and the process of transubstantiation potentizes the medium. The Holy Spirit inspires us with the forces of our own I-being. Like Noah's dove, it serves as a messenger to us from the cosmos, permeating us with the conviction that we lead an eternal existence.

The meditative life is marked with advances and dry periods. When working meditatively with certain contents, the practice can often become wooden and stiff. It seems as if one is simply repeating empty phrases, or that it would be better if we stayed in bed or took our rest instead of meditating. States such as this, and many other variations, are the minima experienced during the potentization process. After such minima, however, the inner sense is as if a new world of possibilities begins to dawn out of the dark night of the soul. This may be the dawning of the next phase of meditation, the highest stage of potencies, in which the medium becomes one with the substance and its archetype.

The bird symbol of the Jupiter stage is the dove, the messenger from above who brings enlightenment and grace to the silent, expectant soul. This shows the influx of grace given to the soul who can continue to practice and fail in silence. Eventually the spirit reveals itself to those who wait—as long as the waiting is permeated with the will to do the inner work, independent of any results.

# THE THIRD PHASE: MEDITATION

### MERCURY
*the third stage*

## THE IMAGE

The Image for the Mercury stage is the waking consciousness which is lifted into the spirit world where the human archetype meets the archetypes which give rise to the sense world. In homeopathy the range of dilutions after the second minimum is considered to be infinite. The substance can be raised to higher and higher dilutions and it begins to manifest powerful effects of transformation on the body and the soul. Likewise, in the alchemical tree, the seventh stage is a stage of profound transformation. In the Venus stage of Imagination, the soul learns to see into the spiritual world. In the Jupiter stage of Inspiration, the soul begins to hear the patterns of becoming which resound out of the archetypes. In Intuition, the Mercury stage, the thinking center moves into the heart region where the cosmic pictures and their music of becoming are integrated into the silent, imageless, warmly luminous experience of archetypal being. The development of such a hearing/seeing in the heart, or what is known to esotericists as the heart eye, marks the onset of Intuition. This state is similar to the ability which the soul exercises in the physical sense world when it is engaged in the activity of discrimination. According to Rudolf Steiner, the ability to determine the correct relationship between a given percept and its concept is intuition. In the seventh stage, however, the Intuition has been consciously developed to extend into the realm of living concepts or archetypes. This reveals living Ideas to the soul and extends the range of waking consciousness into the realms of sleep and dream. It is here that the thinking descends into the esoteric heart. With such a heart vision or spirit vision the student can observe the spirit spaces outside the organism in sleep and dream states while remaining in a coherent waking consciousness. The development of the heart eye in states of Intuition is the *beginning* of a path which goes beyond the subject of this book. However, the heart eye, once firmly established in the daily practice, allows the student to penetrate into the varied experiences which arise in sense perception and to cognize the impact of sensation on the human physiology. Slowly, through intuitive perception exercises, the secret, hidden activity of creative beings in nature becomes at first perceptible and later understood. This stage is the alchemical marriage between the productive soul and the bridegroom, the Christ, who is present in the life forces which animate the world of the senses.

## The Symbol

A woman rises out of a grave with stars overhead. The resurrection of the soul from the grave of the body is another way of expressing the great alchemical marriage. In this symbol, the lifting of the soul out of the substance and the uniting of the soul with the wisdom of the starry cosmos is a reflection of the third level of potentization in which the medium, after becoming sensitive, and the substance, having its ponderables and imponderables loosened from each other, unite finally in a spiritualized substance permeated with great potential.

The medium in this stage of consciousness heals the split incurred when the spirit takes on, by means of a soul, the dust of the earth, thereby splitting apart the primal unity of the cosmos and its corpse, the substance of the earth. To redeem and heal and resurrect this division is the nature of the potentized soul forces found in the third stage of meditation, the stage of Intuition. It is here in the eternal weaving of Cosmos and

Earth that the currents of the caduceus, the healing staff of Mercury, are found.

The bird which represents this high and rare stage of consciousness is the sparrow. An alchemist who has done the great work sees the setbacks and achievements of the stages of the work equally. Like the initiate Christian Rosenkreutz, the alchemist who has cognized the healing mercury holds no expectations, harbors no resentments, champions no causes, and seeks no revenge. The sparrow lives in the community of birds as one among many, content simply to be alive to the great mystery of Creation.

# THE METHOD OF ANALOGY: PHYSICAL ANALOGS FOR SPIRITUAL STATES

The method of analogy is the practice whereby the alchemist seeks to find processes in the natural world which are analogous to soul processes. This approach with its body of techniques is the basis for the Rosicrucian alchemical stream in Anthroposophy. The alchemical tree is an analog of the stages of soul transformation necessary to begin a path of development leading to an understanding of the profound mysteries of the alchemical marriage. We have analyzed in detail the Saturn and Moon stages from a laboratory perspective. The Mars stage of distillation was also presented in detail as the highest stage of the first phase. In the great alchemical work of the transformation of metals, the researcher could develop analogs to depict much higher states of consciousness than the phase of concentration. In the modern world, however, analogs are available in everyday life which can depict these higher states more clearly than the somewhat confusing and subjective analogs generally found in alchemical texts on the great work of the transformation of metals. For this reason, the following descriptions of the contemplation and meditation phases are offered in order to build a bridge from everyday modern life to the teachings of the hermetic masters.

In the previous considerations, the Mars stage represented the distillation process wherein ponderables separated from imponderables and were sublimated to a higher level. Here they condensed into essences in the presence of still more subtle states. This was a model for the gradual spiritualization of matter in its characteristic cycles of resistance, that is, the task of overcoming the earth's matter by spirit. In this process, resistant matter is overcome by the warmth of the will which causes it to transform into subtler states. This is a picture of the psychological phase of concentration.

In the next phase, that of contemplation, the resistance of the material world is present in the Mars stage as the will needed to overcome the material. In this model, however, the resistance, instead of causing a widow of steam, generates a field of electric force. This force field is the characteristic signature of the stage of capacitance.

In order to make this image more understandable it would be useful to look at some attributes of an electric field. When we rub a glass rod with a piece of leather, according to electrical theory, electrons are transferred from the glass to the leather. Losing the negatively charged electrons, the glass becomes positively charged. Gaining negatively charged electrons, the leather becomes negative in relation to the now positive glass. The two substances are mutually polar in their charges where before they were charge neutral—that is, the charges within the glass were balanced and the charges within the leather were balanced. The friction of rubbing the two shifts a charge from the glass to the leather and causes a polarity. With each stroke of the rubbing the charge grows and the polarity of the charges becomes more pronounced. With each stroke the glass is made more positive and will possess a stronger attraction to the negative charge it is losing to the leather: opposite charges attract. The leather, already negatively charged, will tend to repel the negative pole of the glass rod. Finally, it will become impossible to create a greater polarity simply by rubbing the glass with the leather. Potential electrical forces of attraction and repulsion are now present in the relationship between the glass and the leather. The leather and the glass now have the potential to move toward each other attracted by their polar charges or away from each other repelled by a like charge. We could call this state the charged state. It is an analog to the Mars stage where, through effort, a polarity is produced between the desires and drives of the lower self and the potential in the soul for transcendent experience of the True Self.

If we were to suspend a neutrally charged pith ball from a silk thread near the charged rod, then the space around the rod would attract the ball when the rod was rubbed with leather.  But if we let the neutral ball touch the rod, the ball will then be repelled by it.  Under normal conditions both the rod and the leather will be neutral to the pith ball, but when the rod is rubbed a charge moves from the rod to the leather.  We could say it moves from the salt pole to the sulfur pole.

Alchemically glass is salt (silica).  It crystallizes out of a molten solution.  Leather is more sulfur than glass.  It is a product of the metabolic forces.  Salt is antipathetic.  It is a giver of negative charges.  It easily gives its cohesion—to water, for instance.  During friction between glass and leather (sulfur/resin), the leather which is positive (i.e., sympathetic) takes on the negative charge from the glass.  The glass becomes positive and we could say sympathetic in that the glass rod now attracts the pith ball with its overwhelming and seductive positivity.  The negative charge has flowed from salt to sulfur, from glass to leather.  The flow of the negative charge from salt to sulfur can be pictured in an image in which a series of substances are arranged in a continuum from salt/glass to sulfur:  salt, hair, polished glass, wool, silk, frosted glass, rubber, resin, amber, sulfur.  Substances near the salt pole give negative charges to substances to their right.  Sulfur is positive and can absorb negative charges from all substances to its left.  The fundamental polarity is between salt and sulfur or glass and resin.

Since it is the negative charge which moves, the direction of charge between substances is always from salt to sulfur.  Here we can see a fundamental polarity in nature as an image of the dominant soul forces in the sentient soul.  The Moon and Mars nature of these forces is imaged in the antipathetic/sympathetic polarities of repulsion and attraction which dominate the soul in its undeveloped state.

Alchemically the first three stages of the first phase which we have called distillation could also be pictured in these electrostatic relationships.  In the third stage of the first phase (Mars) the antipathy/sympathy polarities are lifted to a higher stage of development.  In electrostatics this would be the induction of a charge into the charged object which is greater than the object's normal degree of charge.  There are several ways to achieve an enhanced capacity to hold a charge.  Since charge flows from a condition of greater charge to the ground, one way to build a greater charge is to prevent the charge from leaking out of the charged object.  Through simple experiment it can be shown that spherical objects will hold a charge which pointed objects discharge.  This can be illustrated in the following diagrams.  In the first diagram we see a negatively charged object (-) and a positively charged object (+) balanced in each other's electric fields.  The field lines represent the forces which the two points have in common, for each object will influence the space around itself with a field of forces.  When they are in balance, two oppositely charged objects share a balanced field between them.

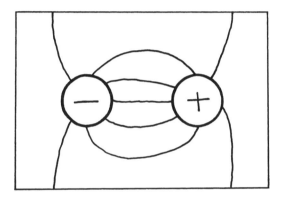

In the next diagram we again see two charged objects, each charged to the same potential, just as we had in the first diagram.  What is different in the second diagram, however, is that the positively charged object is pointed in shape while the negative pole is spherical.  The field lines or lines of force coming from the surface of the negative pole gather together in the point and create a condition of discharge into the field around the positive pole.

In the first diagram the power of the charges in the two poles could be greatly enhanced and there would be no discharge into the lines of force of the field.  In the second case the field lines from the negative pole gather in the point of the positive pole.  Were we to push the point closer to the negative pole, the entire field would collapse into a spark discharge, and the potential power of the field would be lost.  The rule then for building a charge or capacitance is that a pol-

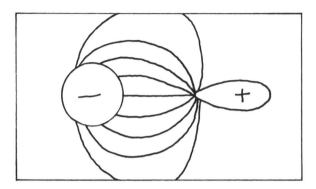

ished spherical surface builds power and a rough or pointed surface dissipates power.

In the inner life this is a picture of the effort of the student to willfully overcome anger, resentment, and other negative emotional states leading to roughness, rudeness, and irritability (prickliness) in order to maintain a rhythmically smooth inner equilibrium. In the pursuit of inner development the production of regular, rhythmic states of equilibrium diminishes the incidence of emotional discharge and allows a field of capacitance to grow around the body of the student. The smoothing of the emotional life is the first stage of the second phase, the phase of contemplation.

Calling this phase "contemplation" may seem at odds with the traditional description of contemplation by mystical writers such as St. Teresa of Avila, St. John of the Cross, and the anonymous author of the *Cloud of Unknowing.* In these works and others, the term contemplation is used to describe a mystical state of union with the godhead in which the thinking of the contemplative is completely extinguished in favor of silent mystical union with God. This total absorption in God is the goal of the tradition of the Christian contemplative. In this tradition meditation is etymologically the thinking of the middle or lower way (medi=middle). To the Christian contemplative the higher state is contemplation. In this work, however, we are pursuing a study of the Rosicrucian path and not that of the Christian contemplative who generally lived in seclusion in order to sustain the necessary distance from life needed to achieve contemplation. The Rosicrucian path requires that the contemplative bring the fruits of contemplation back into the world of daily life in order that the higher stages of existence can be developed here on earth. For this reason the contemplation phase and its three stages must yield on the Rosicrucian path to the phase of meditation, the middle way (as described in Mahayana Buddhism), as the goal of the progressive modern student. The body-free contemplative experience is then structured in such a way that the thinking is maintained but is systematically divested of its thought content until only the pure witnessing attention is present. Concentrated thinking and contemplative willing thus meet and marry in a higher marriage of meditation for the purpose of healing the world.

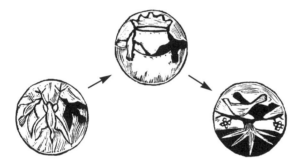

The images present in electrostatic induction can be used as icons pointing toward the transformation of contemplative states into the Imagination, Inspiration, and Intuition states of the meditative phase. We saw earlier that the first state of the phase of contemplation is a Mars state in which our effort to balance the soul forces of sympathy and antipathy allows for a higher charge to build in the electric field around the body of the student. The thinking then begins to be free of stimulus-response, sense-oriented patterns and slowly comes under the self control of the student. We saw how a sphere has a greater capacity to store a charge because its surface has no points where a discharge could occur. This image was given as an analog of the student working to control the emotional life. A higher stage than this is necessary in order for the silence and absorption of contemplation to lift the soul into contact with the spiritual world and its transcendent experi-

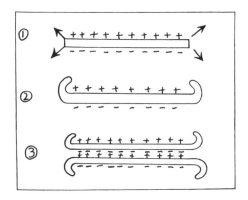

contact with the spiritual world and its transcendent experiences. By using the form of the sphere as an example we can fashion a device which could develop a much greater charge by opening the sphere into a flat plane. From the diagram (1) we can see that the charge would polarize and organize within the plate as positive on one side and negative on the other. With such a flat plane, however, there would be leakage at the edges. To minimize this we could curve all of the edges so that they would resemble the sphere. (2) Such a flat plate with curved edges could take an even greater charge without a discharge. But if we wanted the greatest charge to build up we would arrange for two parallel plates to face each other (3). The two plates then would mutually influence each other, the opposite charges attracting each other in the space between the plates. With such an arrangement a very strong charge can be condensed into the field which the two plates share in common. This condensing of the charge into the field outside of the actual object is the source of the term condenser in electrical theory. Were we to take many such plates and place them together a very large field could be created with a great deal of potential power. Such a device would then be called a capacitor. Capacitors are built to enhance a charge and store it in the field around itself. A capacitor with a strong charge serves as the center of an electric field which extends far beyond its surface.

This is an image of the second stage of contemplation, the stage of the mystical union with the Sun. In the Sun stage the thinking loses its content and enters into a sustained, silent attentiveness to the transcendent.  All cognition is given over to attentive absorptive Beingness.  In such absorptive states time stretches into an infinite sea of light peopled with world creative spiritual beings.  In such a state the thinker, free of the soul and free of cognition, experienced primal unity with the world creator.  In ancient times this state of *samadhi*, of sustained silent contemplation, was the ultimate goal of  adepts who sought liberation in a Nirvana far from the crashing and glittering manifest world.  Such contemplative experiences gave rise to monastic orders who lived by extreme rules and regimens in order to maintain the soul in the optimal condition for mystical union and liberation.

The modern human being, however, has a destiny which must include the transformation of the physical earth and the development of the faculty of individual independent judgement.  For these developments to take place a further evolution of  mystical  union  was  necessary.    The  contemplative needed to voluntarily return from the heights of ecstacy in mystical union and vow to save all sentient beings who were still living in the darkness of ignorance. Personal liberation in the Sun space needed to be given away for the good of the whole.  This mood is the hallmark of the third stage of contemplation where the capacity to sustain a field consciousness gives rise to rhythmical practice.  Such rhythmical practice allows any resistances found in the soul to be the source of the induction of higher truths.  To illustrate this concept let us return once again to electrostatics.

We have seen that a charged capacitor serves as the center of a field which extends beyond the capacitor's surface.  We saw that the repetition of many plates one next to another will dramatically enhance the field strength of the capacitor.  The field lines grow closer together at the periphery showing a loss of force at the edges.  The more repetitions of layers the more power can be stored in the field outside the capacitor. When we place an object into the field around the capacitor the object will interact with the field by drawing field lines to itself.  We saw this earlier in the diagram which showed a sphere and a pointed object interacting with each other to form their common field lines of force. If we place a conducting metal object such as a copper ball in the field around a

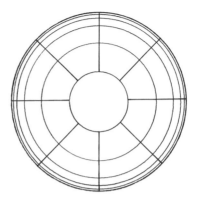

condenser, the copper will draw field lines to itself and induce the potential forces into its surface. The excessive force contained in the field around the condenser will drain off onto the surface of the conducting copper in order to seek equilibrium from the effects of tension brought on by the excessive charge in the field.

In the inner life this is the discharge of energy which can be experienced when a person who has been practicing for a long time falls back into old patterns of behavior. The way down is much easier once a charge has been built and sustained in the fields around the body and the effort to get the charge back up seems to require much more will force. A conductor resists the charge in its center but moves the charge easily along its surface, often resulting in a discharge as the charge seeks the ground or earth. In this conduction the power or potential and its capacity are lost. This is seen in the first diagram as conduction. In the second diagram we can see the way in which a dielectric or insulator would interact with an electric field around a capacitor. Instead of being moved easily across the surface of the conductor, the field lines are drawn into the body of the insulator. The term dielectric which means "electricity goes through it" illustrates this phenomenon.

The ability of a dielectric to pull in field lines and concentrate them is known as induction. Materials with many layers (such as the mineral mica or its common form in schist-like rocks) are very good insulators. Wood is also a good insula-

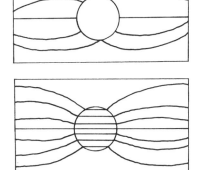

**surface conduction**

**induction of a dielectric**

tor with its many layers of cellulose. In the conductor the charge travels on the surface and remains on the surface. The dielectrics by contrast have a structure or form composed of many *inner* surfaces. The charge travels along these pathways inside the dielectric without building any amperage or discharge which accompanies a flow of current. The charge swells out of the dielectric without breaking across any field lines. As a result the field around the dielectric can have tremendous potential power or voltage because there is no discharge. Any object which is also a dielectric and is placed in the field of a charged dielectric or condenser will also begin to take a charge even though the two objects are not connected in a circuit by a conductor. This ability to take on a charge through simply being in a charged field is called induction. Two capacitors which are tuned to be harmonic in the characteristics of their common fields can augment each other to create more power through resonant induction. In resonant induction we can find an image of the third stage of the second phase of contemplation.

After the contemplative has developed the capacity to enter into a deep contemplative state, the mind comes back down to the waking state. The contemplative in a traditional setting organizes a livelihood and mode of life in which more and more time is devoted to the Sun stage of transcendent mystical union. The modern esoteric Rosicrucian path asks that the contemplative find the transcendent in the phenomena of the world. To do this the contemplative uses inner pictures which have their root in the phenomenal world. Yet when the inner pictures are worked with in rhythmic meditational states, the esoteric student transforms the waking consciousness into a form capable of inducing the spiritual world into the phenomenal world. The rhythms which lie behind the unfolding of a particular phenomenon are the meditative fields into which the worker seeks to induce the creative motion of the archetypal world-creating spirit beings. These world creative spirit beings are the source of the creative movements which are the very genesis of the phenomenon itself. The meditant seeks to establish a charged field of attention which is structured in lawfully perceived creative images. If this work is accurate and devotional, when the meditant returns from the Sun space a spiritual enhancing and rectifying of the living picture of the phenomenon can be induced into the waking consciousness. This heightened awareness of the "becomings" of world phenomena allows the student to induce into the fields around the physical body Imaginations of the genesis of the natural world from spirit world. The process of developing an inductive imaginal consciousness then is the third stage of the second phase.

The traditional contemplative tries to spend more and more time in ecstacy. The meditant on a modern Rosicrucian path strives to induce into daily life the creative motions of the spirit world. In doing so, the modern Rosicrucian strives to be the living and devoted link whereby the spirit and the world can marry each other in an alchemical marriage.

It should be noted that the electrical analogies used to describe the development of capacities are not meant to suggest that the human consciousness is as simple as a machine. The human being seeking the path to contemplation and meditation is not simply emulating a computer. Quite on the contrary, a computer is simply that, a computer. It does not think in a transcendent way. Then why use electrical analogies to describe such a lofty pursuit as contemplation? The careful reader can notice that the analogs given for this phase of the inner life all reside in the field of electrostatics. The study of electrostatics concerns itself with what is known to electricians as *primary electricity*. As esotericists we would call it *pri-*

*mal* electricity. No field lines have been severed in producing an electrostatic field. Electrostatics describe the spiritual being of electricity as a world creating power. When human beings fetter electromagnetic fields for their own use, the primal nature of the power of electricity becomes derivative and subject to conditions which drive it down into a parallel field of activity. It is out of derivative electricity and its technical manipulation that forces counter to the evolution of true human Imaginative cognition are at the present time endangering human evolution. The purpose of this work is to redeem these fallen electrical forces and learn to induce the world-creative Imaginations which foster the progressive evolution of human cultural life.

A student who treads this path learns to rhythmically oscillate between the Sun space, in which the consciousness is focused but empty of content, and the Venus space in which the waking consciousness begins to remember the transcendent experiences in the Sun space. This signals the onset of feelings in which this single lifetime is experientially linked to the lives of all living beings past, present, and future. This mood of cosmic memory is the mood of the first stage of meditation, Imagination.

## THIRD PHASE: MEDITATION

### FIRST STAGE: IMAGINATION
*Universal Salt*—VENUS
*Oscillation/Aggregation*
Substance is liberated through
a rhythmically sensitized medium.
First minimum—the medium
becomes sensitive.

### SECOND STAGE: INSPIRATION
*Universal Sulfur*—JUPITER
*Radiation/Substance*
Substance rays out into its
environment. Second minimum—
the medium becomes the bearer of the
imponderables released from substance.

### THIRD STAGE: INTUITION
*Universal Mercury*—MERCURY
*Potentization/Healing*
Substance and medium become one.

In the phase of potentization we can begin to perceive substance as the activity of hierarchical beings. In the resistance and capacitance phases of human consciousness, substance retains its fallen character of "matter." In the distillation stage, an extract was formed which was still composed of matter. In the capacitance phase, matter is charged to the point where it takes on field properties; this is much closer to spiritualization. However, even in capacitance and induction, matter stays ponderable, while the forces of its genesis remain imponderable. This is an accurate picture of contemplation. In the potentization phase, the forces binding matter are systematically released. As they are released, spiritual "substance" from the hierarchies is simultaneously cognized. In the old literature, this process of moving the ponderable into the imponderable produced grace as a tincture in the soul. The purpose of potentization or dynamization is to rhythmically merge the ponderable and the imponderable, to spiritualize substance. Thus the analogy for the meditative phase of Venus, Jupiter, and Mercury shifts from electrostatics to homeopathy.

In homeopathic practice, the rhythmical shaking or *succussion* of a medium such as alcohol or water makes it possible to transfer patterns of energy from the substance to the medium. There are three distinct stages at which the medium undergoes a transformation, each characterized by a minimum dilution number representing the number of dilution cycles needed to effect the greatest transformation between the medium and the substance. A substance like salt, for instance, is put into ten parts water and rhythmically succussed forty times. This is considered to be a 1X dilution. One part of this dilution is then retained in the shaking vessel. Nine parts diluent are added and shaken again forty times. This is a 2X dilution, or 2D. In many cases, the substance reaches a maximum potency at 6X, and then sharply declines in its effectiveness. This would make 6X a dilution at the first minimum.

However, if the diluting and succussing is continued, a second, higher minimum is usually reached at about 30X. If this diluting and succussing is continued, a long, gradual build-up to a maximum is often possible. As a result, there are considered to be two minima and three maxima in homeopathy. The homeopathic potentization process can then provide a very usable analog for the three meditative stages in the third phase of the work.

In homeopathy the three universals of Salt, Sulfur, and Mercury are released from any substance through step-wise dilution and rhythmical movements. These universal processes are the seed forces in Imagination, Inspiration, and Intuition. In these meditative states, however, each stage of consciousness contains all three universals to greater or lesser degrees. For this reason, even though the ponderables and imponderables can be differentiated in Imagination, they lose their substantiality in the sulfur forces of induction. That is, in the Venus stage of contemplation an oscillation is initiated in the soul which begins to move rhythmically into and out of the spiritual world. In electrical terms, the field around the condenser causes the resistance in the coil to be expanded. This expanding or dissolving of resistance is either a salt substantia or a sulfur process.

In a sulfur process the ponderables and imponderables separate completely. In a sulfur substantia the ponderables and the imponderables remain mingled. In the salt process the ponderable falls out of the imponderable. In the salt substantia the ponderable moves into the imponderable. Mercury keeps the salt and the sulfur in constant interaction. For this reason in the planetary signatures of the potentization phase, Imagination (Venus) has an alchemical salt process due to the formation of an image in the meditant. This image formation is an aggregate or precipitate of the spiritual experience arising in the soul as the meditant oscillates between the spiritual world and the physical world. Imagination also has a sulfur process in that the higher consciousness in which the image originates separates from the salt-like ash image as the meditator cognizes the image in the waking state. Through the continued oscillations of meditative practice, a yearning is produced in the soul to become one with that which is gradually perceived as the source of the imagery. This yearning dissolves the resistances in the salt and sulfur processes so that the beings who are active in the formation of earthly substance begin to reveal themselves as spiritual realities. This Jupiter stage is the stage of Inspiration.

There are three distinct stages of the homeopathic potentization process. In the first stage, there is the character of the polarity between the imponderable medium and the ponderable substance. This stage of the work requires that the medium or diluent be rhythmically agitated so that the salt of the substance is transferred to the medium. In this salt substantia, the initial substance is loosened from its physical form and its pattern of forces impressed into the medium. This process does not reach a completion in the salt phase, because at a certain dilution, the initial substance loses its aggregate form and is expanded or radiated out into the medium.

The forces which were holding the substance together as matter are now spiritualized as a force of radiation. Salt moves to sulfur through mercury. In this, a reversal has taken place. The human consciousness in the role of the medium has both the character of salt and of sulfur. Psychically, this means that the medium can be both matter and spirit. In this way, it is truly mercurial.

In the resistance/concentration phase of the work, the consciousness was distilled into an extract. The mind in this state is the medium of potentization. In the capacitance/oscillation phase of contemplation, the consciousness was transformed into an inductive field. This, too, is the mercurial nature of the mind as the medium. The inductive capacities of the field can support both the ponderables (lines of force or patterns in the field) and the imponderables (the forces themselves).

In the Venus (salt) stage of potentization, the contemplative has begun the process of placing purified images into an oscillating rhythm within the dynamic field of a concentrated mind. This effort begins to loosen the sense-directed aggregates or patterns of knowing from the images. We must cease to know a tree as a physical thing if it is to reveal to us the activity of the beings which stand behind its creative process. Through repeated succussions, the ponderable aspects of the image are slowly, rhythmically, loosened. As this happens, the imponderable aspects of its thingness begin to ray out as insights and creative experiences into the rhythmically moving field of the succussed consciousness. The ponderable is slowly transformed into the imponderable, and matter is becoming spiritualized.

During the Jupiter (sulfur) stage of the potentization phase, the ponderable is induced more and more to reveal to the medium its true nature as a spiritual activity that has come to rest. Images cease to be precipitated as a salt body (Imagination). Instead, the archetypal creative *movements* sublimate the medium as the liberated ponderable elements are induced to radiate in an inspirative way into the medium of the consciousness of the meditant (Mercury).

In the third stage (Mercury) the homeopathically potentized medium of consciousness becomes configured by the patterns which have been liberated from the ponderable into the imponderable. At this stage, the consciousness is transformed into the beings which in the Jupiter stage were raying out their Inspirations and creative sounding activities. Substance and medium both become imponderable.

The consciousness has thus gone through a third stage in which the medium is completely transformed by becoming the field of activity wherein the archetypes which stand behind matter reveal themselves. The human consciousness becomes one with both Universal Salt and Universal Sulfur; the ponderable and the imponderable become one in the alchemical marriage. This phase is known esoterically as Intuition. Alchemically, the consciousness of Intuition is a complete potentization of the latent qualities inherent in the consciousness which links percept to concept in an act of cognition.

In review, then, we can recognize seven alchemical processes which occur in three phases of inner work. The seven processes and their accompanying planetary signatures begin with: Saturn-Combustion; Moon-Solution; and Mars-Distillation, constituting the resistance or concentration phase of inner work.

The phase of contemplation follows, again including Mars. Mars as a distilled extractum, or as the electrical quality of resistance, was a summary of the previous phase. Then in the capacitance/oscillation stage of contemplation, the Mars resistance character becomes the basis for the electrical analogy of a condenser or oscillating capacitance circuit, for Mars is the resistance of the dielectric, the insulative property of the capacitor. Sun is the capacitor itself and its ability to store energy in a field which is outside its own physical limits. At this stage of contemplation the mantrams or visualizations are moved through the consciousness of the contemplative, independent of their connection to the physical body or to sense-perceptible contents. When placed near a dielectric this field can cause the dielectric to induce an electrical charge and build its own electric field. This is a representation of the capacity of a mind in contemplation which begins to induce beings living in the spiritual world. These resonant relationships are the purpose of contemplative disciplines. The Venus stage (induction) of this contemplative phase represents the arising of the harmonies within the expanded field of consciousness of the contemplative.

In the meditation phase, the Venus stage which is a summation of the capacitance/oscillation qualities of the contemplative phase serves as the beginning of a new development. The oscillation necessary for induction serves as a key to the alchemical processes of meditation. We have so far moved from chemistry to electricity in our search for analogs. In the meditative phase with the Venus quality of oscillation, the realm of rhythmic motion is opened. The rhythmic motions of the alchemical process of potentization serve as the analog for the meditative phase of consciousness. In potentization, the polarities of salt (ponderable), sulfur (imponderable), and mercury (the transformative medium) are the basis of the meditative work. Salt represents the stage of Imagination at which the oscillatory movements of the contemplative consciousness begin to induce images from the spiritual world. In homeopathy, the equivalent stage is the dilution of substances by rhythmically sensitizing a medium so that it begins to loosen substance from its aggregate forms. The sensitive medium begins to accept or induce the energetic patterns of

## THE SECOND PHASE: CONTEMPLATION

*Capacitance*
SUN

*Resistance*
*Extractum*
*Distillation*
MARS

*Induction*
*Oscillation*
*Imagination*
VENUS

## THE FIRST PHASE: CONCENTRATION

## THE THIRD PHASE: MEDITATION

*Reflection*
*Solution*
MOON

*Radiation*
*Inspiration*
JUPITER

*Combustion*
SATURN

*Potentization*
*Intuition*
MERCURY

the substance. The substance (ponderable) and its energetic patterns (imponderable) are loosened from each other by rhythmic oscillation of the medium. The inducing of patterns of energy into a sensitive medium is an analog of the stage of Imagination in the phase of meditation. Homeopathically in the second stage of potentization, the ponderable substance loses its aggregate form and begins to ray out into the medium. This is an analog of the stage of Inspiration in meditation. Patterns of energy inherent in the ponderable shift into the imponderable and begin to configure the medium, the rhythmically moving (regularly practicing) meditative consciousness.

In Mercury, the third stage of the meditative phase, the raying-out forces of the ponderable which have been transformed into an imponderable condition in the second stage once again turn toward the ponderable by configuring the medium (consciousness) with their dynamic radiations. The medium and both the ponderable and imponderable become one. In homeopathy, this complete, dynamic union happens in the highest dilution. Here, process and product become one in the great alchemical marriage of the healing mercury.

# 13

## PREPARATION FOR MEDITATION

After an introduction to the alchemical tree, we can now look more closely at the various stages of the work in which the soul is gradually transformed so that it becomes capable of ever finer and more subtle perceptions. The worldview of the alchemists put the four elements of earth, water, air, and fire into a mixed state in plants and minerals. In the mixed state it is impossible to extract essences because the finer qualities often are arranged chemically in such a way that they neutralize each other. The alchemist therefore sought to first separate the various elemental properties and to purify them separately to the highest degree of purity before combining them again into a higher *spagyric* or alchemical marriage. As a result, the division (*solve*) and reintegration (*coagula*) of the purified parts were often separated by long, repetitive periods of laborious purification. During these purifications, any number of things could go wrong, and usually did, until insight was gained into the subtle requirements of heat, moisture, dryness, and so forth, which would permit purification without damaging the inherent pattern of wholeness in the substance undergoing transformation.

The purification/concentration process is based upon the patterns inherent in the four elements. Warmth and air move upwards and are imponderable, while water and earth move downward and are ponderable. In chemistry, Joseph Priestly and others have shown that air is ponderable, and attempts have been made to prove that even warmth is ponderable (the phlogiston theory), but while the weighing of air is a provable fact of modern chemistry, to an alchemist it misses the point. Air as a substance is simply the shadow of an archetypal, imponderable being. Searching for the being behind the element air is the true goal of alchemical laboratory work. This work is a schooling of the perception in such a way that by meditating upon the concepts learned in the laboratory the life of the soul can gradually be penetrated in more and more subtle ways, becoming permeable to the spirit. The alchemist sees analogous relationships between soul states and natural phenomena. The three stages of the work—concentration, contemplation, and meditation—can all be illuminated by studying the relationships among the three universal qualities of Salt, Sulfur, and Mercury and the four elements of earth, water, fire, and air.

In the natural world, systems at rest show the following pattern between the universals and the elements:

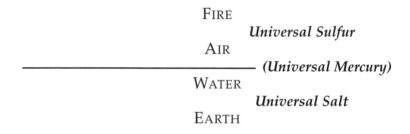

This diagram depicts a state such as is found in the atmosphere at night. The warm air is above the surface of the water which is resting on the earth. This system is stable in that the ponderable elements remain below and the volatile or imponderable elements are above, with a membrane between water and air. Ultimately, however, it is a picture of sclerosis and death in that there is no movement.

The key imaginative process in alchemical thinking is that the motion within the system becomes of paramount interest. By harmonizing inner soul states with the patterns of movements in natural systems, the maximum lawful transformation of both inner and outer systems becomes possible. The movements of the transformation are the goal of the experimental protocol because in order to transform, the soul needs to identify and emulate the lawful movements within the natural system. Of course, the possibilities for error in such work are limitless. However, in spite of such illusions and delusions as becoming rich by manufacturing gold, the alchemical system of thinking presents singular and profound opportunities for self-development through transformation in harmony with nature.

We can see in the first diagram of the elements and universals that Universal Mercury is absent from the pattern. It is in parentheses because it is in a condition known as *en statu nascendi*, in a nascent state, for it is there only in potential.  In order to make it manifest the fire needs to be put below the earth, as in the next diagram:

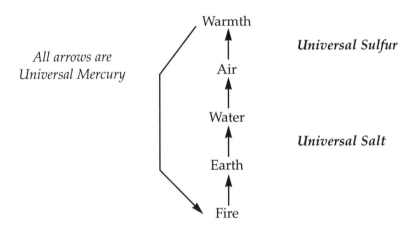

Here, the fire drives upward causing the earth to move toward the imponderable state.  This is the situation in the atmosphere during the day when the sun warms the earth and the water rises to form clouds up in the air.  In chemistry, if we take a portion of garden soil and place it in warm water for a day in order to create a solution, crystals of potassium and sea salt will form out of the solution when it is evaporated.  This is the salt substantia, where the inner nature of the earth is liberated into water through the activity of warmth.  In the inner life, this process of drawing out a salt into water by placing warmth below it is the image of solution—part of the phase of concentration in spiritual science.

In the Great Tree, the first phase of concentration was presented as three sequential stages: Saturn, Moon, and Mars.  In terms of the four elements, Saturn is the process of placing the warmth below the earth. Moon, the second stage, is the process of solution accomplished by placing the burnt earth into warm water where the salt leaves the ash and goes into the water as a solution.  Upon evaporation, the salt falls out of this solution, image-like.  The third stage, Mars, represents the work to purify the salt, an alchemical process known as *dealbation*, *whitening,* or *calcination.* Calcination (from *calx,* or chalk), is the repeated incineration or burning of a plant or mineral in such a way that its salt gradually becomes as white as chalk.

We can now take this sequence of chemical/alchemical processes and apply them to the practice of meditation and the cultivation of the inner life. The ponderable elements of earth and water are pictures of the lower capacities of thought. Earth thinking is sequential logic in which one step must follow another. This form of thinking rests on facts gleaned through thoughtful comparison of cause and effect in relationships found on the physical plane. The thought forms produced are predictable and logical like the axes, cleavage planes, and facets of crystallography. Earth thinking, or logic, is the basis from which all other forms of thinking arise. It is the ground, the root, and the source of all other levels of human consciousness. Without it, there can be no transformation. The very practice of logic is a type of purification of the thinking.

In alchemy, the first process of putting a fire under the earth was always instigated in order to dis-assemble or disintegrate the original substance so that the form or process could be transformed. The substantia and the process are united within the object, but they are not identical. The substantia is a state complementary to the process and comes into being by means of the process. The process sought by the alchemist is an energetic pattern which can be repeatedly developed in order to work on the substantia and move it closer to its ideal form or *star body,* the *iliaster.* This star body was, for Paracelsus, the originator of the lawful movement by which substances arrange themselves into lattices of molecules. In the language of Anthroposophy, the star body is referred to as the etheric body, or the body of etheric forces.

The forms of the etheric body come from the angles and relationships of the planets moving before the fixed stars. The fixed stars are the source of the etheric forces. These astral patterns are the form principles into which the etheric body becomes integrated. The movements of the planets themselves give rise to the etheric formative forces. These are the astrally influenced forces of life, the astral body, or soul. Though broader than the definitions given in Rudolf Steiner's *Theosophy,* these general classifications of the forces involved are workable in an alchemical system.

In a clump of earth, the star forces are adulterated by many other compounds, the *dross* or *corpus* of the alchemist, which prevent the compound from crystallizing. In a crystal, on the other hand, the chemicals and minerals are so purified that they are open to the subtle form forces of the cosmos. As a result, pure solutions form crystals whose bodies are filled with the patterns and forces of the stars. In nature, the earth is purified for the forming of crystals by repeated heating, solution in warm water, filtration through settling of the dross, and re-crystallization of a purer form higher up in the molten mass.

In the human soul, the *content* of a logical thought sequence is the alchemical dross. By contrast, the *activity* needed to think the logical thought sequence is the fire principle. When our will-fire is put under the content of the thoughts and they are put into the boiling flask of the skull, the warmed thoughts begin to move more freely, and the thinking enters the alchemical state of water. It may seem strange that linear logical sequences must be thought in a fluid consciousness, but if all we had were earth consciousness, we would be able to compare one thing with another in endless lists of bits of data, but no sequence would be experienced. In order for us to sequence data, we must put the earth in water and put a fire (will) under it. When we try repeatedly to boil the data in many different ways, this is also fluid thinking. Out of this arises an insight as to which sequence is most correct. The insight falls out of the stream of thoughts in the same way that a salt crystal falls out of a solution.

To form a salt crystal, the proper sequence of substantia and process is necessary. First, we put fire below the earth, or will into the thinking, that is, we only think what we *will* to think. In many traditions, this involves geometric visualizations such as yantras, complex geometric imaginations such as the platonic forms, musical themes, or story lines of poems—in short, anything which requires will to bring the mind to focus on one point. The will warms the consciousness and frees the mind to begin to experience many aspects of the same problem without becoming bored. When we mentally lapse into associative habitual thinking, or if we make an error in our visualization, a higher, more fluid mode is required to reposition the attention or correct the error in logic. This is the placing of the thought (earth) into the water level of the consciousness so that out of the flow a solution can arise in which the crystallizing thought can constellate with the correct sequence or image. The crystallized thought must be dissolved in order for it to recrystallize in the proper form. This warming of thought structures in order to volatize habitual thought into mobile thinking is what Rudolf Steiner calls *morphological thinking*.

In order to carry the analogies between alchemy and meditation further, it may perhaps be useful to give a survey of the alchemical, or *spagyric,* processes commonly used to make a plant or mineral essence. Plants represent the *lower arcanum* in alchemy and concentration represents the lower arcanum in meditation. The following spagyric processes will refer specifically to plant materials unless otherwise noted.

In a spagyric operation it is necessary to take a plant apart (solve). It must then be purified, or whitened, each part separately, and when all parts are pure, they must be reintroduced in such a way that they come together in a higher form. In addition to the residue of earth, a plant's physical body contains salts in its saps, which are used to regulate and harmonize the plant's life forces. There are two forms of alchemical salts: fixed salts which are bound to the earth residue, and volatile salts which can relate to the warmth pole. These volatile salts are the focus of intense labor on the part of the alchemist.

Since volatile salts are related to the fire element, they can be taken up by alcohol and married to the essential oils of the plant in the alchemical marriage. The volatile salts, then, are the first plant parts to be purified. The other two parts which are separated and purified are the alcohol (the plant mercury) and the essential oils (the plant sulfur). The mercury is purified by repetitive distillations and the sulfur is extracted in a steam distillation process. The essential oils come through the still in a pure state. They are easily separated from the water or *phlegm* of the plant through the process of steam distillation. The alcohol comes from the still mixed with phlegm or *evil-water* which weakens its pure fire forces. It must be distilled repeatedly in order to become strong and mercurial. The three essential parts: salt, mercury, sulfur—or volatile salts, alcohol, and essential oils—must be purified separately, then united into a true spagyric essence.

These alchemical processes are analogs to the many indications given by Rudolf Steiner in his books and lectures on the art and science of meditation. The purification of salt, mercury, and sulfur are mentioned in his references to the separation of thinking, feeling, and willing in his book *How to Know Higher Worlds*. This splitting of the soul forces is the initial *solve* necessary for the spagyric marriage (*coagula*) in the soul/spiritual later on. The first part to be purified is the salt, or the thinking pole. A useful analog for the purification of thinking is found in the technical process used to form volatile salts. When a plant is burnt over an open fire, the volatile parts such as the essential oils escape into the air as light and warmth. The water then leaves the plant as vapor, and finally the plant gives up its organic acids and volatile salts. We experience these last elements in the acrid, stinging smoke that burns our eyes when we sit around a campfire. The alchemists, realizing that the salts they were seeking to crystallize were escaping with the acids as they rose in the smoke, would often burn their plants in closed vessels such as clay balls or iron skillets with lids. In this way, the organic acids which help to form crystals of volatile salts are forced back into the ash.

In the life of the soul, the earth element is the habitual thoughts or fixed ideas which, through instinct, determine most of social interaction. The origins of these fixed thoughts are volatile, fluid, mobile thoughts. The mobile creative thoughts need to be liberated from the prison of their fixations. Through exercises in concentration such as the pin exercise given by Rudolf Steiner, or geometric visualizations, the will forces warm the fixed earth element in the thinking into a condition of combustion. Focusing the fire of the will upon the fixed idea patterns causes them to smolder and fume. In the flickering, smoldering light and smoke the shadow contents in our habitual thoughts begin to glow, ignite, and flare into the awakened consciousness of our daytime state. If these shadow contents simply ignite, then our passions will release the psychic energies in fits of rage or sensuality. The potentially creative forces of volatile, mobile thoughts are dissipated. If instead we "put a lid on" our passions by observing or witnessing the smoldering instincts, we can retain the forces of mobility within the ash of the thinking process.

Alchemically, ash is a seed-like substance which has no evident life of its own but can act as a catalyst to life forces. Mostly carbon, ash is a burned out remnant of what was once living. Why is something so devoid of life considered alchemically to be like a seed? There are two reasons. The first is that ash is carbon and carbon is the chemical basis for every compound which is needed for the support of life. All carbohydrates, sugars, starches, alcohols, vitamins, hormones, enzymes, and so forth, have carbon as their base. Carbon is potential life, it is a seed from which life can flourish. The second reason is that ash also contains the salt which was used by the plant to attract the water through which it lived its life. To Paracelsus salt was the life of the plant, the very agent of its being. Ash is the source of salt. The "dust" of the wood is simply the physical facts of its physical existence—so mush carbon and so much hydrogen but no longer imbued with life. Dust must be combusted (rotted or burned) in order for ash to be available for the next resurrection into life. Hidden in ash are carbon, salt, and other constituents held in patterns inherited from the life forms which produced the dust. These substances and patterns become available as the basis for the physical life of the life forms which follow.

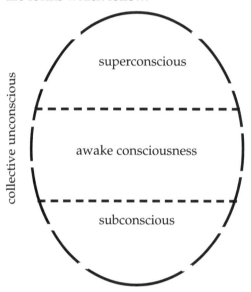

Psychologically these states of matter can be seen as analogs for spiritual development if they are put into the context of Roberto Assagioli's soul egg. Assagioli's concept of the collective unconscious was similar to that of Carl Jung in that for him the unconscious is an archetypal realm of ideas outside of the human waking consciousness. It is the source from which all creation flows. The subconscious is a realm below the awake state, composed of fragments of ideas each of which has its autonomous existence separate from the others. This is the state described alchemically as dust. The subconscious is connected to and composed of unconscious archetypes which have been fixed into dust through instinct, race memory, and habit. The awake state finds an analog to the combustion process which transforms dust into ash. The will employed by a thinker to correct the dust of habits and reactions combusts the sub-personality fragments into ash. The ash is then the seed of the next life, the higher superconscious unconscious state of the meditant. Here thoughts, the salt of thinking, are drawn out of the combusted personality through the warmth activity of the will and are made capable of flying into higher regions of the superconscious state. In the higher meditative consciousness the salt of the awake combustion process is lifted into the silent unconscious superconscious levels of the creative beings of light.  Without the combustion of the dust by the awake consciousness, the sub-personality rules the awake consciousness from below.  Through inner work the personality is combusted and the ash as a phoenix sets the stage for further inner work.  The ash can be experienced directly in exact sense perception, the practice of visualizing a growing plant from seed to flower in the mind's eye.  The visualizing of a plant pattern forward through its growth stages is an analog of the combustion process which produces the ash of the object observed.  This same exercise is also useful to lead to the second alchemical process of solution.

In solution, the ash is placed into water and steeped in order to draw out its salt.  To be more precise in the analogy, we should say that the exercise of imagining the plant's growth from seed to flower with each step following another would be like a combustion process in which the fire of the will is put under the earth, the fixed thoughts about the plant.  The reversal of this image, imagining the plant from flower to seed, is the solution stage that follows the combustive willed thinking.  This backward flow returns the consciousness to emptiness, as the ashes of the thoughts are put into the fluid meditative consciousness of mobile thinking.  Once the fluid water consciousness draws out the salt from the combusted thoughts, the air state of inner repose and silence evaporates the fluid thinking into crystal patterns of ideation, the volatile salts.

In the inner life the mental image is salt.  A mental image is connected to the fixed salt of earth in that it is a picture of a sense object.  It is also connected to the volatile salt of the realm of ideas in that it has an ideal or archetypal existence.  The mental image of a growing plant thus has a relationship both to the individual physical plant and to the ideal spiritual plant.  In the mental image, the earth and the cosmos are united.

The salt nature of the plant connects the dross earth to the living archetype of the plant.  The salt itself has both the earth quality of a fixed salt and the more cosmic quality of a volatile salt.  In alchemy, it is necessary to separate out the fixed and the volatile salts so that the purified volatile salts can, as earth, marry the more volatile natures of the plant mercury (alcohol), and plant sulfur (essential oils).

To release volatile salts in the proper way is one of the most delicate and labor-intensive undertakings in alchemy.  It is accomplished through the process of calcination, or whitening.  The salts as they go into solution from the ash are often impure and of an orange or brown color, showing that the combustion was not complete. The salts often will only form amorphous masses and not shoot into clear, ordered crystals. This happens when the heat is too high during the combustion process and the organic acids are driven off in the smoke. To remedy these defects, the salts need to be whitened through a series of purifications. There are several different techniques of purification, but they all involve a similar process. When the ash is put into solution, fixed salts with an affinity to earth, as well as volatile salts with an affinity to warmth, air, and water, both go into solution.

In the meditative life, when we do an exercise in mentally representing a plant growing and then mentally reverse the image, we are putting into the solution of the soul-spiritual world images which have earthly associations and which are also mental/thinking experiences of the archetype present behind the sense appearance of the plant. Our salt (mental image) is both fixed and volatile.

In alchemical practice, the salt solution is put into a boiling flask and the solvent (water) is boiled off. The evaporated solvent (phlegm) is then collected. After the phlegm has been removed, the salt becomes perceptibly whiter. The phlegm is then reintroduced, the salt solution filtered, and once again set to boil. Phlegm is collected a second time, and the salt is again brought to a dry state. Each cycle of boiling, drying, reintroduction of phlegm, and filtration leaves the volatile salts whiter and purer, while the earth and its fixed salts are removed and filtered. Each phase of this calcination process is known as a *cohobation*. When the volatile salt is the color of snow and forms plant-like shooting crystals, the salt is pure enough to marry the plant alcohol, or mercury. Attaining this degree of purification sometimes takes forty or fifty cohobations. Calcination is a laborious and mentally demanding discipline.

In the inner work, calcination is an analog for the purification of images. We have seen that our mental images possess both fixed and volatile properties. The fixed element of the mental image is found in sense impressions, associative thinking, fixed ideas, obsessions, and pathological fantasies. To assist the formation of volatile salts, the alchemist employs a laboratory procedure of combustion in a closed vessel in order that the ash may retain its organic acids. Effective calcination depends upon good hermetic initial combustion. In the inner work, the will activity used to combust mental images is found in the practice of exact sense perception. The reversal of the exact sense perception places the ash of the thoughts into the water forces flowing through the consciousness. Here in the fluid soul-space the salts produced in the ash of the combustion process are drawn out as meditative images into a silent soul where the mental images are systematically dissolved by thinking them backwards. The silent consciousness then appears to be emptied. What takes the place of the mental images is the archetypal motion behind the images. Esoterically the willful moving forward and backward of images is representative of the soul capacity of Imagination. The dissolving of the images into the water of the soul is representative of the capacity for Inspiration.

In the laboratory rhythmical calcination is an image of the contemplative level of inner work. In contemplation, we rhythmically place the dissolved mental image into the spiritual world. The dissolved mental image is a salt which is sulfur and mercury also, for it is mobile and volatilized. With regular practice the salt nature of thinking becomes purified, brightened, and made creative or volatile.

To complete the alchemical marriage, a ferment is made from the plant to produce a mercury (alcohol). The purified salt is placed into a long process of digestion until the alcohol, through repeated cycles of evaporation and condensation, eventually penetrates it. This was often done by combining the salt and alcohol in a Mary's Bath (double boiler) of boiling water. Through such gentle, moist heat, the volatile salt was "loosened" from its body as it expanded into the alcohol vapors in the still. The loosening of the salt "body" can be seen in the concept referred to by Dr. Steiner as the "loosening of the etheric body" as a preparation for developing a waking consciousness within the spiritual world—a realm wherein we are normally asleep. Through repeated distillations or circulations (contemplations) the loosened etheric body can absorb the volatile salts (creative ideas) which lie behind the manifest forms of nature.

Rather than pursuing the analogy further to alchemical fermentation processes for inner mercury and to steam distillation of essential oils for inner sulfur, I characterized the contemplative stage in the alchemical tree by drawing analogies to field phenomena, and the meditative stage was characterized by analogs to the work in homeopathy. For the development of concentration, however, classical plant alchemical practices are very illustrative. Performing calcinations and extracting salt from plants is a wonderful way to develop insight into the problems of consciousness training for the early stages of the inner work and can also be very quickening for the inner work itself.

# 14

## CONTEMPLATION

The nature of spiritual work is always paradoxical, and the highest truths can best be understood through the contemplation of paradoxes. This truth is present in Rudolf Steiner's descriptions of the goals of the meditative life. In some sources, he clearly states that the esoteric student needs to learn to live consciously *outside* the body. In other sources, most notably in the protection exercises given as a supplement to the six basic exercises and in the main exercise given in *Guidance in Esoteric Training*, Rudolf Steiner describes the perception and cultivation of currents *within* the body of the student. Inner conflicts can arise when a student decides that one or the other source shows the only true direction. A prudent path would be to accept these two sets of directions as poles of a paradox and to work within the polarities to lift them to higher levels of integration.

The purpose of this chapter is to shed light upon these indications of outer and inner currents in the body and to integrate the apparently conflicting statements by comparing Dr. Steiner's comments on the physiological effects of the meditative practice with analogs from natural science, specifically concepts and images connected to the function of capacitors in electronic circuits and antennae. Dr. Steiner himself used such analogies, most notably in the lectures to a philosophical society in Bologna in 1911, in which he compares the function of a coil in a transformer to conditions within human beings in various meditative states. Electronics provides an alchemical analogy which is accessible to modern readers and which goes beyond the physical chemistry models present in classical alchemical studies. The analogy to the electrical phenomena of capacitance is drawn primarily so that a description of field phenomena can be applied to the meditative practice of contemplation, as was sketched out in the chapter on the alchemical tree. It should go without saying that the purpose of these analogies is not to equate a human being with a machine or electrical apparatus.

As a starting point, the many references made by Rudolf Steiner to the fact that the esoteric student needs to learn to live outside the body can be summarized by a passage from Steiner's *Occult Physiology* in which he compares the blood to a tablet which is inscribed on either side by a different set of nerves. On one side the sympathetic system inscribes on the blood the impulses coming from within the inner organs. On the other side the brain inscribes into the blood the impulses it has received from the senses through the central nervous system. This nerve/blood relationship is the carrier of the impulses of the ego in the human being, and it operates primarily in waking consciousness. By means of this relationship between the blood and the nerves, we human beings gain information through the senses, which allows us to orient ourselves in the outside world.

According to Rudolf Steiner, in normal sense-perception the nerve impulses impress themselves on the blood. In concentration, however, the researcher can withdraw the thinking process from the sense impressions streaming in from outside and can live as a consciousness in the nerves of the body alone. Dr. Steiner calls this type of thinking *sense-free thinking*. By isolating the thinking process in the nerves, the thinker does not allow the blood to receive images in the usual way, and images can be experienced which have their origin not in the organs of the body but in the spiritual world. When this happens the sense-free thinking enters the realm of Imagination and contacts the fields of activity working creatively there. This realm of activity was described by Goethe as the realm of the archetypes, and the Greek thinkers called it the *entelechy*.

Recent work in this direction has been done by Rupert Sheldrake in his research into the *morphogenetic field hypothesis*. Sheldrake's work was preceded by the research of Weiss, Burr, and others in the 1930s and 1940s who made electrostatic maps of the low-voltage fields surrounding the bodies of living organisms. Sheldrake believes that the organism receives its ordering information from the fields of energy surrounding it. According to the morphogenetic field hypothesis, these energy fields are ordered and meaningful and are accessible to the organism throughout its life.

In sense-free thinking we learn to live first in the nerves, and when we cease to cognize impressions from outside the body in the sense world, the nerves build a field which induces meaningful pat-

terns from the life field around it.  Dr. Steiner explains this in the following way:

> In the case of the normal consciousness, man feels that he
> takes into himself whatever sort of world happens to face
> him, so that everything is inscribed upon the blood system as
> on a tablet, and  he then lives in his ego with these impres-
> sions.  In the other case [concentration], however, he goes with
> these impressions only to that point where the terminations of
> the nerves offer him an inner *resistance* [italics mine].  Here, at
> the nerve terminals, he rebounds as it were, and experiences
> himself in the outside world. (Steiner, *Occult Physiology*, 46–7)

Steiner goes on to say that the resistance which causes the rebounding
allows us to live in our consciousness only as far inward as the eye
and optic nerve, before eventually going back out of the eye into the
light which is stimulating it.  As a result, we learn to live in the light
outside of and surrounding the body.  Normally when we are present
outside the physical body, the consciousness is in a dream or sleep
state.  During concentration, we remain awake in a place where we
are normally dreaming—in the light surrounding our bodies.  These
concepts have a very clear analog in electronics, in the principle of the
capacitor.  The link to the capacitor is in Dr. Steiner's use of the term
*resistance.*

The material from which a capacitor is made has a great resistance
to the flow of electricity.  Silica is one such substance.  If a current of
electricity is passed over a sheet of glass, the silica resists the flow of
the current.  Because of this property, silica is known as a *dielectric*
material.  A conductor such as iron or copper that allows the current
to flow is said to be *paraelectric*.  In the early days of electrical research,
before the electron theory was developed, researchers referred to
these two properties of resistance and conduction in alchemical terms.
Any substance that resisted electricity was known as *salt* or *glass.*  By
contrast, any conductor was known as *sulfur* or *resin.*  The two types
of electricity were called glass and resin before the terms *negative* and
*positive* were used.  Capacitors are made of substances with the properties of glass.  Glass resists the current, and since there can be no discharge through conduction, the current seeks to collect on the inner
surfaces of the glass and a charge builds there until no more charge
can be held.

Nerves are the representative organ of the silica forces in human physiology. The nerves, the skin, and the sense organs are all associated with an organ-building principle in which fine layers of silica are laid down, one atop the other. The silica layers build up charges on their surfaces, and weak biological voltages can build up in potential. In an electrical circuit such an arrangement of layers of silica would protect the delicate circuitry by regulating fluctuations in the power of currents.

In Dr. Steiner's model the nerve terminals which are formed of layers of silica provide a resistance to the flow of impulses into the blood. The resistance moves the forces of consciousness out to the periphery of the nerves and to the periphery of the body (the eyes or the other senses), and eventually the charge, the potential or capacitance, moves outside the body entirely. In other words, the potential charge is raised in power until the capacity of the dielectric creates a field around the body. In the electric model, the field around a capacitor is an electric field. In the consciousness model, the field around the isolated nerves is a field of awareness. These two are similar in their patterns but are not interchangeable. The field of awareness has the capacity to carry the waking consciousness independently of the brain and the physiology. In the language of esotericism, the term "capacities" refers to the ability of a researcher to sustain a waking consciousness in the dream state. In *How to Know Higher Worlds,* Dr. Steiner uses the phrase "continuity of consciousness." This path, with its focus on the development of sense-free thinking, is intended to develop the capacity to enter the field of imaginations surrounding the human being, making the supersensible world perceptible in a real way. The human being who develops these capacities enters into living relationships with spiritual beings.

In electronics, capacitance is usually linked with another phenomenon in order for far greater fields of energies to arise. By means of capacitance, circuits are ordered and fields are generated. The electrical forces in these fields exist outside the physical limits of the circuit and can cause induction, when no mechanical cause-and-effect relationship is present. When a capacitor is put in a particular relationship to a coil, its field allows for a greater range of power in transmission and reception in an antenna. This relationship is the basis for wireless transmitters, receivers, and the oscillating capacitance antenna which is used on boats and automobiles.

In the language of electronics, the electric field of the capacitor (dielectric) is absorbed by the windings of a coil (conductor). The conductor absorbs the electric field and just starts to move it through itself. This minute movement of electricity through the wire creates a magnetic field around the coil. The coil induces the electrical charge and responds with a magnetic field in motion. As the magnetic field expands, it carries with it electric properties which are resisted by the capacitor. The resistance recharges the capacitor. In this way, alternating electric and magnetic fields oscillate rhythmically. The overall effect of this is an amplification of power. If an antenna is attached to such an oscillating capacitance circuit, the antenna can induce signals from a far greater distance. Space is concentrated and compressed by the oscillating circuit. Transmitters ray out into space and receivers pull in signals from far away as a result of the oscillation between resistance and conduction, capacitance and induction.

In his descriptions of the effects of inner development, Rudolf Steiner has given a number of very precise descriptions of just such an oscillation. In *Spiritual Research: Methods and Results*, he explains the steps to be taken after the development of sense-free thinking (capacitance) as follows:

> We perceive something further: that what we receive from the ordinary sense world through our perception is really only a part of what enters into us from the sense world. The life which enters into us every time we open our eyes is immeasurably richer than can be worked over by us with our ordinary physical bodily nature. Perhaps I may put it this way:— along with our sense perceptions, bounteous life flows into us which is related to a very much greater period of time than is the normal life of the human being. . . . *(Spiritual Research, 102)*

In *World of the Senses and World of the Spirit*, Dr. Steiner characterizes this experience as a perception of the Ruling Will of the Universe. In order to experience this perception, the will of the researcher needs to be in a pure state unrelated to the usually self-oriented nature of the will impulses in normal life situations. Whereas sense-free thinking is really a purification of the thinking life, the states of the soul forces referred to in the preceding quote are experienced on the path towards the purification and transformation of the will—and ultimately the feelings. A further quote may shed light on this contrast.

When pure thinking has been grasped . . . one can strive for something else.  This thinking [sense-free thinking], left in the power of an ego that now feels itself to be liberated within free spirituality can then be excluded from the process of perception.  Whereas in ordinary life one sees color . . . and at the same time imbues the color with conceptual activity, one can now extract the concepts from the entire process of elaborating percepts and draw the percept itself directly into one's bodily constitution. (Steiner, *Boundaries*, 100)

This statement unequivocally points to a further soul development growing out of sense-free thinking.  It may be that a key can be found here to unlock the paradox described at the beginning of this chapter, the polarity between learning to live outside the body and the cultivation of inner currents.  Within the same context as the last quotation, Dr. Steiner alludes to this polarity as follows:

The whole man experiences something in the act of sense perception.  Sense perception, together with its content, passes down into the organism and the ego with its pure thought content remains, so to speak, hovering above.  We exclude thinking inasmuch as we take into and fill ourselves with the whole content of the perception, instead of weakening it with concepts, as we usually do.  We train ourselves specially to achieve this by *systematically* [italics mine] pursuing what came to be practiced in a decadent form by the men of the East.  Instead of grasping the content of the perception in pure, strictly logical thought, we grasp it symbolically, in pictures, allowing it to stream into us. . . . If one desires to do real research concerning human physiology, thinking must be excluded and the picture-forming activity sent inward, so that the physical organism reacts by creating Imaginations.  This is a path that is only just beginning in the development of Western culture. . . . (Steiner, *Boundaries*, 100–101)

Dr. Ehrenfried Pfeiffer *(Notes and Lectures,* 90) gives a picture of the two spinal cords in the body: the physical one of the central nervous system, and the etheric one of the sympathetic nervous system, connected to the lotus flowers of the chakras, the organs of spiritual perception.  The chakras receive a spiritual stimulus and send rays out into the etheric body and stimulate the physical organs via the ganglia of the sympathetic nervous system which are intimately connected to the network of the endocrine glands.  When through correct training the system of chakras becomes able to send out fields to envelop the physical organs of the body, we become conscious of the spiritual world.  It is the particular task of the archangel Michael to help us to link the spiritual world with the physical body.  Dr. Pfeiffer speaks in other places about how the development of the chakras as organs for cognition of the spiritual world is a specific task of modern times.  The reason for this is that the Hierarchies wish to replace materialism with imaginative cognition.

So, here again is an apparent paradox:  in sense-free thinking we must learn to be conscious entirely out of the body, and then we are to enter the body again, passing down into the chakras so that they can spiritualize the physical.  Dr. Pfeiffer's descriptions of the raying out of the chakras seems to be an accurate picture of a field phenomenon.  If we can recall the image of the oscillating capacitance antenna, we may, perhaps, be able to form a symbolic analog to this seeming paradox.

We can recall that the dielectric with its electrical field is placed in juxtaposition to the coil or conductor.  Can we perhaps see the central nervous system as an analog to the dielectric capacitor raying out a field of electrostatic potential?  Could we then imagine the coil, or conductor, to be analogous to the ganglia of the sympathetic nervous system, with the glands inducing this electrostatic field and creating a parallel etheric field of life forces in response?

The central nervous system carries the sense impressions from the outside world, and these impressions are distributed throughout the body.  The sympathetic nervous system is in close contact with the glands and organs of the body.  Perceptions coming into this system originate in the realm of Ideas which stand behind the organs and their formative principles in the entelechy.  In the blood, where the ego lives, these two streams of impressions meet and are cognized.  It is here that the true level of cognition is determined, since the Ego, the I Am, is the site in the soul/spiritual where cognition arises.  We could ask the question:  What is the primary or archetypal form which the blood describes as it moves through the body?  The following image can offer us a starting-point for the formation of an accurate symbol of the integrating function of the ego.

If we regard the circulation of blood within the human body as a totality, the image which arises is that of a vortex ring. If we create a vortex in a container of water, the fluid spinning around the center of the vortex moves in a spiral toward the center, but the water which disappears down the throat of an actively spinning vortex does not go to the bottom of the container. There is a null spot where the throat of the vortex stops as the pressure from the bottom appears to resist the intrusion of the throat. Dye put into the throat of an actively spinning vortex in a container only descends as far as the opening of the throat. If, however, the dye stuff is slightly heavier than water, it will sink to the bottom and gather in a mound. In essence, then, we can regard a vortex in a container as actually two vortices—one above, and one below. The upper vortex has the opening of its throat open to what is above. The lower vortex has its throat open to what is below. All of the water in the container moves in concentric bands around the throat. Materials or dyes put into the water tend to stay within the force lines of the rings. However, these materials will as a unified mass pulse slowly up and down the vertical axis of the throat, even as they continue to spiral around the throat itself. This pulsing movement gradually works any materials placed into the vortex down toward the original termination of the throat. Regarding the movement of a contained vortex, we can say then that there is not just one general circulation but rather a series of interrelated pulsations and divisions within what appears to be a uniform circulation.

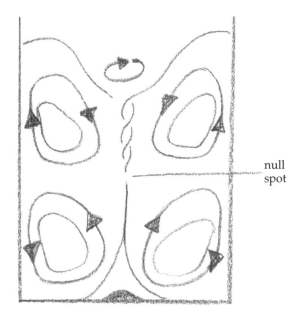

null
spot

This image of the double vortex with its interrelated pulsations is echoed in the form and movement of the heart and bloodstream within the human body. The movement is upward and outward in the upper arterial blood flow, and downward and outward in the lower arterial circulation. The return movement is downward and inward in the upper, venous circulation, and upward and inward in the lower. From this, we can see that the archetypal movement of the blood is from center to periphery and back, simultaneously upward and downward, with a division or exchange in the center. This is also an accurate image of the flow of energies in the earth's geomagnetic field, where a *Bloch wall* at the equator divides the magnetic field into upper and lower vortices. The same is true for the circulation patterns of the world winds and for the currents in the oceans and beneath the earth's crust.

Rudolf Steiner has described a soul configuration in which the pure thinking of the ego hovers above and the pure sense perception passes down into the organism. It is possible then that these descriptions represent two movements of the ego within one vortexial system. In this representation, the actual vortex throat and its concentric ring organization constitute the upper ego vortex of pure thinking. The gradual descent of the "dye" of the pure sense impressions slowly works its way down to the lower sympathetic vortex of the chakras. The two vortices meet in the heart of the etheric body, as the pulsations from the ideal world and the cognized sense impressions from the world of Ruling Will surge through the sensing heart organization. Using such a fundamental phenomenon of nature as an analog for the inner development of soul capacities is an alchemical approach to the problem of esoteric schooling and seeks to address the further development of anthroposophical meditative practices which are directed toward the establishment of a new Michael culture. The road to this goal is through imagination which has been made exact. It is hoped that these contributions are seen as a modest beginning for the destiny of Anthroposophy in America, which has as its task the transformation of materialistic thinking into imaginative cognition.

# 15

# THE NEW YOGA

In the lecture series *The Archangel Michael: His Mission and Ours*, Rudolf Steiner introduces a new yoga of the senses based upon will forces that have been penetrated by the activity of human-induced living thinking. Dr. Steiner contrasts this new yoga-will with the ancient yoga-will by saying that the ancient adepts were searching for their spiritual life forces in the element of air and sought to concentrate the soul element *(prana)* of the air in themselves through rigorously controlled breathing exercises. In the present time, however, the soul element is not found in the air, but in the light, and if a new yoga based upon Christian mysticism is to develop, our task, our training for healing the soul, will be to create inner organs which can breathe light. The organs referred to are not the eyes or lungs, but the subtle organs of the soul, the chakras.

What is the nature of these organs and where are they? The main ganglia of the sympathetic nervous system are located in the approximate positions of those areas known to ancient adepts as the chakras. To this extent there is a physical nervous organ forming the basis of each chakra. But the physical organ is present in all human beings while not all human beings have fully functioning chakras. In order for the chakras to be developed, a systematic training is necessary. This training is the purpose of yoga. However, if the Christian esotericist wishes to breathe light into the chakras, then physical breathing exercises performed in order to take prana from the air are not particularly effective.

Breathing light into the chakras is the basis of Christian esotericism. In order to breathe light, we must school ourselves to maintain an intact waking consciousness outside the physical body, in a place where we are normally asleep. The rudiments of this schooling are in the six basic exercises given by Rudolf Steiner in the fifth chapter of *How to Know Higher Worlds*. This path is not undertaken without danger.  Accompanying the six basic exercises, therefore, are protection exercises given to establish a safe practice for esoteric students.  As an introduction to the schooling of the imaginative consciousness, we will review the six exercises and pay particular attention to the protective exercises because they form a doorway into understanding the development of the chakras.

We have actually already encountered the first basic exercise in the first stage of the alchemical tree when we observed the pin or button.  By daily holding thoughts about the object, or preferably, for the training in breathing light, by representing the exact image of it in the mind's eye, a feeling of stabilization in the inner picturing process can be experienced.  If this exercise is continued for a month and the image of the button is maintained each day for five minutes or so, then the next, more imaginative phase of the exercise can be undertaken.  This second phase of the concentration exercise involves recognizing that a feeling of firmness in thinking, or a feeling that we are in control of the thinking, has arisen in the brow chakra and can be experienced at the root of the eyebrows as a sensation of fullness in the front of the brain.  In order to develop and protect this feeling, Dr. Steiner advises us to let the feeling wash across the brain and down the spinal marrow in a current.  Physiologically, since thinking in general, and image-forming in particular, employ the inner light of the brain, the moving of a sensation of fullness in thinking through the brain and down the spine by means of the student's attention stimulates the nerves which affect the blood and connects the blood and nerves in a harmonious way.

Doing such an exercise in concentration is actually a standard daily occurrence in science or mathematics.  What is different here is that the feeling arising from the exercise is cognized as an event within itself, irrespective of the content of the exercise, and the conscious movement of this feeling or sensation across the brain and down the spine stimulates the whole nerve network.  How is this a protection, and why does this activity of concentration even need a protection?  These questions are far-reaching in their implications.  The exercise is a protection because we are doing it consciously.  We choose to concentrate, we consciously observe the sensation as it arises, and we consciously move it through the chakras.  There is no place in this sequence where an alien or adversarial consciousness can enter into the process.

Mental concentration yields light and in time moves us slightly out of our physical bodies. When we sleep, we move out of the physical body with our consciousness, but we are protected in this nightly breathing by our angels who wait near our sleeping bodies as we visit the higher worlds. Through concentration, or trauma, or drugs, we can also leave our bodies, but the angel cannot so easily protect these exits because we are, by divine plan, destined eventually to be under our own recognizance. That is, we must learn to consciously excarnate and still maintain the experience of being in the body. To rely upon an outside stimulus which causes us to excarnate puts us *unlawfully* outside the body. As a result the angel who looks over us has no ability to stand watch. We could ask, Why do we always get such naughty thoughts when we daydream?—or drink too much? Why does trauma or abuse leave such deep emotional needs in the soul? The answer to these questions could generally be that when we are "absent without leave" from the body, other types of consciousness can enter into our unattended life forces or physical bodies and set the seeds for habits, urges, instincts, and drives to develop within our consciousness. Unattended, consciousness is the consciousness of the trance medium and is a serious danger in modern esoteric training. Thus, one goal of contemporary esoteric development is to learn to live consciously outside the physical body in a protected and harmonious way.

An expanded consciousness creates a field around the vehicle it is connected to. The time-lag created in the life forces by such an expansion must be accounted for, or else it becomes fair game to adversaries. The field of *prana* or ether (life forces) developed by any sort of concentration constitutes such an expansion. In the everyday world no thought is given to protecting an act of concentration. Its force dissipates and is no longer available after a certain period of time. The esotericist must do something consciously with such forces in order for the inner organs of cognition, the chakras, to be strengthened and harmonized.

In the Golden Legend we saw how the pituitary gland could be seen as an image of Cain and Abel. We saw where the impulses of cosmic warmth and light from the cerebral cortex and the senses streamed through the gland into the rest of the body. The pituitary gland sits behind the two-petalled lotus in the center of the brow. This gland unites the nervous sense impulses of the cerebrum with the will forces in the metabolism. The brow chakra thus becomes the door of the first basic exercise because it allows the fruits of concentration in the form of warmth and light impulses to be breathed down and out through the rest of the body, spreading warmth and light to all other organs and glands in a protected and harmonious way.

The second basic exercise is devoted to the conscious development of the nerves on the other side of the blood stream—the sympathetic nervous system. This exercise consists in performing at the same time every day a simple meaningless action of no consequence, such as standing on a chair or turning a ring on your finger. When the meaningless exercise is remembered and performed on time the student has touched a deeper level of the will with the waking consciousness. After a time, add another non-essential task to the first one, and so on. Do this for a month. When the will forces, in which we are primarily asleep, begin to be penetrated with wakefulness, a subtle feeling or sensation of an inner soul activity can be perceived as an impulse. Take this sensation or feeling and let it pour down out of the head and stream over the heart. This movement acts as a protection for the concentrated attention which is developed in the exercise.

Again, a repeated activity in concentration results in a feeling which is then guided out of the head and down into the body. Again there is a breathing of warmth and light to produce a current, but this time it is associated with doing things, with will impulses. There is a phase of esoteric study in which students become painfully aware of two things: one, that they have very little personal control over their own will impulses, and two, that the world is made up of will impulses having their origin in a whole universe of spiritual beings. This second perception is one in which the student recognizes the Ruling Will behind the phenomena of the world. The problem for the esoteric student is to penetrate the sleeping forces in the personal will with clear, wakeful thinking until the impulse arises in the soul to transform or reverse the personally-directed will forces, making them resonant with the Ruling Will of the Godhead and the Hierarchies.

In order to develop such a surrendering will, the student needs to remove all personal desires from deeds done in life. This, then, is the source of the advice to practice non-essential actions. If they are non-essential, we can have no desire or compulsion to perform them, and the will can act freely out of the purest of motives. This briefly reverses the will current, and the student gets a brief glimpse of how life could be if human beings chose to do the good out of freedom. By

regularly performing non-essential acts, the will is rendered unconditional, and can then serve as the true basis for love.

But what has the protection exercise to do with the reversal of the
will?  In the Golden Legend, after Cain slew Abel, Seth undertook an
act of selfless devotion for his father Adam.   To do this, Seth had to
reverse his own will to serve another.  In the protection exercises we
practice transforming a current in or around the body which is normally associated with personal goals and desires.  Through the second basic exercise we permeate this current with attention and purify
reactive and automatic thought patterns.   Reactive instinctual patterns and the glandular responses which they generate are saturated
with self-willed drives and urges.  In the protection exercise we consciously guide the expanded and purified fields of awareness resulting from the basic exercise into areas in and around the body in which
we are habitually self-willed in normal life.  The protection exercise
reverses our self-will, allows us to practice living consciously outside
the body, and offers to the soul an enhanced aura of pure thought on
the basis of which we can work to build a higher body of light.

Seth is the archetype of these practices.  He had to journey to
Paradise to obtain the oil of mercy.  Earlier, we saw Paradise as mirrored in the brain in the region of the cerebellum and diencephalon,
and Seth as the activity of the pineal gland.  Physiologically, the pineal
gland has a most profound relationship to the sympathetic nervous
system.   Even though it is situated in an area where ocular and
cochlear nerves impact the cerebrospinal fluid which surrounds the
gland, its own nerves have numerous links to the great cervical ganglion which covers the first few vertebrae in the neck, behind the
spine itself.  It has extensive connections to the nerves and the blood
vessels of the neck, the larynx, the pharynx, the tongue and vagus
nerve, and the jugular nerve.  These nerves are in turn woven into a
plexus of sympathetic ganglia surrounding the heart.  We can see
from this picture in physiology that the path of the protection exercise
of the second basic exercise leads from the head to the heart.

Rudolf Steiner also gives indications similar to those of this second exercise in his book *Guidance in Esoteric Training* in which he
speaks of currents which are experienced as moving from the brow
chakra to the throat chakra, to the arms and hands, and finally out to
the skin.  In these exercises the consciousness appears to be trained to
circulate the light generated when the student focuses a sustained
attention on a given chakra or part of the physiology.  The image of a

light circulation is further enhanced by the third basic exercise in which thoughts of equilibrium in the soul are radiated from the heart out to the periphery in the hands and feet. In the next basic exercises, currents of attention are drawn from the heart back into the head, out of the eyes, and into the space around the body. In the final basic exercise the space around the body is expanded and enlivened.

In both the six basic exercises and the main exercise the focus of the "yogic practice" (Steiner's term from the *The Archangel Michael: His Mission and Ours)* is to breathe in light from the surroundings, move it through the chakras, and circulate it once again outside the body. Pictured analogously, this is an image of the movement of fields around a capacitor. Seen alchemically, it is an image of the circulation of a substance in a digestive rhythm or *digestio.* The purpose of a digestio is to effect the coagula, or re-marriage, of the separated and purified parts into an essence or *quintessence.* The quintessence contains the parts of the plant in their correct relationships but at an extremely subtle and penetrating level. The circulation of the substance brings out its harmonies and healing forces and connects the physical properties present in the essence with the spiritual archetype behind the plant with which the alchemist is working.

In the Imaginative (Venus) stage of the meditative phase in the alchemical tree, the key concept was oscillation and induction. In the oscillating capacitance antenna, the field around the apparatus induces signals from distant sources and amplifies them. Similarly, in the early alchemical work, circulation is carried out in a vessel known as the *philosophical egg.* The contracted substance in the egg is gently heated until it expands to the periphery where it condenses and falls back down into the bottom of the egg. All of these analogs point to the concept of a "body" or field capable of circulating refined substances in a vortexial fashion. Such a body, if given a specific name borrowed from alchemy, would be called the *soul.* From the inner etheric currents in organs and glands through the blood and nerves out into the space around the body and then back again into the eyes and other senses to return to the chakras once again, the etheric/astral body can be imagined as a philosophical egg, or a sphere with its circulating, vortexial, pulsating rhythmic currents both inside and outside the physical body. A symbolic picture such as this, based on numerous scientifically approachable ideas, can serve as a symbol which can be worked with in a contemplative way. Ultimately the components of the various exercises given by Dr. Steiner can be experienced as a wholeness rather than as isolated exercises.

The philosophical egg with its field of movements is harmonic with structures in the spiritual world.  It is the shape and form of galaxies and of cells.  It fits the descriptions of Ezekiel's wheels as images of the hierarchies.  In working imaginatively with such a symbol, many apparent paradoxes seem much more approachable.

In circulating the light outside the body, a membrane can be experienced beyond which the Ego consciousness seems unable to penetrate.  Exploring this membrane with the witnessing Ego consciousness can reveal that at certain times of day a potential or charge is present.  In meditative states it is possible to experience that the membrane is charging from the periphery of the cosmos.  This may be due to the harmonic between the field edge of the astral or philosophical egg and the periphery of the cosmos.  It should be noted that the fluctuations of the electrostatic image of this charge can actually be monitored with a very sensitive voltmeter and saline solutions in cups in which the subject dips his or her index fingers.

Outside of the realm of bioelectric phenomena, the charge can also be experienced in imaginative cognition as the ability to stay focused on the symbolic image one has placed in the mind.  When sufficient time has elapsed at the periphery of the astral egg, the protective exercises or the main exercise can be done (without the physical breathing indications, for we are trying to breathe light, not air).  If we are sufficiently concentrated, and a calm, rhythmic attitude governs the inner-outer oscillation, a warm, deeply reverential feeling pours down the chakras like a waterfall.  The feeling is one that the universe is intelligent and moral and that in our meditation activity we are deeply harmonic to its farthest and nearest regions.  Such an experience seems like a blessing from a holy fire.

Working with such a symbol as the philosophical egg in the imaginative realm requires that great efforts be made on the part of the researcher to establish both the ability to sustain sense-free thinking and the capacity for thought-free sensing (the ability to sustain attention in a sense experience without the intrusion of a concept).  In a series of lectures on the mystery centers, Dr. Steiner makes yet another plea for the re-establishment and renewed development of this kind of mystery wisdom based on the transformation of the senses. He says:

A knowledge of the world was the result of the forces which predominated in the Mysteries. That gave man the impulse to carry over to Asia [Alexander the Great] what was then this natural science.  Then in a weakened diluted form it later came across over Spain, through Europe.  One can still trace it in what Paracelsus, Jacob Boehme, Gichtel, and various others wrote and taught, culminating in such spirits as Basilius Valentinus and others.  But at first, that which was clothed in mere thought-forms, in mere logic, had to transcend all else, and the rest had to wait.  The time has now come when this other has fulfilled its task of waiting, when it must again be found as the sum total of natural knowledge.  (Steiner, *Mystery Centers*, 100)

Dr. Steiner here refers to the development and cultivation of imaginative cognition, i.e., the ego hovering above and outside the physical body consciously sending warmth and light down into the body in the form of sense impressions cognized in the system of chakras. The true basis for this work starts with the cultivation of sense-free thinking.  Sense-free thinking is thinking which is not a result of a direct sense impression, that is, thinking not generated as a reaction to some sensation.  Rather, it occurs just in the soul with no response to outer stimuli.

When the stimuli are not present, the impressions arising from within are sustained in the memory as mental images.  Further work with mental images creates an inner capacity to induce images which arise neither from the body nor from any sense impression but which come solely from the archetypal realm as creative imaginations.  To do this the student must be able to form and hold a mental image at will and to dissolve it at will.  In *Spiritual Research: Methods and Results*, Dr. Steiner places the ability for the soul to remember and work with images as the basis for inner work.  By continual concentration on certain symbolic mental images, the sense-like nature of the symbol is transcended, and the researcher experiences autonomy as a thinker in the realm of pure thinking.

The symbol can either be a prescribed symbol such as the Rose Cross meditation, or if imaginative cognition in general is the goal, the symbol can be a sense impression chosen from the realm of nature. By repeated concentration on the mental image of, for instance, a plant growing, the sense data is transcended and we approach the archetype of the plant. This procedure is Goethe's exact sense perception. In and of itself, this practice establishes sense-free thinking in the Ego, independent of the body. Imaginatively, we could say that an outer field of warmth and light around the upper body is established, with a vortex coming down through the chakras from above, approaching the region of the heart.

By practicing what Dr. Steiner calls *thinking backwards* (in *Learning to See into the Spiritual World),* we can think the mental image of a flower backwards until it is no longer present in the mind's eye. When we sit in the silence thus constructed, we establish a meditative state with a direct relationship to the archetype which stands behind the object of our contemplation. The movement pattern of the natural object helps to pattern and form the inner movements of the chakra. The next time we observe the plant, if we refrain from elaborating our percept with concepts, the light streaming into us through our eyes can be directed into the chakras which are already harmonic with its movements.

Over a period of time, such practice connects the outer Ego field and the inner chakra field in a rhythmic, outer-to-inner, lemniscatory movement of warmth and light, very similar to breathing. One can then experience the Imagination leading to Inspiration, the breathing in of cosmic warmth and light. The movement of the light from outside to inside and back again is a motif found in most of Rudolf Steiner's indications for inner development. The imaginative contemplation of the vortex ring and its lemniscatory movement can serve as a very useful meditative symbol for those who wish to practice spirit vision.

# 16

## THE ALCHEMY OF
## GOETHE'S FAIRY TALE

I t is known from Goethe's biography that he had a keen interest in the study of alchemy. Some biographers contend that he actually cured himself of a sudden illness in his late teens by making an alchemical medicament from crystals. Whatever the case, it is clear from his *Fairy Tale of the Green Snake and the Beautiful Lily* that Goethe was very conversant with alchemical practice. His interest in minerals and mining alone would have put him into contact with the lore of metals and their generation—a pervasive theme in the fairy tale. If we examine the figures of the fairy tale's four kings, we may be able to get a clear picture of how the alchemy of transformation of metals can serve as an analog for the transformation of the soul life. We must first discuss in detail, however, certain key concepts in alchemy before we can approach the fairy tale in a discriminating way.

The central idea in alchemy, the concept of mercury, is also the most arcane. Mercury has a thousand different alchemical names—it is a stone; it is fire; it is the seed of metals; it is a thick liquid, yet is dry and warm; it is living gold; it kills and it gives life; it destroys and it heals; it is everything yet is nothing. Clearly, the term "mercury" does not just apply to the metal, quicksilver. It is rather the medium which unites all metals. It is the spiritually living potential which becomes manifest metal. From a lexicon of alchemy published in 1612, we learn that "the mercury of philosophers is not the common mercury," and from the first canon of Paracelsus' *Coelum Philosophorum*, we read:

> All things are concealed in all. One of them all is the concealer of the rest—their corporeal vessel, external, visible, and movable. . . . For the vessel is a living and corporeal spirit, and so all coagulations or congelations enclosed in it, when

prevented from flowing, are not therewith content.  No name can be found for this liquefaction . . . still less can it be found for its origin.  And since no heat is so strong as to be equalized therewith, it should be compared to the fire of Gehenna [hell].  A liquefaction of this kind has no sort of connection with others made by the heat of natural fire, or . . . coagulated by natural cold.  These coagulations, through their weakness, are unable to obtain in Mercury. . . .  Elementary powers, in their process of destruction, can add nothing to, nor take away anything from, celestial powers . . . nor have they any capacity for operating.  (Paracelsus, I, 5)

The philosophical mercury thus stands outside the elemental spheres and the operations of manifest nature.  Universally, alchemists understand that this state of mercury is the source of the seven metals and that they have a deep and intimate kinship with it.

The monk Basil Valentine describes this relationship in the following evocative passage from his *Last Will and Testament.*

It is seen by all the works that are undertaken about Metals, that there is nothing so volatile as Metals are, and so nothing stirs and moveth more subtly than it; but this stirring and moving I will call here the Ferch of Metals [Latin:  *fera,* to carry], by reason of its continual proceeding [becoming], and incessant moving. . . .  Seeing Ferch is a perpetual living and forthgoing thing, one might admire and say, of what condition is Metal then, which we behold with our eyes, and feel with our hands . . . ?  (Valentine, 1)

This question is central to the alchemy of transformation of metals.  The ferch is the life of metals.  It is that which keeps metals growing in the bowels of the earth.  It is this volatility and movement, this mercury principle in metals which is the basis for all transformation.

However, the life or mercury of metals does follow its own cosmic laws.  These laws are the goal of the alchemical work, for without them, all labor is in vain.  From the *Sixth Canon* of Paracelsus, we hear:

It is not useful to transmute what is perfect into what is imperfect. . . .  Nevertheless, it is well to know what is the material of Luna [silver], or whence it proceeds. . . .  What is Luna?  It is among the seven metals which are spiritually concealed, itself the seventh, external, corporeal, and material. For this seventh always contains the [other] six metals spiritually hidden in itself. And the six spiritual metals do not exist without one external and material metal. . . . The seven corporeal metals mix easily by means of liquefaction, but this mixture is not useful for making Sol [gold] and Luna. For in that mixture each metal remains in its own nature, or fixed in the fire, or flies from it. . . . For example, mix . . . [all seven metals]. It will not thence result that . . . the other five . . . will become Sol and Luna. For though all be liquefied into a single mass, nevertheless each remains in its nature whatever it is. This is the judgement which must be passed on corporeal mixture. But concerning the spiritual mixture and communion of the metals, it should be known that no separation or mortification is spiritual. . . . Though the body should be taken away from [the metals] . . . they would always acquire another much more noble than the former. And this is the transposition of the metals from one death to another . . . from a lesser degree [of purity] into one greater and higher, namely, into Luna; and from a better into the best and most perfect, that is, into Sol, the brilliant and altogether royal metal. . . . The six metals always generate a seventh, or produce it from themselves clear in its *esse* [essence]. (Paraceslsus, I, 8–9.)

If we link this concept of the transformation of metals with the initial concept of the mercury or ferch of metals, we can see an image of a state in which each separate stage of metalline existence is connected holographically with the other states. They are all connected to the becoming of the mercury as a cosmic process. The seven metals need the spiritual wholeness of the six, or the Being of Metalness, as well as the manifestation of the particular metal in order to exhibit a wholeness. When we only cognize the silver or copper, then we lose the ability to connect with the mercury process streaming through them all, the "becoming" of the metal. The manifest metal is volatile or fixed, depending upon its contact with the living mercurial fire in which all metals live. Perhaps an image from Paracelsus' *Treasure of Treasures* can aid our understanding.

Now, I assert that in this mineral [metal] are found three principles, which are Mercury [spirit], Sulfur [soul], and . . .
Mineral water [or Salt (body)]. Spagyric science [alchemy] is
able to extract this last [body] from its proper juice [solution]
when it is not altogether matured, in the middle of the
autumn, just like a pear from a tree. The tree potentially contains the pear. If the Celestial Stars and Nature agree, the tree
first of all puts forth shoots in the month of March; then it
thrusts out buds, and when these open the flower appears,
and so on in due order, until in autumn the pear grows ripe.
So it is with the minerals. These are born, in like manner, in
the bowels of the earth. (Paracelsus, I, 36)

From this we see that the metals, like the pear, exist first in the
celestial spheres as potential (mercury). The potential contains all of
the metals. The manifest metal is an image of the cosmos growing
down into the earth and into matter. To do this, mercury (spirit) needs
a sulfur (soul) with which it can combine. Neither the mercury nor
the sulfur is manifest. They are in potential and in continuous movement. In the formation of metals, the mercury and sulfur exist in the
form of a vapor or gas. This gas would be in the form in which the
famous chemist Van Helmont originally perceived matter to exist.
His use of the word *gas* comes from the Greek *chaos*, or potential. For
Van Helmont, the gaseous state was neither a material one, nor was it
"nothing," so it was seen as a gas. To the medieval mind, the term
*vapor* for the mercury and sulfur seems to carry this in-between quality of the original word "gas." According to Martinus Rulandus
(*Lexicon of Alchemy*, 388–90), vapors meet in the cosmos and are drawn
into the earth by water and air. In the earth, they meet and mingle
with a saline fluid and are sublimated back to the surface by the central fire of the earth which is their life. Here they meet with sulfur
compounds in underground caverns or caves, and metals arise. All
metals have a common seed. It is the place of their birth which causes their difference. If the mercury meets the sulfur in a warm and
pure place, gold is the result. If the mercury meets the sulfur in a cold
and impure place, lead is the result. Copper results when the earth
through which the mercury is moving is pure, but there is an abundance of sulfur. The vapor which contains the seed of the metal contains the spirit of light of fire, and is of the nature of celestial bodies.

In this view then, gold is a manifestation of cosmic potential, or star influences, united with light and placed into the earth to be nourished. If the nourishment is imperfect, then imperfect metals arise. The alchemist, by taking note of these relationships, can step in where nature has not provided the proper metalline nutrition, and through repeated rhythmical purification he can transform imperfect metals into perfect ones. This concept stands at the foundation of Goethe's fairy tale, especially in the conversations among the Green Snake, the Old Man with the lamp, and the four kings.

The four kings represent the two purest metals (gold and silver), an alloy (brass), and a mixture of all other metals. There is an impure nutrition in the mixed king. Brass is only made by human beings, as zinc and copper do not alloy in nature. It is produced through an alchemical process known as cementation. Zinc is very volatile and flies off when heated, so the alchemist mixes the ore with a flux and cements thin plates of copper together with it. The plates are put into a very hot, closed fire so that the zinc bubbles up into the copper. The brass king thus points to alchemy. The silver and gold kings are the noble metals which are the goal of alchemical transformation. They are found in a cave where the vapors of mercury and sulfur meet the salt.

The snake in alchemical imagery represents earth wisdom arrived at through the senses. The old Rosicrucian image of the snake going into the cave of the skull, winding in one eye and out the other, is an image of the instruction given to the soul through the senses. We will return later to this motif.

The Gold King asks the Snake, "From where do you come?" She answers, "In the chasm where the gold dwells." The gold was shaken into the chasm by the two will-o'-the-wisps who had eaten it and then cast it off. Alchemically, the image of the will-o'-the-wisps has the aura of mercury about it. These beings are vapors which are flame-like. We have seen this flamelike vapor as the source of metals in the mercury-plus-sulfur vapors. But why do they eat gold? In the chemistry of will-o'-the-wisp phenomena, it is generally recognized that marsh gas, or methane, can form in unusual ways which allow a phosphor-sulfur flame to arise and ignite the gas. This chemical reaction changes the methane ($CH_4$) into a sulfur radical known as mercaptan ($CH_3 CH_2 SH$). It is this which gives the rotten egg smell to marsh gas. The term *mercaptan* is a shortening of the Latin words *corpus mercuriam captans,* or "capturing the body of mercury." If we recall the alchemical saying that mercury is the spirit of the light of the fire, we can connect these will-o'-the-wisps with the mercury which both destroys and produces the seven metals. The will-o'-the-wisps are an image of mercury, the seed of metals, the spirit, the primal matter.

Mercury is also the image in the questions which the Gold King asks the Green Snake.

> King:   What is grander than gold?
> Snake:  Light.
> King:   What is more refreshing than light?
> Snake:  Speech.   [Word/Logos/Mercury]

In this famous passage, Goethe carries us from the cosmic Logos-nature of mercury, through light, to the manifestations of gold as a metal in the earth. This sequence connecting gold, light, and Logos (mercury) will later become the wisdom with which the Old Man with the lamp will call the Gold King to give his gift to the Young Man.

The Silver King does not speak but shows to the world a fine appearance. This is the quality of silver (Luna), the quality of the formation of images. Silver is the metal used to coat glass in the production of mirrors. It is also the metal which forms the basis for light-sensitive photographic emulsions. The Snake cannot have a conversation with the Brass King or the Mixed King, because the Man with the Lamp enters the cave. In many alchemical texts the Man with the Lamp is seen following blindly in the footsteps of the beautiful maiden Natura, holding the lamp of the intellect. The alchemist can only see Natura's footsteps because he is blinded by his own intellectual light.

The Gold King then asks of the Old Man, the alchemist, "Why do you come here? We already have light." The alchemist replies, "You know that I may not enlighten what is dark." That is, the intellect can only cognize Logos beings and events. The Silver King (image) asks, "Will my kingdom [imagination] end?" Says the alchemist, "Late or never." That is, there is no end to the place from where imaginations arise. The Brazen King asks, "When shall I arise?" That is, when can I be transformed into silver and gold? This refers to the doctrine of the ascension of metals into more noble forms. The answer is "Soon." With whom shall I combine?" asks the Brazen King. "With thy elder brothers," replies the alchemist. This again is the doctrine of the transformation of metals, where all metals are the same in their Mercury (Logos) nature and only differ in the location of their development.

"What will the youngest do?" asks the Brazen King about the Mixed King. "He will sit down," answers the alchemist. That is, his forces will be diminished. Says Basil Valentine in his *Last Will and Testament:* "For if a mineral [and its metal] is exsicated [dried out], then it has no more the strength to run forth [Ferch], but grows tough, and is dried up sinking into the ground" (Valentine, 47). This happens when the metal loses its connection to its cosmic nutriment, the starry forces borne through the earth by surface water percolating downward. The Mixed King has no cosmic nutrition and no forces of integration. Many experiments by Lily Kolisko have shown that the ability of two metals to form an alloy is highly dependent upon cosmic parameters which support the amalgam. Without this cosmic connection, all the metals can do is mix together without entering into a marriage with each other. This is the problem of the Mixed King.

This problem of the cosmic nutrition of metals is found again later in Goethe's fairy tale when the Kings give their gifts to the Youth. The Brass King gives a sword with the advice "The sword on the left the right free." This points to the marriage of volatility and fixedness hidden in the alloy brass. In brass, the alchemist's princely metal, a marriage of the fixed malleability of copper and the manifest volatility of zinc gives strength and luster to the alloy so that it shines with a golden hue: volatility and fixedness, freedom and strength, the perfect advice for youth. The Gold King gives the youth his oaken garland, the headdress of the priests and seers. With this gift, he tells the youth to "understand what is highest." Clearly this points to wisdom won through thinking.

It is the Silver King, however, who gives a most puzzling piece of advice. He gives the youth his scepter, his symbol of power as a king, and with it comes the admonition, "Feed the sheep." Taken on a simple, exoteric level, this could mean to rule his kingdom in a benign and generous way. Taken at a deeper level, however, the advice to "feed the sheep," coming from the Silver King, the king who represents the realm of the moon, can point to the whole esoteric task concerning the alchemy of the cosmic nutritional stream.

Earlier, the idea was put forward that the basis of alchemical thought rested on the perception that processes in the natural world were analogs for inner soul processes in the human being. If this is so, what soul processes are analogous to the transformation of metals, and what does this have to do with silver and feeding the sheep? In answer to these questions, we can turn to Rudolf Steiner's work at the Goethe Archives in Weimar and to the culmination of his research into Goethe's morphological ideas. His book *Goethean Science* addresses the problems Goethe wrestled with in his scientific works. In the chapter "Goethe as Thinker and Investigator," Rudolf Steiner addresses the concept of the archetypal phenomenon. He does so by comparing the human experience of the sensation of "red" to the scientific explanation of the sensation. Steiner states that between the stimulus and the inner cognition of "red" in a human being there are many states of existence which are described by natural science. Science can describe the wavelengths of red, the pigment itself, the chemical changes in the pigment, the motion of waves or particles in the medium which is carrying the sensation, the action of the sense organs in response to the stimulus, and the chemical and electrical changes in the body and brain of the perceiver. Yet nowhere in this chain of transformations can we point to a phenomenon and say clearly that here the sensation becomes a cognized perception.

> The sensation is present at every point, from the stimulator to the brain, but not . . . explicitly, but rather in a way corresponding to the nature of the object [state] existing at each point. . . . What do I experience from the investigation of a thing caught up in a process that appears in my consciousness as sensation? I experience no more than the way that thing responds to the action which issues from the sensation, or, in other words the way a sensation *expresses itself* in some object or other of the spatial-temporal world. It is far from the truth to regard such a spatial-temporal process as the *cause,* as that which causes the sensation *in* me; something quite different is the correct view: The spatial-temporal process [color wavelengths, brain chemistry, etc.] is the *effect* of the sensation within a thing that has extension in space and time. (Steiner, *Goethean Science*, 209)

This concept is reminiscent of Basil Valentine's concept of the ferch as well as Paracelsus' analogy of the pear tree. Sensation is the mercury, the potential existing in freedom as archetype which then manifests into the world in order to seek nutrition and grow. It is the seed of metals, the primal matter of the world.  Again from Rudolf Steiner we find:

> By [scientifically] following the perception [sensation] from its stimulus to the organ of perception, we are investigating nothing other than the continuous transition from one perception to the other. . . .  The perceived world is therefore nothing other than a sum total of metamorphosed perceptions. (Steiner, *Goethean Science*, 210).

Dr. Steiner goes on to say that the causal relationships of such perceptions which are revealed by science do not address the reality of the existence of the sensation "red" which exists outside of time and causal relationships.  What we study in science is how the essential being of a sensation comes into manifestation in time.  This is its causal ontology, its line of emergence.  Time, however, has very little to do with essential or archetypal being, since it belongs to the manifest and phenomenological world.  Dr. Steiner continues:

> Only someone who cannot manage, in his train of thought, to go back from the phenomenon to the essential [archetypal] being will hypothesize time as something preceding the facts. Then, however, he needs a form of existence that endures beyond the changes. He conceives indestructible matter to be just such an existence. He has thereby created for himself a thing to which time can do nothing, something that abides amidst all change. Actually, however, he has only shown his inability to press forward, from the temporal phenomenon of the facts, to their essential being, which has nothing to do with time. . . . The essential being of a thing [Mercury] cannot be destroyed; for, it is outside of all time and itself determines time. With this, we have shed light upon two concepts . . . for which but little understanding is still to be found:  upon *essential* being . . . and *outer manifestation*. . . . The sense-perceptible world picture [image] is the sum total of metamorphosing perceptual contents without an underlying matter. (Steiner, *Goethean Science*, 213–4)

In these quotations can we not see a distinct parallel between the thinking of Rudolf Steiner and the alchemical world-view?  We need only substitute "sensation" for the concept "mercury, the seed of metals," or "the spirit of the light of fire," to find which processes in the human soul are analogous to the transformation of metals. The soul in its growth uses sensation as a stream of cosmic nutrition. The colors and forms of the sense world are the various streams of "metals" which arise within the soul as images. It is through these mental images arising out of the cosmic nutritional forces present in sensation that organs arise which enable the soul to live and grow. Behind all sensations (metals) stands the archetype of sensation (mercury), the great "becoming." By working to purify metals, the alchemists were feeding their souls with lawful cosmic sensations of the mercurial movement of the spirit. Through constant immersion in and purification of the sense life in the realm of manifestation, the Ego, or true Self, was formed in the soul-spiritual realm as a sensing organ for cosmic patterns of light.

Once existence through thinking independent of the body becomes a reality, it is then possible to truly explore the metals (senses) and purify them systematically so they can eventually become like gold (mercury cemented by light). Such purified senses can then serve the soul as cosmic nutrition so that the senses themselves can grow back into the spiritual world, just as the earthly metals grow into the body of the earth. The purified senses find the nutrition they need in the production of pure mental images, which in their silvery, moon-influenced energies enabled the Young Man to "feed the sheep."

The challenge represented by this great alchemical task of transformation lies at the very source of the mission of the archangel Michael. Its import for the future is enormous, as anthroposophical work must enter the world at large through deeds of earthly transformation. A final quote from Rudolf Steiner, outlining the nature of this alchemical work, comes from his book *The Boundaries of Natural Science:*

> Whereas in ordinary life one sees color . . . with conceptual activity, one can now extract the concepts from the entire process of elaborating percepts [purification] and draw the percept itself directly into one's bodily constitution. Goethe undertook to do this and has already taken the first steps in this direction. . . . [For Goethe] the whole man experiences something in the act of sense perception. Sense perception, together with its content, passes down into the organism, and

the ego with its pure thought content remains, so to speak, hovering above.  We exclude thinking inasmuch as we take into and fill ourselves with the whole content of the perception, instead of weakening it with concepts, as we usually do. We train ourselves specially to achieve this by systematically pursuing what came to be practiced in a decadent form by the men of the [Eastern mystery traditions].  Instead of grasping the content of the perception in pure, strictly logical thought, we grasp it symbolically, in pictures, allowing it to stream into us as a result of a kind of detour around thinking.  We steep ourselves in the richness of colors, the richness of the tone, by learning to experience the images inwardly, not in terms of thought but as pictures, as symbols.  Because we do not suffuse our inner life with the thought content, as the psychology of association would have it, but with the content of perception indicated through symbols and pictures, the living inner forces of the etheric and astral bodies, stream toward us from within, and we come to know the depths of the consciousness and of the soul. . . .  If one desires to do real research concerning human physiology, thinking must be excluded and the picture-forming activity sent inward, so that the physical organism reacts by creating Imaginations.  This is a path that is only just beginning in the development of Western culture, but it is the path that must be trodden if the influence that streams over from the East, and would lead to decadence if it alone were to prevail, is to be confronted with something capable of opposing it, so that our civilization may take a path of ascent and not of decline.  (Steiner, *Boundaries*, 100-101)

In order to send picture-forming inward to create Imaginations, the adept needs to be awake outside the body in a coherent consciousness.  The capacity to do this is the attainment of spirit vision. The methods and techniques given to the student need to be practiced faithfully for a longer or shorter time so that complete detachment from the results of the work becomes the natural mood of soul.

There are, of course, many pitfalls, setbacks, and trials for each practitioner in such a path of development.  In the final chapter of this book, the challenges to humanity as a whole in the activity of seeking spirit vision will be addressed.  For better or worse, it is just in this time that many souls will be called to seek the spirit through the faculty of Imagination.  In these times the results of an individual practice must be consciously transferred to the whole.  This is the requirement of the new alchemical mysteries and is the guiding tone of the challenges they will have to confront.

# 17

## SEEING THE DOUBLE

In previous chapters the creation of a field consciousness was discussed as a stage of esoteric development. This stage of contemplation is possible once the student has developed a thinking process which is independent of the physical sensation/response patterns of the physiology. It should be noted here that this development is not without its dangers due to the profound implications of the body-free state of consciousness. These dangers do not only apply to the esoteric student, for they can also be found in everyday life as the roots of neuroses and other soul pathologies. Levels of even more ominous and sobering insight can be gleaned from trying to characterize more advanced inner work. To understand this it is useful to think about the levels of esoteric development in relation to their trials and levels of mastery. The first level is that of the student and is characterized by the pursuit of knowledge and the accompanying struggle to think clearly in the process of ordering that knowledge. Trials at this level often involve mistrust of teachers and denial of the validity of the knowledge or, as a polarity, uncritical acceptance of concepts which cannot be proved or disproved by the student.

What is required to advance beyond the level of student in a given tradition is the search for and acquisition of personally effective techniques. Using effective techniques in the meditative or alchemical work develops in the student the consciousness of the alchemical artist. The artist is a worker, an experimenter, a student who is not content with hearing about knowledge but who develops a commitment to researching experiences and techniques for furthering the knowledge. The trials of the artist are inflation and delusion when the work is going well and self-doubt and depression when it is not. Through practice the artist transcends the knowledge gained as a student and begins to enter the spiritual world. The alchemical artist also begins to have significant experiences of creative yet unsettling higher states of consciousness. Eventually these altered states begin to intrude into the waking consciousness; through practice and rigor they can be integrated into the waking consciousness in a systematic way. This is the challenge of the level of the adept.

In the adept, knowledge and technique must be gracefully surrendered to attain prolonged spiritual experience beyond the reach of the intellect. The accomplishment of the adept is the ability to maintain a focused attention which is structured in strong intent but has no content. Such a consciousness was known to alchemical adepts as the *stone*, for the path from student to artist to adept is the gradual forming of a full attentive consciousness as coherent as a stone. The artist's processes of distillation, combustion, and precipitation are shifted by the adept into analogs for inner psychological or psychic phenomena. The goal of the adept is then the complete transformation of the soul faculties of thinking, feeling, and willing.

The gradual consolidation of the faculties of concentration in the thinking and a selfless powerful will was seen by the alchemists as an analog for the process known to Paracelsus as *embryonation*. Paracelsus considered that crystalline minerals were formed similarly to embryos, with the greatest concentration of gems or pure minerals at a center surrounded by layers of "embryonates" or more generalized mineral-bearing soils. The image which Paracelsus often refers to is the structure of a walnut. The gem or pure mineral at the center is the "stone" formed out of the "nutriment" layers around it. To the alchemists the process of the forming of the stones in nature was analogous to the process of physical incarnation. The stone was any *process* moving inevitably and immutably toward a pure crystal form. The stone was a cosmic process in which the human "salt of the earth" precipitated into physical incarnation. The student would learn the knowledge particular to earthly incarnation, the artist would develop thinking techniques for willing the various levels of the incarnating stone, and the adept would work to infuse the heart with the fluid and mysterious healing mercury imaginations which had been made stable. In the language of alchemy the stone was a fixing of the purified mercury so that its fluid purity became immutable in the soul.

The paradoxical fixing of the mercury was the last phase of a very long and arduous process. It can be seen diagrammatically as a gradual descent of fluid cosmos into the Earth. This is the path of the human being incarnating out of cosmic existence into life on Earth. Nature and the descent of life forces into matter is another evolution described by such a descending curve. Rudolf Steiner has characterized such a descent from the spirit into matter in a series of planetary stages. The most primal stage, during which all matter which is now substantially solid was in an expanded warmth state, is called *Old Saturn*. Through the activity of cosmic beings during the evolution of Old Saturn, warmth gathered into differentiated states.

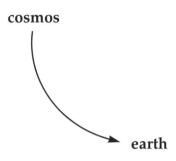

This is similar to modern scientific descriptions by physicists of the plasma state. By differentiating more warmth from less warmth, the Old Saturn stage is also an analog for the first formation of a differentiating membrane in biology. This quality of differentiating and individualizing is the greatest tool of the alchemist. In the alchemical language Saturn individualizes and creates the possibility for gradients.

Biologically, as a result of the gradient-forming forces of Saturn, there then arises the possibility of an organism which separates itself from its environment. The Saturn process then is the first stage in the separating out of the organism in evolution. As an analog for processes in nature, Saturn sets the stage for the forming of membranes and out of this arises forces of resistance. Saturn creates an inner and an outer. What is in resists what is out. Psychologically, at the student level in the inner planes, the student resists the work needed to assimilate and differentiate the knowledge needed to develop concentration. At the next level resistance often arises while the artist is trying to overcome the inertia developed through a glut of information. It takes great force to sublimate this information into creative forms. For the adept, resistance is the alpha and omega, the sum total of the work, the primal force which needs to be overcome on the path toward surrender. Symbolically, resistance is the ouroboros or tail biter, the simultaneous tool and problem of the worker. The adept becomes a master at resisting the unconscious tendency to resist. For the adept the way and the goal are one.

For this reason it is said in the myths that Saturn must eat his children. Saturn and the resistance which accompanies the whole process of ego individuation must eat the lower ego, i.e. its own image (resistance), in order to develop. In the alchemical texts Saturn is often seen as a crippled man on crutches. The crippling egoity of the student must be overcome and completely assimilated in the adept in order for there to be the possibility of initiation into the mysteries of the higher ego or True Self.

These concepts of the return to the Saturn state for the purpose of transforming or consuming egoity are characterized by the alchemical language as the stages of *multiplication* and *projection*. Both are processes undertaken at the later stages of the work when the artist and adept have actually formed a body of energy with which work can be done in the spiritual world. This energetic body or light body or etheric body is composed of life forces of warmth and light which are accessible to the worker in meditation. In the stage of projection, techniques are practiced which allow the soul forces to be used independently by the researcher. That is, the thinking and feeling and willing are split into separate forces and used consciously by the alchemist. In projection the goal is to get outside of the body by splitting the soul forces from their habitual patterning (multiplication) and projecting them out of the body consciously and coherently (projection).

For the artist who works in the laboratory the technique of multiplication involves taking a small amount of highly purified metal in which the mercury forces were previously highly refined alchemically. The alchemist would obtain this highly refined metal from an adept who had mastered the transformation of metals. With such a "starter" an artist could affect metal transformation by simply multiplying the "starter" through a simple process of layering it with very thin leaves of a baser metal in a process of *fermentation* or *cementation*. The refined mercury substance or "white gold of the philosophers" would then transform (multiply) the base metal into a more noble condition. This process was also known as cementation. If the refined mercury substance was sufficiently pure then the quality of cementation would be termed alloying. That is, the whole mass of the metal would be transformed by the powerful mercury of the ferment. In the process of multiplication a complete transformation of the whole mass of a base metal into gold was not accomplished all at once, but rather small alloys were performed to move a metal into its next stage. A complete transformation from base metal to noble metal without the help of the "starter" needed the greater forces of transformation present in the higher stage of projection. Here the alchemist worked "from scratch."

There were two levels in the projection stage, the yellow (lower) and the red (higher). At the yellow level, the highest degree of transformation possible was the equivalent of what we today would call electroplating. In yellow projection the process of transformation was only on the surface, it was an *image* of complete transformation. To go to the higher red projection stage the transformation of the entire substance of the physical form needed to be accomplished. This required a much more intense level of warmth, or Saturn. The Saturn forces had to be turned upon themselves and "reverberated" so that the warmth could be intensified into a warmth capable of red projection. We could call this red state Saturn squared or $\saturn^2$. In the original Old Saturn warmth state the many manifestations arise out of one homogenous state of cosmic warmth. In $\saturn^2$ the many manifestations are systematically led back to the primal unity state, an all-pervading warmth in constant flow.

As we have seen in the early alchemical doctrines, the process of incarnation from the original cosmic Saturn stage into the manifest world is the focus of "the Work." The traditional concept of the stone as an alchemical goal is predominantly an incarnating salt process. The opposite process of lifting the stone back into warmth states was not the goal of the alchemists. They historically preferred to render the volatile elements into the fixed state. But if alchemy is to offer any psychological ideas for the future, this incarnating stone-forming force from Saturn needs to be researched in the red projection phase and not just in multiplication or cementation, as is mostly discussed in alternative psychology today. To illustrate this research into projection perhaps a view of a few myths compared with some modern inventions would be useful.

As was stated earlier, the forces of Saturn are the forces of the process of individuation. In this Saturn process individual organisms form a membrane or barrier with which they can resist the environment. This membrane allows the organism to separate off from the flowing life of the environment and to establish an autonomous energy economy. The most common example of such an energy economy is a single cell living within the general flowing forces of life in the surrounding environment. In this image Saturn can be seen to represent the cell's forces of resistance to the flow of the cosmos. Once Saturn (or Chronos) established such a resistance against cosmic flow, the door to the possibility of the human drama was opened. One of the first goddesses to experience the forces and feelings of resistance to the flow of the cosmic life was none other than Demeter, the goddess of the flow of cosmic life. She experienced the pangs of resistance when she lost her daughter Persephone to the god Pluto in the underworld. At this loss she began to mourn, resisting her task of bringing abundant life to earth and refusing to allow the flowing cosmic life, which animates the changing seasons, to manifest.

The Greeks had two terms which they used to describe the two faces of Demeter. Demeter as cosmic life (the etheric plane) flowing freely through the universe, they called *Zoe*. Demeter as life contained in an organism was known as *Bios*. Bios arises as the forming of the outer membrane of an organism gradually resists the flow of Zoe. As the complexity of membranes in an organism increases, it develops a higher resistance, an increased hardening against the flow of cosmic life. Ultimately, through resistance to the flow of life, an organism produces electricity. Modern science has come to identify the electrical forces in organisms with life. As we will soon see in the image of the battery, electricity is but an *image* of life, created when a flowing life process is resisted. Zoe becomes Bios through the gradual resistance of the membrane. The cosmically flowing Zoe is cast down through the membrane of resistance into Bios. The biological life is still flowing but is restricted in its degree of freedom by the forces kept in balance as a function of its separation from the environment. In the following descriptions the degree of freedom of the energies in a system is the fundamental consideration.

The Greek term *pleroma* or *plenum* can be used to describe the free cosmic potentials of Zoe. The pleroma of free creative forces of Zoe is the realm of primal light, or *lux*. Lux creates forms in constant flux. It is outside of space in an ever proliferating *time.* By contrast, the fallen light, or *lumen,* is an image of flux which reveals objects with discrete fixed boundaries. Some objects have fallen so far that they fall out of life completely and are inanimate. Objects which have fallen out of the lux but still retain the generative form-producing forces of life are in the realm of Bios. Bios is more free than fixed matter but less free than Zoe. The falling of the light out of time and into space and matter is the action of Chronos. As a result, bodies in space have a *particular* degree of freedom for their energetic economy. This is determined by the surfaces of the object which are, as we have said, manifestations of the forces of resistance of Saturn. In science this restriction on an organism is known as the law of minimal surface. It is what keeps the size of the cell in a mouse the same size as the corresponding cell of a whale.

To summarize, lux, the creative light of the pleroma of the Godhead, animates the void beyond space with the formative potential of Zoe. The light falls from time into space, and an image of the primal light arises as visible light which casts shadows (images). The ability to make images or cast shadows is an inherent unmanifest nonlocal attribute of Zoe. Lumen, visible light, is an image of lux, Creative Light. Lumen brings life to Bios by making images of Zoe in visible light. Lumen also falls in doing this. Matter arises as the image of the falling of lumen. Zoe is resisted by Saturn and falls as an image into Bios. The organism in turn resists the Bios and an *image* of the flowing Bios forces arises out of the falling Bios forces. This *image* is biological electricity.

Saturn resists Zoe and the *image* of Zoe arises as Bios or biological life. Bios is in turn resisted by the membranes in an organism until the *image* of life arises in the space above the membrane, the biological electric field. The fallen life forces (Bios) are thus imaged in or accompanied by electricity. In a cell the membrane arises out of a dynamic movement between two different conditions. In water which is in motion in even the slightest degree, innumerable sensitive inner membranes arise between regions in which a movement gradient exists. The same is true for temperature gradients, chemical gradients, or viscosity gradients. Any difference is accompanied by a sensitive boundary which is an *image* of the place where the two gradients are in the process of interacting. In cell biology certain substances move into this sensitive boundary area where the forces of differential gradients interact. These substances are deposited in the dynamic interstices between the dynamic gradients. After a while these substances form the physical membrane of a cell, a material image of the falling of the primal light into substance through the agency of time. Biologically these substances which form the image of the activity of the fallen light are known as *phospholipids*—solidified light and warmth. This membrane of fallen light is the site of myriad minute electrical reactions, most of which are based upon hypothetical models of pore size and molecular bonding reactions to explain the mysterious flux of life in which the cell is embedded. The energies released by the cell in the activities of life, if taken together, represent a field of electrostatic potentials in the environment of the cell.

This field is read by biological electrical engineers as the source of life. From another perspective, however, it is not the source of life but an *image* of the life which has died into matter. Since we have no instruments to measure the quantum-like energies of the pleroma all we can register is the image of the dying life as it hits the electrode in our probe.

Esoterically, electricity is light that has fallen out of life and is caught in an existence below the level of Bios. It is a force which has its genesis in the cosmic process of resistance. It accompanies life like a tracer or sign post, pointing to where we might look to catch a glimpse of life as it moves mysteriously through the organism. To confuse electricity with life is to confuse our own face with our reflection in the mirror. Perhaps a practical description of this fundamental esoteric problem concerning the relationship between life and electricity can be seen in the image of the galvanic cell or storage battery.

The typical galvanic cell consists of two different metals, such as carbon and zinc, placed in close proximity to each other in the presence of an electrolytic fluid. The electrolytic fluid, or electrolyte, causes a chemical reaction or combustion to take place in each metal. In the case of the carbon/zinc polarity the electrolyte is a saline (salt) solution. To an alchemist a metal is a unique form of mercury. All metals have a common mercury principle which is the basis of the alchemical transformation of lead into gold. In this view, carbon and zinc are both mercury. Carbon however has an electrochemical yearning to become zinc. In modern chemistry we would say that between carbon and zinc there is an electrolytic potential. This means that the metal will lose ions if placed into a solution of its own salts. In an electrolyte the solution aids the migration of ions from the surface of the metal, enabling the ions to pass into solution and release heat. The heat which is released is a form of combustion or oxidation of the metal. The metal decays or "burns" in the electrolyte. The latent heat in the metal is released as the heat of the reaction, and an oxide is formed as an ash. This is known as electrolysis and is present as a process among all metals in an electrolytic series. The electrolytic series of metals starts with carbon as the most sulfur and moves through the noble metals to the base metals to the salts such as sodium, calcium, and potassium.

To an alchemist carbon yearns to flow through zinc into potassium. However, in a galvanic cell the ionic flowing of carbon into potash is altered and resisted by the presence of zinc. The zinc hampers the complete electrolysis (combustion) of the metals in the cell. The normal formation of heat caused by the oxidation of one metal flowing completely toward the other metal is resisted. The resistance is gauged to restrict the total release of heat present in complete oxidation, and instead of heat arising in the cell, the reaction is designed to manifest as an *image* of the complete potential combustion. This *image* or reflection of combustion is an individualized potential combustion or power unit which shows up as a charge on the surface of the metal poles instead of flowing away as heat. The individualized potential combustion *image* registering as a charge on the surface of the metal is an analog for the process which we saw earlier when creative life (Zoe) fell into Bios, the *image* of life.

In a living cell the *image* of life (Bios) is further resisted by physical membranes and substances and falls further into an *image* of an *image* of life. Modern science identifies this twice fallen image as the source of life itself and calls it bioelectricity. The relationship is: resistance to life produces an *image* of life. The *image* has the force patterns of life but not its beinghood. The cell of a battery is a fallen *image* of the cell in a living organism. Ironically, the relationship between flow and resistance in the fallen life force in the living cell is measured abstractly as power, or potential electrical voltage, as it is found in a battery cell. In a battery, when this power is directed through a wire to a bulb, the electricity is combusted and levity (light and warmth) is released as work. In a flashlight, the warmth of combustion is seen as a waste product of entropy since the warmth is lost to the atmosphere. In the lighting of the bulb in work the true origin and biography of the being of electricity itself is not grasped. Rather, what is grasped is an *image* of the countenance of Bios as it is first resisted and then combusted or consumed. In its coming into being through enhanced resistance, electricity shows itself to be a fallen *image* of life which accompanies the consumption of life but is not life itself. This would perhaps suggest a way of thinking about the often confusing relationships found in debates about the damaging effects of electrical currents on biological systems.

Looked at from another direction, we could say that in a galvanic cell, electricity is a non-spatial *image* of the transformation of the actual metal in space. The resistance built into the relationships within the battery causes electricity to arise as an *image* of the combustion or warmth process. The warmth reappears when we finally consume the *image* (the electrical field) in the light bulb. In the battery there is a continual building and collapsing of the *image,* the electrical field, until the metals can no longer support the tension of the electrolyte. In the battery, a chemical reaction which would happen in a specific space (for instance, the chemical/physical transformation of two metals and the production of heat) is shifted into the partial transformation of two metals with an electric *image* of the warmth generated into the field around the physical metals. Through resistance, the chemical reaction is pushed out of the physical spatial realm into the nonspatial existence of the electric field. To accomplish this the physicochemical combustion of the metal with its attendant warmth process must be hampered in its usual mode of operation. The enhanced resistance set up in the cell retards the normal combustion found in the separation of warmth and ash.

As we have already seen, the warmth in a battery cannot escape the chemical reaction but travels to the surface of each metal where it appears as the charge or electrical potential of the cell. In a battery this rhythm of initiating a chemical combustion and then resisting it into the form of an image of combustion in an electrical charge (power) is multiplied into the power charge of the battery through multiple repetitions of the building and retarding process. In this way the heat which would normally be released is lifted off of the materials and exists as a non-spatial field of power. Here we could say that the electrical field is a densified and fallen warmth. Here the relationship between electricity, an image of life, and Bios or life itself is contained within the boundaries of an organism. Bios is the alchemical force of multiplication, that is, the splitting of the primal unity (reproduction). In an organism this pattern of Bios or biological multiplication of organisms is accompanied by an analogous but not functionally comparable phenomenon such as is found in electrical field generation.

The cell wall, the tissue in the pleura of an organ, and the outer skin of an organism with its sensory organs, are all biological examples of the principle of resistance through the production of membranes. Such skins of organisms are *images* of the Saturn incarnating process, and the membrane-forming process gradually results in a physically manifest organism. This process in alchemy is the great descending, precipitating process of salt. It is a tempering process which eventually creates a hardened, formed organ or organism. In fact this picture is present in the Demeter myth when the mourning

Demeter visits the hut of a shepherd and his wife Metaneira. Metaneira has a son named Triptolemus whom Demeter nurses for the mother.   She nurses Triptolemus with her flowing milk (Bios=flow), but at night Demeter holds Triptolemus over the fire to harden him (resistance) and make him into an immortal.  One night the mother finds Demeter holding her son over the fire and prevents the completion of the hardening process with the result that Triptolemus eventually must die.

The hardening of the Bios force into resistant form is, as we have said earlier, the alchemical motif of the forming of the immutable stone, the goal of many alchemical texts.  This inner soul reality is present also in the forming of a biological "stone," or organ.  This stone-forming process in biological systems is present most strongly in the physiology of the human sense organs.  The eye is actually layered silica sheaths built very much on the pattern of a crystal.  It has lost its own growing and swelling life (Bios) and serves simply as a mechanical device.  The nerves which serve the senses have also lost their own proliferating Bios and, being structured of conducting and resisting membranes, serve in the body as electrical/chemical devices. Since the lens of the eye and the sheaths of the nerves have so little life we might wonder what the life source is, out of which the nerves and senses have precipitated.

Alchemy would call this source the healing mercury force. We could also call it the etheric or life field.  The Greeks called it Zoe.  If the nerves and senses have indeed fallen out of life, is it their destiny to be forever devoid of life?  The alchemical doctrine of the stone as immutable fixed volatility would seem to say yes.  The present technological and material world view has arisen out of such thinking as the alchemical forming of the immutable stone.  The death forces generated by this world view are apparent everywhere.  We have seen earlier how this process of stone formation by the splitting into multiples through the activity of membranes is a pervasive force in nature.  In our technology we have taken this natural salt process of individuation one step further into the realm of what Rudolf Steiner calls *sub-nature.*  A simple technical device can illustrate the nature of this concept.

The origin of a silica crystal out of a fluid matrix is an example of salt in nature.  The crystal precipitates out of an expanded liquid form into a hardened, solidified state.  In this sequence we see the activity of a stone formation in nature.  If, however, as a technical process we

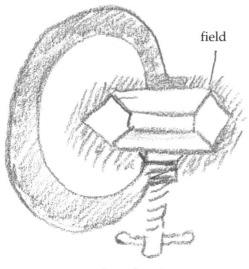

field

**piezoelectric**

go one step beyond nature, we can put a clamp onto a crystal and press it down into an even more concentrated form, in effect pushing the crystalline form into a condition "below" its natural form. The crystal resists this intrusion, and in its resistance some of its latent heat is pressed out of the crystal in the form of an electrical charge. Through pressure we have created a discontinuity in the natural form and force field of the crystal. Out of this discontinuity or resistance a field of electrical charge arises (the piezoelectric effect).

This electrical effect can also appear when heat is applied to the crystal. In this case a discontinuity arises when the inner planes of the crystal are expanded out of their natural spatial order. The result is once again a discontinuity followed by a resistance followed by an electrical field. Such discontinuities are continually happening in nature as the Sun heats up mountain ranges or the water in the atmosphere. In the case of the artificially compressed crystal, however, human beings take the resulting electrical field and use the electricity in devices such as crystal radios, rectifiers, and resistors in feedback circuits. Hidden in this technical ability lies the key to the difficulties facing humanity in the future as more and more devices are built to convert the cosmic forces of life into the fallen forces of electricity. This results in the construction of a humanly-conceived evolutionary stream parallel to nature but discontinuous from it. This parallel, discontinuous, or resisting evolutionary stream is an *image* of nature made over again in the *salted* form of the human being. (The human being is the salt of the earth.) As such it is based upon resistance to life. This parallel stream flowing below nature is now threatening the Bios sphere. To expect that a series of technical inventions will solve the problems of technology is to deny the true root of the problem which lies in the forces of resistance present in the individuating organism.   Perhaps a look at a concept from the warmth course of Rudolf Steiner can serve to illustrate the problem inherent in the tendency for human beings to transform nature into sub-nature.

In the warmth course *(Title,* 31ff), Rudolf Steiner points to a conveniently overlooked mystery in the process of heating a solid until it melts.  When we follow the temperature curve of lead, for instance, as it is being heated we can see that the lead steadily rises in temperature as it approaches its melting point.  At the melting point, however, the temperature of the lead ceases to rise as first one place in the solid liquifies and then another until finally it is completely liquid.  Only then does the temperature once again begin to rise.  During the time of the transformation from the solid state to the liquid state the heat which is doing the transformation ceases to be sensible in the lead even though the lead is absorbing heat at a constant rate.  Rudolf Steiner points out that in physics this latent heat is not taken into account, and a graph of the temperature curve of lead from its solid to its liquid state normally shows a consistent rise in temperature. The same phenomenon is repeated when we further track the temperature rise of the liquid into a gas, and it occurs yet again in the transformation from the gaseous to the pure warmth state.  At each transformation more heat is absorbed by the material than is recorded by the recording instruments.  Where does this heat go?  In what condition does it exist that it cannot be measured?  Rudolf Steiner's answer is that it goes into the realm in which heat or warmth is the original state.  It goes out of physical space into the original or counter space, the etheric realm beyond the periphery of Saturn (etheric warmth), which we have come to know as Zoe.  The archetypal warmth state touches the transforming matter at the Saturn membrane to allow it to transcend its fixed elemental form.  Modern science has very few descriptive possibilities for this realm.  We have known it earlier as the realm of flowing life or Demeter or as the eternally healing forces of the alchemical mercury.  The metal lead, when going from solid to liquid, is undergoing a mercurial transformation.

With every step of transformation the latent heat, the cosmic warmth from the archetype inherent in the incarnated being, is released from its connection to matter.  Simply rubbing our hands together gives a quick experience of the transformation of Zoe or latent heat into Bios or sensible heat.  Friction can be thought of as a micro-combustion process.  By the friction in the act of rubbing, physical substances are rendered into extremely fine states known alchemically as "dust." As particles of "dust" get smaller and smaller they approach a size where their surface becomes greater than their mass can support and they begin to approach levity states. Their peripheral surface or Saturn force begins to dominate. It is at the periphery of the organism that the forces of life (warmth and levity) are induced by the organism, and it is also at the periphery that cosmic forces are released into the space around the organism.

In friction the surfaces being rubbed together produce finer and finer particles. The ratio between the mass and surface of a particle is fixed into a peculiar relationship known as the law of minimal surface. This law states that the mass of a particle grows by cubes while the surface grows in squares. In other words the growth of a cell is limited by the numerical ratio between its contents (mass) and its surface. Inversely, the surface of a particle becomes stronger in its influence the smaller the particle becomes. The tiny particle begins to lose its levity to the space around it, first as a tendency to deny the field of gravity. This can be seen in the dust motes floating in a sunbeam. Later this is found in the actual release of latent warmth into sensible warmth (combustion) in the phenomenon of spontaneous combustion. Similar release of heat can be experienced in the compression of a gas where the compression or resistance to the natural space the gas wishes to occupy can create a spontaneous combustion in the diesel effect. In each of these cases the spatial relationship present in the natural state is altered and a resistance boundary is formed where there is a gradient between one spatial configuration and another. In each case the resistance to the spatial change causes the levity or warmth in the material state to be released into the space around the material, forming a warmth gradient in this space. In this pattern the surface area is the place where the warmth transformation takes place.

The pattern of gradient formation in the physical world is an image of the Saturn process in the supersensible world. Since ancient times the Saturn process and its gradient-forming forces have been the *image* into which life has flowed in the formation of an organism. The esoteric biological law states that an organ is formed by supersensible beings who use supersensible forces and that once the organ is formed the forces which formed it are manifest in the *function* of the organ. These forces and the patterns of their manifestations are called Creative Imaginations by Rudolf Steiner. Esoterically, the realm of these Creative Imaginations is a space which is outside the physical organs yet which influences their formation. This space around the organ is known in alchemical esoteric language as the *pleroma* or etheric field. The etheric field of Imaginations is known to the discipline of projective geometry as *counterspace* or *negative space.*

Counterspace is a mathematically provable domain in which *neg-entropy* prevails, the opposite of entropy. While entropy is the gradual heat death process in the physical universe, a neg-entropic universe would give birth to warmth as a counter movement to heat death. The unmeasureable heat which is present in the transformation of solid lead into molten lead can be considered to enter the state of being in which manifest heat once again becomes nascent or creative heat. In approaching this heat state, lead reverts back through its incarnating stages from solid to liquid to gaseous to pure warmth by being led rhythmically into neg-entropic patterns. The unmeasureable warmth from re-entering a nascent state exists as a field of potential around the object being transformed. This primal warmth field was recognized in alchemy as the source of the archetypal form through which a substance manifests in nature. The warmth field exists outside the physical perimeter of the object as a coherent or meaningful supersensible pattern. This pattern has been called the morpho-genetic field by Rupert Sheldrake and has been known to esotericists since antiquity as the etheric body. A more articulated subtle body than the etheric body was known to alchemists as the astral or star body. These subtle bodies are capable of existing free of the physical body, but through interaction with the physical they are the source of the physical body's forms and animation. The coherent, organized patterns of warmth found in the subtle bodies of organisms can be thought of in terms of organized combustion processes which support cognition, digestion, and the capacity to make willful motion. In combustion, rarified substances are led into etheric fields in the counterspace of an organism. The patterns of warmth in the counterspace of an organism have been known to esotericism as the aura of the organism. The aura has different densities of warmth or "colors" which are images of the various qualities of combustion arising from the physical organs.

Normally, in complete combustion processes warmth is released upward and an ash falls down. This is an analog of the physiological, catabolic phase of digestion. In physical chemistry, once warmth is released from matter it can become a problem such as we can see in the thermal pollution of the greenhouse effect that results from the incomplete combustion of carbon based fuels. However, it is important to realize that warmth as combustion is not the only modality in which warmth can be considered. In a materialistic technical world combustion is of prime importance. It is however a catabolic warmth state. In living organisms an anabolic warmth phase must follow each catabolism. Death in an organic system is simply the cessation of anabolic warmth states which yield to an overwhelming and terminal catabolic combustion. "From dust ye come and to dust ye shall return."

However, as we have shown before, the most fundamental warmth state arises when through friction a levity state is induced in a small particle. In this friction process resistance is the key element. When the resistance is great the generated heat is liberated from the surface of the particle, and it moves into the counterspace where an elemental transformation takes place.

Resistance, then, yields combustion and the release of warmth as a waste product. However, by carefully controlling the resistance the complete combustion can be held in check, and what arises is the *image* of combustion, the electric field. If we now refer back to Rudolf Steiner's comments about the mysterious non-spatial nature of warmth, when a solid becomes a liquid or a liquid becomes a gas, we can remember that warmth occupies a non-spatial plane of existence. This non-spatial quality can easily be experienced in heat conditions by the radiant heat given off by a source in which the medium can be much cooler than the warmth which is moving through it. Rudolf Steiner illustrates this effect by making a lens out of ice which can condense sunlight to ignite a paper while itself remaining untouched by the warmth. In warmth and light the phenomena are beyond the confines of physically determined space and begin to exhibit the quality of simultaneous appearance. Such simultaneous non-spatial effects can be found in the current physical exploration of quantum relationships and superconduction in which extremely low temperatures play a key role in allowing warmth to approach the non-local condition of spatially free simultaneity.

Electricity and the devices which use it also approach this level of simultaneity in non-spatial relationships. Telephones and electrical transmissions using fiber optic cables allow simultaneous or near simultaneous conversations over great distances. At this point, however, it is useful to consider the evolutionary direction in which such devices are heading, since as has been said, in today's physiological studies the dominant electrical model of the body and the electrochemical model of biology can be seen from an esoteric perspective as a case of mistaking an *image* of warmth for the true nature of warmth in the human organism.   This apparent error has profound moral implications for the future.

We have already seen that the freeing of levity as light or warmth is connected to the phenomenon of resistance.  In the human organism the structure of the sense organs, glands, and nerves is patterned upon the repetition of membranes which build up the organs.  In a gland, impulses coming through the sense organs trigger responses through the resistance in the layers of membranes.   The gland responds by enacting a micro combustion process of secretion.   In endocrine pathways a secretion, a corpus or salt, "falls" in the body, and the liberated levity rises in the consciousness of the organism in the form of inner *images* (emotions or instinctual responses).   The inner *images* are elctrochemical in nature and constitute the primary content of instinctual soul life.  What these electrical *images* lack is true warmth of being.  We could say that the warmth they lack is the psychological faculty of will.  The arising of automatic instinctual inner images composed of electrochemical impulses is in essence an automatic pattern devoid of cognition or directed will on the part of the organism experiencing the pattern.  There is no active involvement of the true self in such instinctual responses even though these may be intense inner images.  There is no soul warmth or enthusiasm for the deed being done but merely the unfolding of a stimulus/response pattern in an electrochemical circuit.  That many leading neurophysiologists use such hormonal responses to explain such things as human love, altruistic behavior, or moral conscience is from a spiritual perspective a profound error, for it mistakes an effect for a cause.  It would be like trying to explain the moral content of a telephone conversation between two people on the basis of observing and analyzing the quantity of electrical impulses generated, or the forms of the circuitry in the equipment.

In esoteric physiology a distinct difference needs to be established between the purely electrical response to a stimulus in and around an organ and the conscious activity generated in and around an organ by the enthusiastic attention of a true Self.  We can gain a clearer picture of this distinction if we recall the earlier description of the transformation of a crystal through pressure into an electrical generating substance.  The original crystallizing crystal moving alchemically from the warmth state through the gaseous to the liquid to the solid is following its evolutionary path through lawful formal motion. When the human being further compresses the crystal, the crystal creates around its physical form an electric field. This field gives the space around the crystal some of the characteristics of matter. Space has been materialized into a condition which Rudolf Steiner calls sub-nature. The character of this matter-laden space is electrical. In an organism, a gland, organ, or nerve reacts to the stimulus of sensation through a sense organ by creating around itself a minute electro-chemical field. Paracelsus called such endocrine fields the clouds of sweat of an organ. The charge and configuration of this field are the realm of the dubious union of psychology and biology so dominant in today's universities. Contemporary research has found that the patterns of such fields are predictable and specific to species and even individuals. The development of drugs such as Prozac attest to the capacity of researchers to map these fields. In life the organism learns to divine the movements of these fields as the source of inner instinctual imagery, and the appropriate conditional response to the appropriate stimulus is thoroughly documented by modern research. However, the automatic nature of the conditioned behavior and the habitual construction and divination of conditioned inner imagery induced in the electric fields around the organs is not the highest state of consciousness to which a human being can aspire. Human love is not simply a chemical reaction which generates the appropriate electrical field response. To equate the two is to push the organ into the realm of sub-nature where it simply becomes apparatus.

To an esotericist the impact of a sensation on an organ causes the field around the organ to be permeated with light and to be patterned in the formative motions which originally formed the organ out of warmth, gas, and liquid movements in its original genesis in the organism. Such movements are creative organ imaginations which, when forced out of the organ under a stimulus, arise in the consciousness as patterns such as fight or flight. In an animal the pattern of the creative imagination present around the organ is the source of the uncognized complexes of responses seen in instinctual urges and drives. If a human being becomes capable of accessing these organ imaginations, the result is a belly or organ clairvoyance filled with wisdom but entirely unfree. Phenomena such as spiritism or channeling point toward such conditioned induction or organ clairvoyance. In such organ clairvoyance the human being is literally outside the body in the space around the organ, flowing with instinctual consciousness along the paths of the creative imaginations present in the incarnating stream of the organ.

In decadent spiritual traditions the body-free state is often achieved by driving the True Self out of the organ through drug ingestion, fatigue, illness, or dubious spiritual practice. Such practices are dubious because being driven out, the True Self is not present with its self-cognizing warmth forces of upbuilding anabolic creativity. Only the lower self is present, analyzing the unconscious catabolic effects of stress and/or response patterns. Undoubtedly the great adepts of the past made much use of these practices. In a modern scientific consciousness, however, it is necessary to penetrate the altered states with an analytic method. The most widespread method for such research today is in the bio-chemical approach to neurology and epistemology. Certainly, the panorama of electrochemical wisdom of the automatic stimulus/response patterns is wondrous to contemplate in neuro-physiology. However, when the results of such scientific contemplation suggest that human moral ideals and creative or religious inspiration finds its genesis in automatic chemical-electric patterns a mistake is being made intellectually which severely limits the future potential for creative insight into human development.

As we have seen, the production of an electric field around a crystal through the application of an external pressure is analogous to the production of an electrical potential around an organ, gland, or nerve when stimulated by the pressure of a sensation. With the crystal we can place a wire in the field at a particular place and connect the wire to an amplifier. We can then hear the radio signals which the crystal is inducing. Likewise, when a gland or organ receives a stimulus from the sense world we can learn to induce its "signal" as a patterned response in the instinctual life. Philosophers call this production of an inner image the mental image.

When human beings observe an object, the sensation comes through the eye and into the body. Depending upon which organ we habitually use to store the impression, the stimulus triggers activity within that organ. Reductionist science sees the memory being stored in the brain. Esoteric science sees the brain as the reflecting organ for mental images (memories) which are stored throughout the body. Recent discoveries in neuro-physiology are tending to show support for the more esoteric view (multiple brain theories). Sense activity creates an electrical field which in turn creates a sensory impulse in the nerves. This we can then monitor in the soul as the mental image connected to that particular sensation.

A mental image usually emerges far below the soul's capacity to consciously identify the source of the mental image. To consciously remember the original stimulus we must either apply will in attention to the sensation or apply will in attention to the thoughts we have about the sensation. In either case the warmth in the willed attention allows the consciousness to have access to the emergence of the mental image. Mystical or visionary consciousness has its roots in the development of an ability to be aware of the particular organ around which the mental images arise. Esoteric exercises such as rhythmic breathing, fasting, chanting or repeating actions into states of exhaustion entrain the consciousness into the electric field around a particular organ. The practitioner can then read the arising mental images as the content of an oracular message. The electrical field is encoded in the logos or language of the incarnation of the organ. Practitioners typically see this incarnating or becoming process in a dream or trance state. They read the electrical potential and learn through practice and tradition to interpret the imaginations contained in the field. Such practitioners become in effect multiple personality transducers. They can select certain organ channels through which they can learn to bring in information from the supersensible worlds.

This reading of the electrical field of the multiple organs is characteristic of alchemical yellow projection. As we saw earlier yellow projection is a kind of electroplating process whereby the metallic surfaces of objects migrate to the metallic surfaces of other objects or metals suspended in an amorphous electrolyte. By passing a current through one pole, the metals in the solution are induced to migrate to the other pole of the circuit. Through yellow projection we can make a copper rod appear to be made of gold. Through mystical yellow projection we can turn a personal memory habit into a lucrative career as a seer or medium.

In the alchemical state of red projection, a higher state of consciousness, the entire actual substances of the metals in the process are completely transformed. This is the true nature of the search to turn lead into gold. Red projection is a much higher and more exacting alchemy than either yellow projection or multiplication. Likewise imaginative cognition or spirit vision is a much higher seeing than soul tripping, mystical fantasy, or trance channeling. The difference lies in the relationship which the practitioner's transcendent True Self has to what is known in esotericism as the *double,* or the *electric double.*

In order to understand the nature of the electric double and its role in projection it is helpful to imagine that esotericists can cognize, independent of the physical organs of the body, a model of the incarnating force field around each organ. Seen together as a whole field of patterns, these forces would constellate into a cohesive subtle body of encoded forces. For instance, if all of the forces which animate the senses were gathered into a whole, this body of forces would appear to the inner eye as a phantom or double of the human being, composed entirely of impulses flowing through the physical sense organs. This encoded force body of nerve potentials and fields of endocrine responses would be an *image* of the incarnating imaginations used by the human being to build the organs of the physical body. It would also be a double, or *image,* of the human body consisting of patterned and entrained electrical fields. This way of seeing puts us into the general neighborhood of the electric double.

In mystical multiplication and in the lower yellow phase of projection, the mystic has direct perception of this *image* body of electrical fields. In lower forms of alchemical projection the light of the True Self, which is in a very smothered or darkened etheric condition, faintly shines through these conditioned *image* fields. This is hiding one's light under a bushel. The conditioned *image* fields are spiritually more opaque and therefore more of the nature of electricity because they arise in the realm of sub-nature as *images* of a life process. The forces in the organ are *forced* out of the organ by habitual or stressful sensation, and they densify the surrounding space into an *image* of the primal creative imagination which is forming the organ from the spirit world. The forced imaginations densify the space around the organ into the spiritually opaque fallen *image* of life, into electricity.

The True Self, which exists as warmth in the spiritually more rarified and dynamic atmosphere found in human blood, is more radiant and creative than the densified electrical spaces around the organs. The True Self, or Ego, experiences the denser electrical patterns as a kind of rind or plating (armor) on its radiant, warm, and dynamic periphery. In stress or trauma the True Self is also pressed out as warmth through the rind into the space around the organs. Being forced out, however, the True Self cannot exist in its true state of anabolic warmth and creative enthusiasm. Warmth, the vehicle of the True Self in the body, always seeks to transform matter into the condition of counterspace or the levity state. We saw this image earlier in the difference between nascent heat and sensible heat in the transformation of a solid into a liquid or a liquid into a gas. Warmth forces seek the cosmic periphery and its continual state of transformation.

The cosmic periphery is the native state of the True Self or higher Ego, and the True Self finds its greatest transformative activity at the periphery of the organs in a state of warmth. In an organ which is under stress the True Self is forced to excarnate into a warmth state outside of the organ. In lower instinctual patterns this forced warmth excarnation is an *image* of creative imagination. It produces a secretion or excretion as an analog of the alchemical corpus or ash while the formative Imaginations which lie as the pattern of the organ are squeezed out along with the warmth into counterspace. The True Self finds itself in a forced excarnated modality outside the organ in a warmth sheath composed of the ordered patterns of the creative Imaginations which formed the organ in the first place. In this situation, the True Self is in a place where it normally belongs lawfully only in the dream state. The human being who possesses the stressing organ experiences the production of the formative Imaginations streaming through the True Self and its warmth sheath as inner dreamlike mental images of dimly perceived creative Imaginations. In daily life we call this a daydream. This process happens continually in the semi-awake human being and serves as the basis for most automatic instinctual patterns of behavior. Since in this condition unconscious arising of mental images as a response to sense stimuli is not under the free conscious control of the True Self, it cannot serve as the basis for the life of reason in the human being.

Training is needed in order to develop in the True Self the capacity to awaken to the arising of forced automatic patterns in the process just described. Ancient cultures provided mythos as a method of educating the human being who was striving toward an awakened consciousness instead of an instinctual consciousness. In the esoteric mystery schools much effort was devoted to developing techniques whereby students could be made aware of the production of organ imaginations within the body. The old clairvoyance is totally based upon these techniques. However, to recognize the *production* of the inner organ dreams is not the same as being able to cognize the *meaning* of the organ dreams. To dream into the field of forced imaginations around an organ is not the same as being freely conscious in the awake state in an organ dream. This is a later development in the evolution of consciousness and is the primary focus of the Rosicrucian alchemical adept. It is not sufficient for a being who possesses an intellect to simply read the forced instinctual images produced by an internal organ. The personal nature of the images connected to personal shadows woven into the organ pattern must be consciously purified and distilled alchemically in order for a higher vision at the stage of Imagination or spirit vision to develop.

As we have already seen, this difference of higher and lower vision is pictured in the difference between the two processes of yellow projection and red projection. In yellow projection the forced image produced from the organ stress simply radiates into and densifies the surrounding space. We saw this as the electric *image* of potential warmth. In yellow projection a kind of psychic cement is formed out of the electric *image*. It is this cemented *image* which is psychically/alchemically at the root of the neurotic syndromes and fixed ideas found in pathological soul states. The forced quality of the electric *image* in the warmth sheath is not *cognized* but simply experienced or "read" out of the warmth sheath of the organ. Through usage and over time such projected electric *images* multiply in the sheaths around the organs and serve as the basis for species or race memory. When this projection is firmly cemented in the psyche, unconscious memory dominates the soul life and the true conscious perception of a stimulus unelaborated by instinctual memories becomes impossible. This is the life of instinct and the basis for the neurotic condition in which the soul is terribly certain of the absolute depth of its pathology. On one side, the densification of the habitual excarnation causes the fixed conditioned response in the life of the soul. On the other side, the fixed mental images find their physical counterparts in the secretions and excretions which issue from the organs as a physical accompaniment to the shadow projections in the soul. Both the secretions and the neurotic forced mental images represent a hardening, or rind in the essentially fluid warmth condition of the True Self. These rinds or soul calluses are discontinuities in the energetically integrated whole of the warmth of the True Self. It is between such rinds or energetic discontinuities of an electrical nature that the human double finds access to the soul.

The human being experiencing the forces related to sensation has an analog in the processes connected to flow and resistance. The sense organs transmit impulses to the nerves which in turn transmit impulses to the glands. The glands resist the sensations and secrete their substances into the blood. These substances stimulate the life organs and their excretions. This whole process of the gradual forming of the organs and their excretions can be seen alchemically as a salt process. The myriad membranes and skins of the glands, nerves, and sense organs, composed primarily of siliceous materials, can be thought of as analogous to capacitors. That is, they resist the flow of the forces contained in the sense impulses. The resistance builds a field around the organ, and the Imaginations produced in this field arise inwardly as mental images of the process of flow and resistance. This process becomes critical when a person sleeps or lives over a mass of stone such as a buried boulder. Under such conditions the person will experience the distortion of the fields around his or her organs as a precondition to illness. When we consider the constitution of a boulder as a mass of conducting and resisting minerals we can easily see how such a mass would form its own field structure and radiations. In a human being, if the fields around the organs are inserted into a strong outer field, they would tend, especially during sleep, to configure to the larger dominating field rather than to the archetype of the human organ field. The organ field would be displaced by the boulder's stronger field and would deny the physical organ access to the archetypal human forces it requires during sleep. If the boulder under the bed were also submerged in a spring or flowing water source, the human organ field would be further stressed and have a tendency to adapt its forms to the flowing field of the water course. Prolonged exposure to such overwhelming distorting fields and radiations often will seriously weaken the life forces and rest patterns of a human being and will lead to serious illness.

In the course of esoteric development the human being learns to gradually and consciously loosen the life fields around the body's organs in order to experience the spiritual dimensions of a body-free consciousness. This loosening of the life force fields presents a distinct challenge to the student, artist, or adept who undertakes esoteric development. Living in the fields around the physical organs causes them to be much more susceptible to the distorting influences of other fields. As a result, after development of the subtle bodies certain foods can no longer be tolerated since they cause the archetypal field to excarnate strongly from the distressed organ. Substances which could be easily tolerated before such esoteric practices were undertaken suddenly provoke sensitive allergic reactions. Again the Imaginations are driven out of the organs and arise as instinctual patterns of forced reaction such as inflammation or sclerosis. Such personal reactions can be overcome by further practice in which the artist or adept learns to excarnate meditatively into the field around the organs and around the body consciously and at will. Such constant conscious excarnation places the meditant in the exact place in which the ancient belly clairvoyants found their inspirations. The modern clairvoyant, however, is awake in the organ field as a result of his or her capacity to experience the awake perception of having a coherent but subtle body while in the spirit world. This experience of the regulating effect of the physical body outside the actual physical body is developed through the active participation of the awake consciousness in the state of excarnation in the organ field. In such a state the day clairvoyance gives a firm foundation to what would otherwise be a forced disembodied ejection of the soul into the organ field.

The tremendous importance of this distinction in modern esoteric training cannot be over-emphasized, for the contemporary bombardment of unlawful images through the sense organs denies the soul the capability of attaining a controlled awake excarnation into the fields around the body. A particularly potent example of this problem can be found in an article by Michael Kneissle in the June 1997 bulletin by the Waldorf Education Research Institute (Vol. II, no. 2). Kneissle cites research done in Germany by distinguished researchers at the Institute of Medical Psychology at Tübingen and the Rational Psychology Association (GRP) in Munich. Researchers at these institutes have discovered what appears to be a profound physiological adaptation which human brains have made since 1969 in response to the tremendous onslaught of sensory input and conflicting images given to modern human beings through the media. It appears that the "new brains" refuse to be aware of sense stimuli which exist below a "thrill" level of sensation. Nerves from senses have lost the capacity for integration with other senses in the majority of people born after 1969. In such people the brain, in order to protect itself from invasion, refuses to bring contradictory pieces of information into any kind of relationship with each other. Young people with such brains have grown up within an environment of stress stimuli and conflicting images. The brain has adapted to this by reducing the cross-linkages which serve as the neurological base for creative thinking and by producing instead an analog of parallel circuitry which simply stores uncognized sensation as bits of information. Such a neurological pattern creates in the person's soul a tremendous feeling of indifference to stimuli. This in turn induces a mass unconsciousness which is the equivalent of a state of shock. This is the new normal state of consciousness through which the brain tries to adapt to electronic stimuli which overwhelm it at every turn. This causes the ordering system which is responsible for coordinating sense impressions and conscious activity to shift into a spastic, unconscious mode of perception.

Untrue or violent images cause a spasm in the subtle bodies with a strong forced discontinuity in the organ fields. These fields become structured with dense, solidified, and opaque patterning which is not permeable by the waking consciousness. We could say that the fields become polarized, fibrous, and hardened in response to such stress-producing sensations as images from virtual reality, images of violence, or simply the evening news on TV. In America such electronic influences are doubly effective because the geology of America from Denver to the West Coast is an enormous mass of geological discontinuities. Each mountain range is composed of rocks different from the adjacent range, having migrated from very different sources in the Pacific in the earliest geologic periods. As a result, tremendous anomalous fields of charges dominate the geology of North America. Where the bedrock rises to the surface as it does in the front range of the Rockies, or where volcanic dikes create dense vertical lenses underground, the geological forces flowing along fault lines move abruptly to the surface. We could say that such masses of rock and ore are organs in the earth body which react to planetary motions and tensions by producing fields of imaginations around the organs of rock. Human beings living in such fluctuating fields are continually receiving influences from below which cause geopathic stress on their physical organs. They are forced to excarnate unconsciously under the influence of such stress and their own organ fields seek to adapt themselves to the larger field characteristics of the upflowing geological forces. As if this were not enough, according to some sources, the great electrical interstices which supply the power grid for the western United States have purposely been placed along such fault lines by dowsers. Since the early days of telegraphy it has proved advantageous to run power lines along discontinuities. Electricity has an affinity for discontinuities and flows along them with a minimum of resistance.

If we look at the contemporary possibility of an American eating devitalized, or worse, synthetic food which stresses the organ to cause excarnation, and if we place this person along an electrically and geo-pathically active geological discontinuity, we can begin to imagine a situation of constant forced unconscious excarnation. If we then have this person play video games or watch violent shows on TV or absorb themselves in the spasms encountered in virtual reality program-ming, we can see a subtle body which is hardened into layers in which the collective electrical double forces of human beings can create a permanent abode. The spaces contained in such a subtle body would be an actual parallel universe not of this earth and not directly acces-sible to the consciousness of the awake human being or to the con-sciousness of the Hierarchies who created human bodies. Such a par-allel universe would be characterized by a constant acceleration of the forces of resistance. This would be experienced as a titanic and prodi-gious capacity for competition and innovation. Forces of pressure, compartmentalization, and paranoia would dominate the waking consciousness. Technical memory and information would be highly valued, and meditation and creative exploration would be sup-pressed. This is the realm of the forces of the electric double. It is a chilling and aggressive destiny for the human soul who is spastically forced into the distorted, enormous field lines of a materialized and densified soul space, hard and unyielding, resistant and inflexible, which will gradually suffocate the tender and delicate soul currents which bring life and color to the human being.

The ominous portents of this vision are present in abundance in contemporary life. What can be done to heal and soften the devastat-ing compulsion of this dilemma? Two forces present in the human soul are available to directly defy these destructive tendencies of con-temporary life. The first, thinking backwards, is seen by some to be the highest, most coherent force of human consciousness on the plan-et today. Fundamentally, any thought which we can think forwards becomes much more dynamic, warm, and infused with potential life when we think it systematically and exactly in the reverse order from which it was originally thought. Such a practice removes the rigidi-fying and automatic patterning which sets the stage for the hardened layering of the electric double in the subtle bodies. Through thinking backwards the will moves our waking consciousness out of its habit-ual patterns in the physical and sense organs and excarnates us con-sciously into the field of Imaginations. Thinking backwards provides a specific technique for softening and unwinding patterns of instinc-tual thinking present in habitual excarnations in an unconscious manner. Through thinking backwards an esoteric artist becomes an adept at living consciously in the space outside the physical body.

Once adepts are in the space outside the body in a conscious manner they must cultivate the experience of inner silence in order to dissolve any ill effects encountered through the double and its electric forces. Silence builds power, power that is dissipated in the flow of daily life. Silence dissolves resistance. Silence allows the excarnated soul to hear the sounding of the universal forces which lie behind the world of the senses. In silence the word-like nature of the creation can be devotedly heard before it manifests into the fallen deluge of empty words present in contemporary life. The vast potential forces of silence give the soul of the adept a confidence that life exists death in the silent infinitely expansive state which is freely entered into in every act of meditation. With such confidence in the continuity of consciousness the daily life with its disappointments and trials becomes a much greater cosmic striving for truth, beauty, and flexibility of soul. In such transcendent, silent luminous states the soul experiences itself as a spiritual being among other spiritual beings. It takes its place as a creative spirit fully awake while seriously engaged in the playful dreaming of new worlds. Silent, aware, and structured in meaning, the spirit makes sense of even the meeting with the double. By cultivating silence, fear and doubt are replaced by empathy and capacity for selfless action. Anxiety and the tendency to mock what we do not understand yield to acceptance and the strength to allow ourselves to fail. Acceptance of our own failures fosters compassion for the failures of others.

The Imaginations of the spiritual beings who have created the visible world out of spirit need to be perceived by human beings who are willing and able to complete this great work of the creation of the universe. To do this we must touch the earth in a new way. To heal the abstract nature of thinking, the most valuable technique is thinking backwards. Through this practice, intellect becomes reason and the capacity to understand. The will, the driving force of the self-made human being, is also reversed in thinking backwards so that the will is applied with no thought of outcome.

In our time the heart is hardened by the materialistic half-true imaginations of a fallen creation. This hardening is reversed by being silent even when we know the answer. It is the heart sitting in silence which is the ultimate goal of the new esoteric tradition. But the heart thinking in silence does not arrive at better answers. Rather, the thinking heart seeks better questions. It seeks them in the warm luminous layers of silence from which creative Imaginations flow toward humanity from the light-filled realms of world-creating spirit—if only we take the time to cultivate a vision which can seek the spirit.

# BIBLIOGRAPHY

*Artists on Art: from the XIV to the XX century.* comp. and ed. by Robert Goldwater and Marco Treves. New York: Pantheon Books, 1972.

Assagioli, Roberto. *The Act of Will.* New York: Viking Press, 1973.

Hoppal, M., ed. *Shamanism in Eurasia.* Gottingen: Herodot, 1984.

Damasio, Antonio R. *Descartes' Error: Emotion, Reason and the Human Brain.* New York: G. P. Putnam's Sons, 1994.

Goethe, Johann Wolfgang von. *Goethe's Fairy Tale of the Green Snake and the Beautiful Lily.* New York: Steiner Books, [n.d.].

―――. *Metamorphosis of Plants.* Kimberton, PA: Bio-Dynamic Farming and Gardening Assn. Inc., 1993.

*Gray's Anatomy.* ed. by P. Williams, R. Warwick, M. Dyson, L. Bannister. 37th ed. Edinburgh and New York: Churchill Livingstone, 1989.

Harner, Michael. *The Way of the Shaman.* New York: Harper & Row, 1980.

Kniessle, Michael. "Research into Changes in Brain Formation," *Research Bulletin.* Spring Valley, NY: Waldorf Education Research Institute. Vol. II, No. 2. June 1997, pp. 30–33.

König, Karl. *Earth and Man.* Wyoming, RI: Bio-Dynamic Literature, [n.d.].

*The New Painting: Impressionism 1874–1886.* An exhibition organized by the Fine Arts Museums of San Francisco with the National Gallery of Art, Washington. San Francisco: The Fine Arts Museums of San Francisco, 1986.

Nicholson, Shirley, comp. *Shamanism: An Expanded View of Reality.* Wheaton, Ill.: Theosophical Publishing House, 1987.

Paracelsus. *The Hermetic and Alchemical Writings of Paracelsus the Great. 2 vols.* ed. Arthur Edward Waite. Edmonds, WA: Alchemical Press, 1992.

Pearce, Joseph Chilton. *Evolution's End: Claiming the Potential of Our Intelligence.* San Francisco: Harper San Francisco, 1992.

Pfeiffer, Ehrenfried. *Notes and Lectures, Compendium #1.* Spring Valley, NY: Mercury Press, 1991.

Querido, René M. *The Golden Age of Chartres: The Teachings of a Mystery School and the Eternal Feminine.* Fair Oaks, CA: Rudolf Steiner College Press, 1987.

Rulandus, Martinus. *A Lexicon of Alchemy.* Kila Mt.: Kessinger Publishing Co., 1612.

Steiner, Rudolf. "The Ancient Yoga Culture and the New Yoga Will" (Dornach, Nov. 30, 1891) in *The Archangel Michael: His Mission and Ours.* Hudson, NY: Anthroposophic Press, 1994.

———. *The Archangel Michael: His Mission and Ours.* Hudson, NY: Anthroposophic Press, 1994.

———. *The Boundaries of Natural Science.* (Dornach, Sept 27–Oct 3, 1920). Spring Valley, NY: Anthroposophic Press, 1983.

———. *The Evolution of Consciousness as Revealed through Initiation-Knowledge.* (Penmaenmawr, August 19–31, 1923). trans. V.E.W. and C.D. London: Rudolf Steiner Press, 1966.

———. *Goethean Science.* Spring Valley, NY: Mercury Press, 1988.

———. *Guidance in Esoteric Training.* London: Rudolf Steiner Press, 1998.

———. *How to Know Higher Worlds.* Hudson, NY: Anthroposophic Press, 1994.

———. *Learning to See Into the Spiritual World: Lectures to the Workers at the Goetheanum, June 28–July 18, 1923.* trans. Walter Stuber and Mark Gardner. Hudson, NY: Anthroposophic Press, 1990.

———. *Mystery Centers.* (Dornach, Nov. 23–Dec. 23, 1923). Blauvelt, NY: Spiritual Research Editions, 1989.

———. *An Occult Physiology.* (Prague, March 20–28, 1911). London: Rudolf Steiner Press, 1983.

———. *A Road to Self Knowledge* and *The Threshold of the Spiritual World.* trans. H. Hollison. London: Rudolf Steiner Press, 1975.

———. *Spiritual Research: Methods and Results.* ed. Paul M. Allen. Blauvelt, NY: Steinerbooks, 1981.

———. *The Temple Legend.* London: Rudolf Steiner Press, 1985.

———. *The Warmth Course.* Spring Valley, NY: Mercury Press, 1998.

———. *Wonders of the World, Ordeals of the Soul, Revelations of the Spirit.* (Munich, August 18–27, 1911). London: Rudolf Steiner Press, 1963.

———. *The World of the Senses and the World of the Spirit.* (Hanover, Dec. 27, 1911–Jan. 1, 1912). Vancouver: Steiner Book Centre, 1979.

Valentine, Basil. *Last Will and Testament.* San Jose, CA: English Grand Lodge, Rosicrucian Order, AMORC, 1993.

Tromp, S.W. *Psychical Physics: A Scientific Analysis of Dowsing, Radiesthesia, and Kindred Divining Phenomena.* New York: Elsevier Publishing Co, 1949. (Borderland Science Foundation, P.O. Box 429, Garberville, CA 95440-0429)

ISMAEL 1/99